Fifth Edition

NorthStar 2

Listening & Speaking

Author: Laurie Frazier

Series Editors: Frances Boyd
Carol Numrich

NorthStar: Listening & Speaking Level 2, Fifth Edition

Pearson Education, 221 River St, Hoboken, NJ 07030

Staff credits: The people who made up the *NorthStar: Listening & Speaking Level 2, Fifth Edition* team, representing content creation, design, manufacturing, marketing, multimedia, project management, publishing, rights management, and testing, are Pietro Alongi, Stephanie Callahan, Gina DiLillo, Tracey Cataldo, Dave Dickey, Warren Fishbach, Sarah Hand, Lucy Hart, Gosia Jaros-White, Stefan Machura, Linda Moser, Dana Pinter, Karen Quinn, Katarzyna Starzynska - Kosciuszko, Paula Van Ells, Claire Van Poperin, Joseph Vella, Peter West, Autumn Westphal, Natalia Zaremba, and Marcin Zimny.

Project consultant: Debbie Sistino
Text composition: ElectraGraphics, Inc.
Development editing: Debbie King
Cover design: Studio Montage

Library of Congress Cataloging-in-Publication Data

A Catalog record for the print edition is available from the Library of Congress.

Printed in the United States of America

ISBN-13: 978-0-13-523266-8 (Student Book with Digital Resources)
ISBN-10: 0-13-523266-X (Student Book with Digital Resources)

ISBN-13: 978-0-13-522696-4 (Student Book with MyEnglishLab Online Workbook and Resources)
ISBN-10: 0-13-522696-1 (Student Book with MyEnglishLab Online Workbook and Resources)

1 2019

CONTENTS

WELCOME TO NORTHSTAR

A Letter from the Series Editors

We welcome you to the 5th edition of *NorthStar Listening & Speaking Level 2*.

Engaging content, integrated skills, and critical thinking continue to be the touchstones of the series. For more than 20 years *NorthStar* has engaged and motivated students through contemporary, authentic topics. Our online component builds on the last edition by offering new and updated activities.

Since its first edition, *NorthStar* has been rigorous in its approach to critical thinking by systematically engaging students in tasks and activities that prepare them to move into high-level academic courses. The cognitive domains of Bloom's taxonomy provide the foundation for the critical thinking activities. Students develop the skills of analysis and evaluation and the ability to synthesize and summarize information from multiple sources. The capstone of each unit, the final writing or speaking task, supports students in the application of all academic, critical thinking, and language skills that are the focus of unit.

The new edition introduces additional academic skills for 21st century success: note-taking and presentation skills. There is also a focus on learning outcomes based on the Global Scale of English (GSE), an emphasis on the application of skills, and a new visual design. These refinements are our response to research in the field of language learning in addition to feedback from educators who have taught from our previous editions.

NorthStar has pioneered and perfected the blending of academic content and academic skills in an English Language series. Read on for a comprehensive overview of this new edition. As you and your students explore *NorthStar*, we wish you a great journey.

Carol Numrich and Frances Boyd, the editors

New for the FIFTH EDITION

New and Updated Themes

The new edition features one new theme per level (i.e., one new unit per book), with updated content and skills throughout the series. Current and thought-provoking topics presented in a variety of genres promote intellectual stimulation. The real-world-inspired content engages students, links them to language use outside the classroom, and encourages personal expression and critical thinking.

Learning Outcomes and Assessments

All unit skills, vocabulary, and grammar points are connected to GSE objectives to ensure effective progression of learning throughout the series. Learning outcomes are present at the opening and closing of each unit to clearly mark what is covered in the unit and encourage both pre- and post-unit self-reflection. A variety of assessment tools, including online diagnostic, formative, and summative assessments and a flexible gradebook aligned with clearly identified unit learning outcomes, allow teachers to individualize instruction and track student progress.

Note-Taking as a Skill in Every Unit

Grounded in the foundations of the Cornell Method of note-taking, the new note-taking practice is structured to allow students to reflect on and organize their notes, focusing on the most important points. Students are instructed, throughout the unit, on the most effective way to apply their notes to a classroom task, as well as encouraged to analyze and reflect on their growing note-taking skills.

Explicit Skill Instruction and Fully-Integrated Practice

Concise presentations and targeted practice in print and online prepare students for academic success. Language skills are highlighted in each unit, providing students with multiple, systematic exposures to language forms and structures in a variety of contexts. Academic and language skills in each unit are applied clearly and deliberately in the culminating writing or presentation task.

Scaffolded Critical Thinking

Activities within the unit are structured to follow the stages of Bloom's taxonomy from *remember* to *create*. The use of APPLY throughout the unit highlights culminating activities that allow students to use the skills being practiced in a free and authentic manner. Sections that are focused on developing critical thinking are marked with 🔍 to highlight their critical focus.

Explicit Focus on the Academic Word List

AWL words are highlighted at the end of the unit and in a master list at the end of the book.

The Pearson Practice English App

The **Pearson Practice English App** allows students on the go to complete vocabulary and grammar activities, listen to audio, and watch video.

ExamView

ExamView Test Generator allows teachers to customize assessments by reordering or editing existing questions, selecting test items from a bank, or writing new questions.

MyEnglishLab

New and revised online supplementary practice maps to the updates in the student book for this edition.

THE NORTHSTAR UNIT

1 FOCUS ON THE TOPIC

Each unit begins with an eye-catching unit opener spread that draws students into the topic. The learning outcomes are written in simple, student-friendly language to allow for self-assessment. Focus on the Topic questions connect to the unit theme and get students to think critically by making inferences and predicting the content of the unit.

UNIT 1

Offbeat Jobs

LEARNING OUTCOMES

- Infer the use of humor
- Take notes with key words
- Recognize contrast
- Use descriptive adjectives
- Use word stress
- Show interest

Go to MyEnglishLab to check what you know.

2 UNIT 1

1 FOCUS ON THE TOPIC

1. Look at the photo. What is happening? What is the person's job?
2. Read the title of the unit. *Offbeat* means "unusual." A bike messenger has an offbeat job. Can you think of other offbeat jobs?
3. What is most important to you when choosing a job? Think about things like salary (how much money you make), hours, interest, safety (how safe or dangerous it is), workplace (indoors, outdoors, home, office), education, and number of job openings (how easy it is to find a job). Compare your answers as a class.

Offbeat Jobs 3

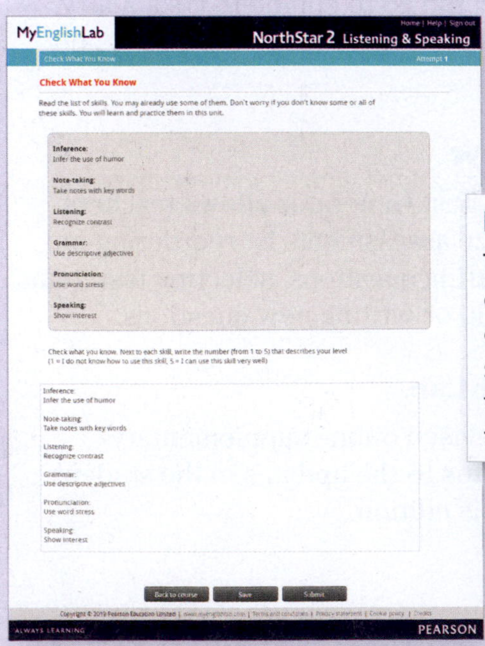

MyEnglishLab

NorthStar 2 Listening & Speaking

Home | Help | Sign out

Check What You Know Attempt 1

Check What You Know

Read the list of skills. You may already use some of them. Don't worry if you don't know some or all of these skills. You will learn and practice them in this unit.

Inference:
Infer the use of humor

Note-taking:
Take notes with key words

Listening:
Recognize contrast

Grammar:
Use descriptive adjectives

Pronunciation:
Use word stress

Speaking:
Show interest

Check what you know. Next to each skill, write the number (from 1 to 5) that describes your level (1 = I do not know how to use this skill, 5 = I can use this skill very well)

Inference:
Infer the use of humor

Note-taking:
Take notes with key words

Listening:
Recognize contrast

Grammar:
Use descriptive adjectives

Pronunciation:
Use word stress

Speaking:
Show interest

Back to course | Save | Submit

ALWAYS LEARNING PEARSON

MyEnglishLab

The "Check What You Know" pre-unit diagnostic checklist provides a short self-assessment based on each unit's GSE-aligned learning outcomes to support the students in building an awareness of their own skill levels and to enable teachers to target instruction to their students' specific needs.

2 FOCUS ON LISTENING

A vocabulary exercise introduces words that appear in the listenings, encourages students to guess the meanings of the words from context, and connects to the theme presented in the final speaking task.

Go to MyEnglishLab lines indicate when additional practice is available online.

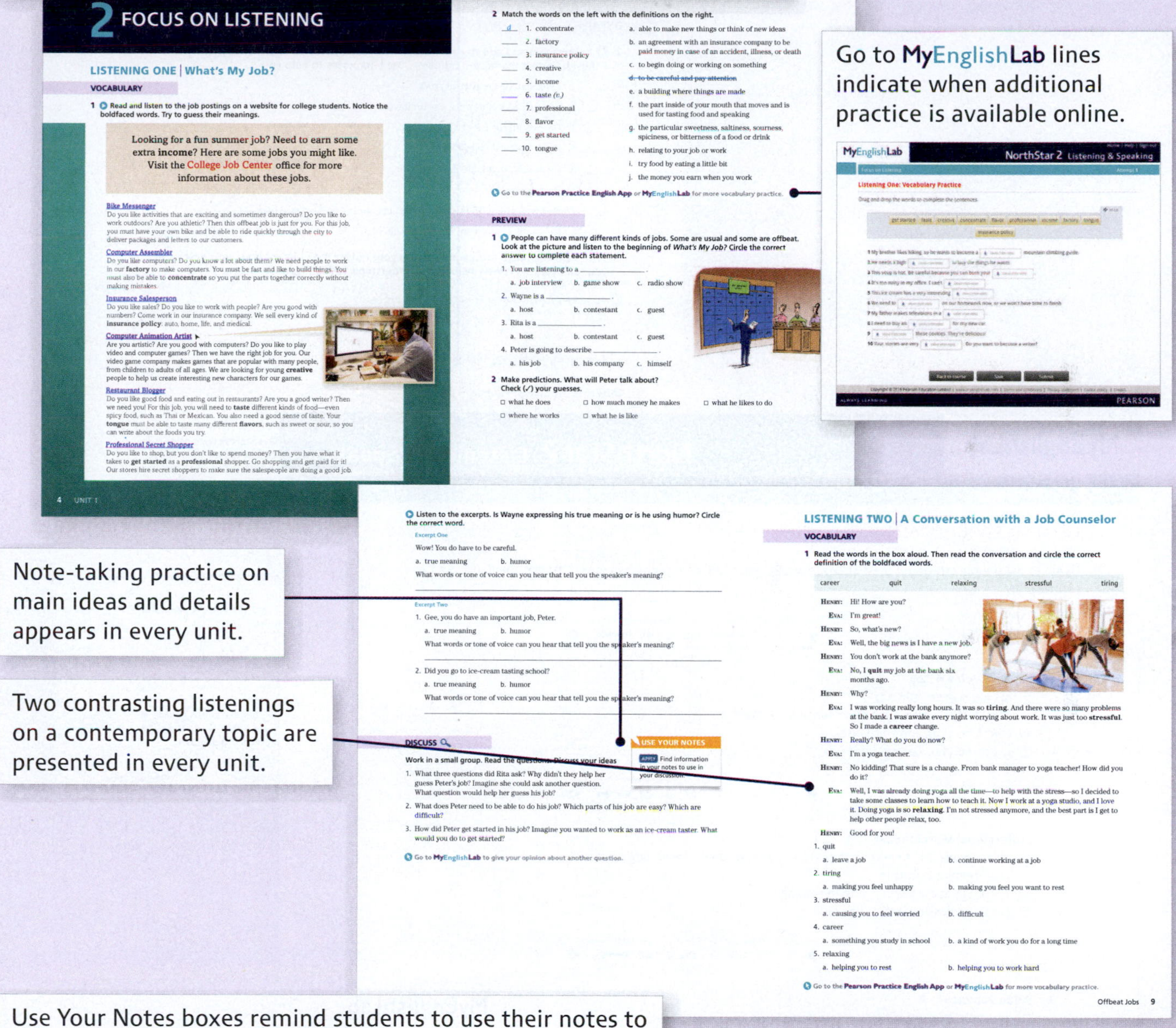

Note-taking practice on main ideas and details appears in every unit.

Two contrasting listenings on a contemporary topic are presented in every unit.

Use Your Notes boxes remind students to use their notes to complete exercises that support language, academic skills, production and critical thinking.

Every unit focuses on noting main ideas and details and features an additional note-taking skill applicable to the listenings. Activities are designed to support students in successfully completing the final speaking tasks.

EXPLICIT SKILL INSTRUCTION AND PRACTICE

Step-by-step instructions and practice guide students to move beyond the literal meaning of the listenings. 🔍 highlights activities that help build critical thinking skills.

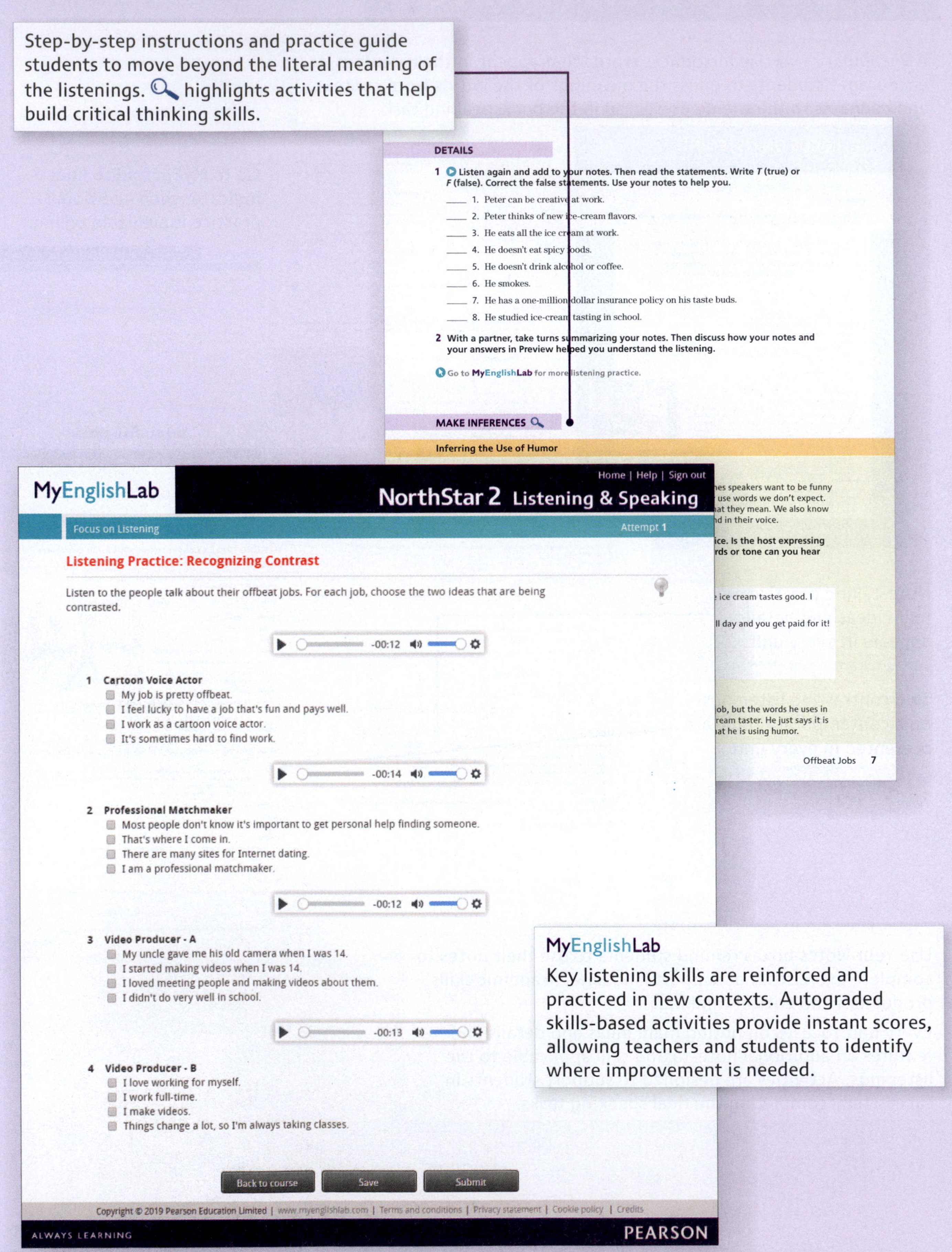

MyEnglishLab
Key listening skills are reinforced and practiced in new contexts. Autograded skills-based activities provide instant scores, allowing teachers and students to identify where improvement is needed.

3 FOCUS ON SPEAKING

Productive vocabulary targeted in the unit is reviewed, expanded upon, and used creatively.

3 FOCUS ON SPEAKING

VOCABULARY

REVIEW

Match the statement on the left with the best response on the right.

__b__ 1. My friend went to school to learn to cook. She just got her first job cooking in a French restaurant. She loves her job.

____ 2. Working for myself isn't easy. I have a lot of work to do.

____ 3. I don't like my job. I want to get a new job.

a. It sounds like you want to **quit**!

b. ~~You're so lucky your friend is a **professional** chef! Does she ever cook for you?~~

c. Wow, having your own business sounds **stressful**.

d. You're very **creative**.

Grammar presentations focus on skills that are used in the listenings and applied in the final speaking task. A concise grammar skills box serves as a reference point for students throughout the unit and beyond.

GRAMMAR FOR SPEAKING

1 Work with a partner. Read the conversations aloud. Look at the underlined words. Then answer the questions.

1. **A:** What's your job like?
   B: My job is interesting.

2. **A:** What kind of person are you?
   B: I'm a friendly person.

a. Look at the answers to the questions. What is the verb in each sentence?
b. What is the noun in each sentence?
c. Which words describe the nouns? Where do they come in the sentences?

Descriptive Adjectives

ADJECTIVES DESCRIBE NOUNS.	
1. Adjectives can come after the verb *be*.	*My job **is tiring**.*
2. Adjectives can also come before a noun.	*Artists are **creative people**.*
3. When a singular noun follows an adjective, use *a* before the adjective if the adjective begins with a consonant sound.	*This isn't **a high-paying job**.*
4. When a singular noun follows an adjective, use *an* before the adjective if the adjective begins with a vowel sound.	*Peter has **an offbeat job**.*

2 Some words describe a person, some describe a job, and some describe both. Write the words in the correct box. If the word can describe a person and a job, write it in both boxes.

boring, dangerous, friendly, hardworking, interesting, offbeat, safe, tiring, creative, difficult, happy, high-paying, low-paying, relaxing, stressful

WORDS ABOUT PEOPLE	WORDS ABOUT JOBS
a(n) ____________ person	a(n) ____________ job

18 UNIT 1

MyEnglishLab

Auto-graded vocabulary and grammar practice activities reinforce meaning, form, and function. Meaningful and instant feedback guides students to self-correct and provides students and teachers with essential information to monitor progress.

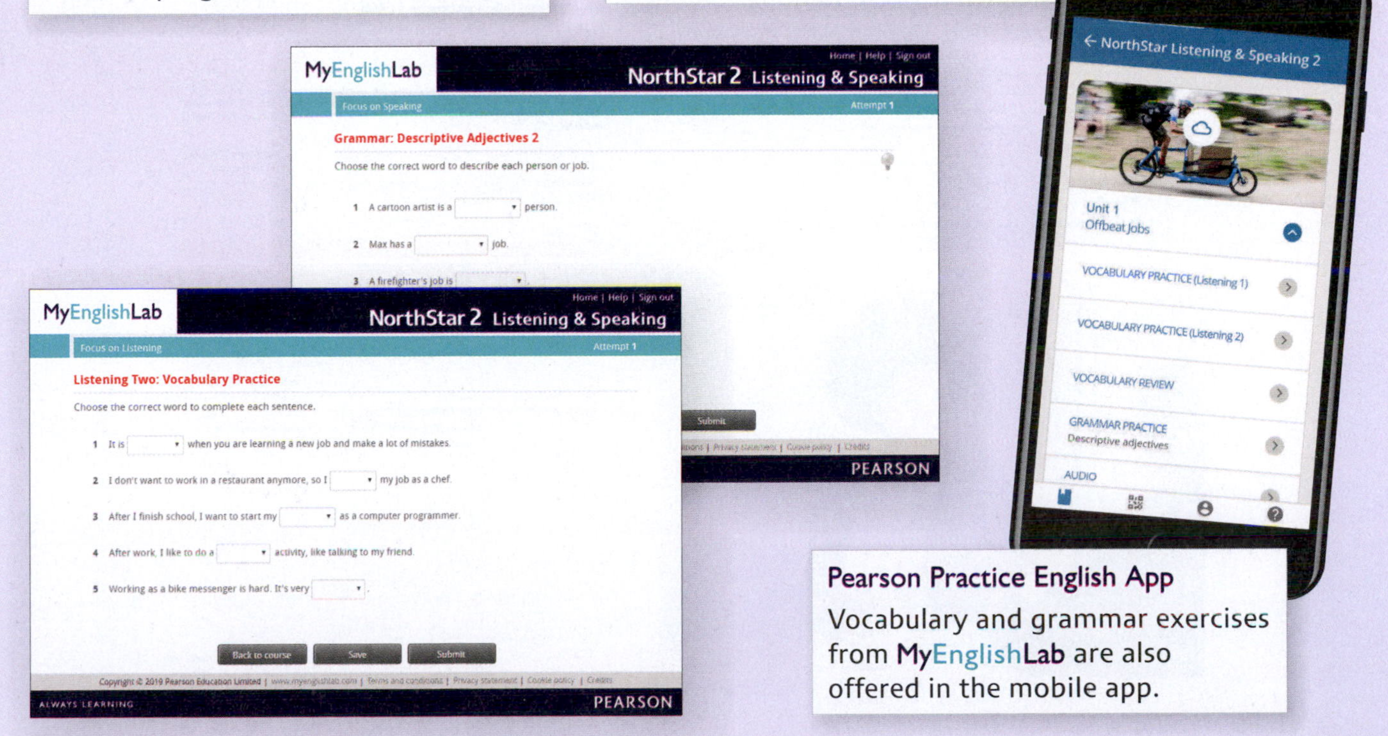

Pearson Practice English App

Vocabulary and grammar exercises from **MyEnglishLab** are also offered in the mobile app.

A TASK-BASED APPROACH TO PROCESS WRITING

3 Work with a partner. Take turns making statements using the nouns and adjectives provided. React by saying, "I agree" or "I don't agree. / I disagree." If you don't agree with a statement, correct it.

Example

Restaurant blogging / dangerous

A: Restaurant blogging is dangerous.

B: I don't agree. Restaurant blogging isn't dangerous. It's safe.

1. a bike messenger's job / tiring
2. an ice-cream taster / creative person
3. selling insurance / stressful
4. computer animation /offbeat job
5. window washing / interesting job
6. a game show host / hardworking
7. a professional shopper's job / relaxing

4 APPLY Make a list of your top five favorite jobs. Discuss them with a partner. Use descriptive adjectives to describe the jobs on your list.

Go to the Pearson Practice English App or MyEnglishLab for more grammar practice. Check what you learned in MyEnglishLab.

PRONUNCIATION

Using Word Stress

In words with multiple syllables, one syllable is stressed. Stressed syllables sound longer than unstressed syllables. They are also louder and higher in pitch than unstressed syllables.

Listen to the examples.

Example One

careful creative

A compound noun is formed when two nouns are used together as one noun. In compound nouns, the stress is stronger on the stressed syllable in the first word in the compound.

Example Two

bike messenger salesperson

When an adjective is followed by a noun, the stress is usually stronger on the noun.

Example Three

A professional shopper A good salary

Pronunciation and Speaking Skill tasks are focused on learning outcomes which are later used in the final speaking task, helping students develop their professional and academic public speaking skills.

SPEAKING SKILL

Showing Interest

When we speak to others, it is polite to show interest in the other person and in what he or she says. We can show interest with our words and also with body language.

ASKING SOMEONE QUESTIONS	TALKING ABOUT YOURSELF	SHOWING INTEREST	
		WITH WORDS	WITH BODY LANGUAGE
What do you do?	*I'm not working right now.* *I'm a (student / chef / homemaker).* *I'm retired.*[1]	*Oh . . . really?*	Make eye contact. (Look at the person.) Nod your head up and down to show you are listening.
How do you like it?	*It's great.* *It's interesting.*	*Good for you.*	Smile at the person.
	It's all right, but . . . *I don't like it at all.*	*Oh, I see.* *Oh, why not?*	Use a facial expression to show concern.
What do you like to do in your free time?	*I like to (listen to music / play tennis).* *I enjoy (reading / playing computer games).*	*That's interesting.* *That's nice.* *Really? Me, too!* *Oh, yeah?*	Raise your eyebrows to show you are pleasantly surprised and interested.

[1] retired: no longer working at a job, usually because of age

Showing concern

Showing pleasant surprise and interest

Offbeat Jobs 21

APPLY calls out activities that get students to use new skills in a productive task.

The Final Speaking task incorporates themes and skills from the unit in a final productive task that engages students in a variety of public speaking genres, from interactive role-plays to academic presentations.

A: Hi. My name's ____________.

B: Hi. I'm ____________. Nice to meet you.

A: Nice to meet you, too. So what do you do?

B: I'm ____________.

A: ____________. How do you like it?

B: ____________. How about you? What do you do?

A: ____________.

B: ____________. So what do you like to do in your free time?

A: ____________. How about you?

B: ____________.

Go to MyEnglishLab for more skill practice and to check what you learned.

Using the right body language helps make a good impression during a job interview.

22 UNIT 1

FINAL SPEAKING TASK: A Job Interview APPLY

In this activity, you will take part in a job interview. You will choose a job that you would like to have. Your partner will interview you for the job.

STEP 1

Choose one job from the list below or another job. List the reasons you want to have this job. Then list the strengths and skills you have that will help you to do that job. Use words and phrases from Review and Expand. Give examples of times you used those strengths and skills.

computer animation artist	bike messenger	restaurant blogger
insurance salesperson	computer assembler	game show host
window washer	ice-cream taster	professional shopper
other: ______		

Example

JOB: COMPUTER ANIMATION ARTIST		
Why do you want this job?	*like to work with computers* *like cartoons* *want to work indoors in an office*	
What are your strengths?	*creative* *hardworking* *team player*	*Examples:* *think of my own characters and cartoons* *finish my school work on time* *work with other students on group projects*
What skills do you have?	*good with computers* *good with my hands* *good at drawing pictures*	*Examples:* *know computer animation programs*

Offbeat Jobs 23

STEP 2

APPLY Use the vocabulary, grammar, pronunciation, and speaking skills from the unit. Use the checklist to help you.

- ☐ **Vocabulary:** Read through the list of vocabulary on page 25. Which words can you include in your notes from Step 1 to make it clearer and more interesting? Choose at least three words or phrases to use and add them to your notes.
- ☐ **Grammar:** Scan your notes for descriptive adjectives. Are they in the correct place? Do you need to add *a* or *an* in front of them?
- ☐ **Pronunciation:** Look for examples of compound nouns and adjectives + nouns in your notes. Which syllable should you stress in each? Underline it.
- ☐ **Speaking Skill:** Review ways to show interest in the other person with words and body language.

STEP 3

1 Work with a partner. Student A, you are the job interviewer. Greet your partner and ask questions to find out if they are the right person for the job. Take notes of your partner's answers. Student B, you are interviewing for a job. Answer the interviewer's questions. Then switch roles.

2 Report back to the class. Do you want to hire (choose) your partner for the job? Why or why not?

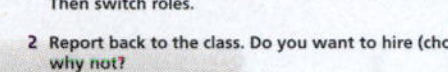

24 UNIT 1

ALTERNATIVE SPEAKING TOPIC

APPLY Discuss the questions. Use the vocabulary, grammar, pronunciation, and speaking skills you learned from the unit.

1. Why do you think some people like offbeat jobs?
2. How do you think most people get started in their offbeat jobs in the first place?
3. What job skills do you think are the most difficult to learn? Why do you think they are difficult?
4. What skills do you think are most important for students to learn so they can find a job or start a career in the future?

CHECK WHAT YOU'VE LEARNED

Check (✓) the outcomes you've met and vocabulary you've learned. Put an X next to the skills and vocabulary you still need to practice.

Learning Outcomes	Vocabulary		Multi-word Units
☐ Infer the use of humor	☐ career	☐ professional AWL	☐ get started
☐ Take notes with key words	☐ concentrate AWL	☐ quit	
☐ Recognize contrast	☐ creative AWL	☐ relaxing (*adj.*) AWL	
☐ Use descriptive adjectives	☐ factory	☐ stressful AWL	
☐ Use word stress	☐ flavor	☐ taste (*v.*)	
☐ Show interest	☐ income AWL	☐ tongue	
	☐ insurance policy	☐ tiring	

Go to **MyEnglishLab** to watch a video about an offbeat job, access the Unit Project, and take the Unit 1 Achievement Test.

Offbeat Jobs 25

At the end of the unit, students are directed to MyEnglishLab to watch a video connected to the theme, access the Unit Project, and take the Unit Achievement Test.

Academic Word List words are highlighted with AWL at the end of the unit.

MyEnglishLab

Home | Help | Sign out

NorthStar 2 Listening & Speaking

Focus on Speaking — Attempt 1

Speaking Practice: Showing Interest

Drag the words and phrases to complete the conversation.

Move

Me, too! | Oh, really? | What do you do? | Oh, I see | It's great! | It's all right | Good for you! | freetime | yeah | interesting

A: Hi, I'm Carolina.
B: Nice to meet you, Carolina. I'm Fatemah. So, what do you do?
A: I'm a dentist.
B: [DRAG ITEM HERE] How do you like it?
A: [DRAG ITEM HERE], but sometimes it's stressful. Most people don't like going to the dentist!
B: [DRAG ITEM HERE]. I can understand how that would be stressful.
A: How about you? [DRAG ITEM HERE]
B: I'm a student at City College. I'm studying business.
A: That's [DRAG ITEM HERE]! How do you like it?
B: [DRAG ITEM HERE] I love my classes.
A: [DRAG ITEM HERE] So, what do you like to do in your [DRAG ITEM HERE]?
B: I like to go jogging in the park.
A: Oh, [DRAG ITEM HERE]? [DRAG ITEM HERE]
B: Well, then we should go together sometime.
A: Sounds good!

Back to course | Save | Submit

MyEnglishLab

Key writing skills and strategies are reinforced and practiced in new contexts. Autograded skills-based activities provide instant scores, allowing teachers and students to identify where improvement is needed.

COMPONENTS

Students can access the following resources on the Pearson English Portal.

- **Classroom Audio and Videos**

  Classroom audio (the readings for the Reading & Writing strand and the listenings and exercises with audio for the Listening & Speaking strand) and the end-of-unit videos are available on the portal.

- **Etext**

  Offering maximum flexibility in order to meet the individual needs of each student, the digital version of the student book can be used across multiple platforms and devices.

- **MyEnglishLab**

  MyEnglishLab offers students access to additional practice online in the form of both auto-graded and teacher-graded activities. Auto-graded activities support and build on the academic and language skills presented and practiced in the student book. Teacher-graded activities include speaking and writing.

- **Pearson Practice English App**

  Students use the **Pearson Practice English App** to access additional grammar and vocabulary practice, audio for the listenings and readings from the student books, and the end-of-unit videos on the go with their mobile phone.

INNOVATIVE TEACHING TOOLS

With instant access to a wide range of online content and diagnostic tools, teachers can customize learning environments to meet the needs of every student. Digital resources, all available on the Pearson English Portal, include **MyEnglishLab** and ExamView.

Using MyEnglishLab, *NorthStar* teachers can

Deliver rich online content to engage and motivate students, including

- student audio to support listening and speaking skills, in addition to audio versions of all readings.
- engaging, authentic video clips tied to the unit themes.
- opportunities for written and recorded reactions to be submitted by students.

Use diagnostic reports to

- view student scores by unit, skill, and activity.
- monitor student progress on any activity or test as often as needed.
- analyze class data to determine steps for remediation and support.

Access Teacher Resources, including

- unit teaching notes and answer keys.
- downloadable diagnostic, achievement and placement tests, as well as unit checkpoints.
- printable resources including lesson planners, videoscripts, and video activities.
- classroom audio.

Using ExamView, teachers can customize Achievement Tests by

- reordering test questions.
- editing questions.
- selecting questions from a bank.
- writing their own questions.

SCOPE AND SEQUENCE

	1 Offbeat Jobs Pages: 2–25 Listening 1: What's My Job? Listening 2: A Conversation with a Job Counselor	**2 Where Does the Time Go?** Pages: 26–49 Listening 1: Student Success Workshop Listening 2: A Student Discussion
Inference	Inferring the use of humor	Inferring the purpose of questions
Note-Taking	Taking notes with key words	Taking notes with questions
Listening	Recognizing contrast	Identifying disagreement
Grammar	Descriptive adjectives	Simple present
Pronunciation	Using word stress	Identifying stressed and unstressed words
Speaking	Showing interest	Using your voice effectively
Final Speaking Task	Role-play: job interview	Presentation: strategies for student success
Video	An offbeat job	Creativity
Assessments	Pre-Unit Diagnostic: Check What You Know Checkpoint 1 Checkpoint 2 Unit Achievement Test	Pre-Unit Diagnostic: Check What You Know Checkpoint 1 Checkpoint 2 Unit Achievement Test
Unit Project	Research and present information on an offbeat job you'd like to have	Research and present more strategies for student success

3 A Penny Saved is a Penny Earned Pages: 50–71 Listening 1: A Barter Network Listening 2: The Compact	**4 What Happened to Etiquette?** Pages: 72–93 Listening 1: What ever happened to manners? Listening 2: Our Listeners Respond—Why is there a lack of manners?
Inferring feelings from intonation	Inferring contrasting ideas
Taking notes with symbols	Organizing your notes
Recognizing and understanding emphatic stress	Recognizing and understanding summaries and paraphrases
Comparative adjectives	*Can / Could / Would*
Pronouncing numbers and prices	Using rising and falling intonation in questions and statements
Making suggestions and coming to an agreement	Making polite offers and invitations
Role-play: bartering and negotiating	Role-play: situations involving etiquette
Money	Etiquette
Pre-Unit Diagnostic: Check What You Know Checkpoint 1 Checkpoint 2 Unit Achievement Test	Pre-Unit Diagnostic: Check What You Know Checkpoint 1 Checkpoint 2 Unit Achievement Test
Comparison shop for something you'd like to buy and report back on data for two similar items	Conduct a study about etiquette (door test, document drop, customer service test)

SCOPE AND SEQUENCE

	5 The Sounds of Our Lives Pages: 94–117 Listening 1: Sound Experience Listening 2: Music With A Purpose	**6 Everyday Heroes** Pages: 118–143 Listening 1: The Subway Hero Listening 2: Psychology Lecture—Altruism
Inference	Inferring meaning from context	Inferring feelings from tone and word choice
Note-Taking	Taking notes on cause and effect	Organizing notes with numbers
Listening	Recognizing incomplete and complete ideas	Recognizing and understanding definitions
Grammar	Simple present and present progressive	Simple past
Pronunciation	Linking sounds	Pronouncing *-ed* endings
Speaking	Showing confidence	Using signal phrases in presentations
Final Speaking Task	Presentation: a favorite piece of music	Presentation: everyday heroes
Video	Color psychology	Heroes
Assessments	Pre-Unit Diagnostic: Check What You Know Checkpoint 1 Checkpoint 2 Unit Achievement Test	Pre-Unit Diagnostic: Check What You Know Checkpoint 1 Checkpoint 2 Unit Achievement Test
Unit Project	Research and present on the effects sounds in our environment have on us	Research and present information on an organization that tries to help others

7 Take Care of Yourself Pages: 144–169 Listening 1: Self-Care Listening 2: Let's Hear from our Listeners	**8 Endangered Languages** Pages: 170–197 Listening 1: Language Loss Listening 2: My Life, My Language
Inferring a speaker's assumptions	Inferring a speaker's viewpoint
Taking notes with abbreviations	Taking notes on reasons and examples
Recognizing and understanding clarification	Recognizing and understanding pronoun reference
Should / Ought to / Have to	Modals of possibility: *Can / Could / Would*
Using reductions	Pronouncing contractions of *will*
Asking for and expressing opinions	Using pauses effectively
Group discussion: healthy habits	Presentation: an endangered language
Health problems	Endangered cultures
Pre-Unit Diagnostic: Check What You Know Checkpoint 1 Checkpoint 2 Unit Achievement Test	Pre-Unit Diagnostic: Check What You Know Checkpoint 1 Checkpoint 2 Unit Achievement Test
Research and present information on technology used to help people lead healthier lives	Research and report back on an endangered language and culture

ACKNOWLEDGMENTS

I would like to thank everyone at Pearson who helped to make this book possible. Special thanks to Debbie King, whose support and editorial insights were invaluable to me. I would also like to thank Stefan Frazier for his contributions to the audio.

—Laurie Frazier

REVIEWERS

Chris Antonellis, Boston University – CELOP; Gail August, Hostos; Aegina Barnes, York College; Kim Bayer, Hunter College; Mine Bellikli, Atilim University; Allison Blechman, Embassy CES; Paul Blomquist, Kaplan; Helena Botros, FLS; James Branchick, FLS; Chris Bruffee, Embassy CES; Joyce Cain University of California at Fullerton; Nese Cakli, Duzce University; Molly Cheny, University of Washington; María Cordani Tourinho Dantas, Colégio Rainha De Paz; Jason Davis, ASC English; Lindsay Donigan, Fullerton College; Mila Dragushanskaya, ASA College; Bina Dugan, BCCC; Sibel Ece Izmir, Atilim University; Érica Ferrer, Universidad del Norte; María Irma Gallegos Peláez, Universidad del Valle de México; Vera Figueira, UC Irvine; Rachel Fernandez, UC Irvine; Jeff Gano, ASA College; Emily Ellis, UC Irvine; María Genovev a Chávez Bazán, Universidad del Valle de México; Juan Garcia, FLS; Heidi Gramlich, The New England School of English; Phillip Grayson, Kaplan; Rebecca Gross, The New England School of English; Rick Guadiana, FLS; Sebnem Guzel, Tobb University; Esra Hatipoglu, Ufuk University; Brian Henry, FLS; Josephine Horna, BCCC; Judy Hu, UC Irvine; Arthur Hui, Fullerton College; Zoe Isaacson, Hunter College; Kathy Johnson, Fullerton College; Marcelo Juica, Urban College of Boston; Tom Justice, North Shore Community College; Lisa Karakas, Berkeley College; Eva Kopernacki, Embassy CES; Drew Larimore, Kaplan; Heidi Lieb, BCCC; Patricia Martins, Ibeu; Cecilia Mora Espejo, Universidad del Valle de México; Oscar Navarro University of California at Fullerton; Eva Nemtson, ASA College; Kate Nyhan, The New England School of English; Julie Oni, FLS; Willard Osman, The New England School of English; Olga Pagieva, ASA College; Manish Patel, FLS; Paige Poole, Universidad del Norte; Claudia Rebello, Ibeu; Amy Renehan, University of Washington; Lourdes Rey, Universidad del Norte; Michelle Reynolds, FLS International Boston Commons; Mary Ritter, NYU; Ellen Rosen University of California at Fullerton; Dana Saito-Stehiberger, UC Irvine; Dariusz Saczuk, ASA College; Miryam Salimov, ASA College; Minerva Santos, Hostos; Sezer Sarioz, Saint Benoit PLS; Gail Schwartz, UC Irvine; Ebru Sinar, Tobb University; Beth Soll, NYU (Columbia); Christopher Stobart, Universidad del Norte; Guliz Uludag, Ufuk University; Debra Un, NYU; Hilal Unlusu, Saint Benoit PLS; María del Carmen Viruega Trejo, Universidad del Valle de México; Reda Vural, Atilim University; Douglas Waters, Universidad del Norte; Emily Wong, UC Irvine; Leyla Yucklik, Duzce University; Jorge Zepeda Porras, Universidad del Valle de México

LEARNING OUTCOMES

- > Infer the use of humor
- > Take notes with key words
- > Recognize contrast
- > Use descriptive adjectives
- > Use word stress
- > Show interest

Go to **MyEnglishLab** to check what you know.

UNIT 1

Offbeat Jobs

1 FOCUS ON THE TOPIC

1. Look at the photo. What is happening? What is the person's job?
2. Read the title of the unit. *Offbeat* means "unusual." A bike messenger has an offbeat job. Can you think of other offbeat jobs?
3. What is most important to you when choosing a job? Think about things like salary (how much money you make), hours, interest, safety (how safe or dangerous it is), workplace (indoors, outdoors, home, office), education, and number of job openings (how easy it is to find a job). Compare your answers as a class.

2 FOCUS ON LISTENING

LISTENING ONE | What's My Job?

VOCABULARY

1 **Read and listen to the job postings on a website for college students. Notice the boldfaced words. Try to guess their meanings.**

Looking for a fun summer job? Need to earn some extra **income**? Here are some jobs you might like. Visit the College Job Center office for more information about these jobs.

Bike Messenger
Do you like activities that are exciting and sometimes dangerous? Do you like to work outdoors? Are you athletic? Then this offbeat job is just for you. For this job, you must have your own bike and be able to ride quickly through the city to deliver packages and letters to our customers.

Computer Assembler
Do you like computers? Do you know a lot about them? We need people to work in our **factory** to make computers. You must be fast and like to build things. You must also be able to **concentrate** so you put the parts together correctly without making mistakes.

Insurance Salesperson
Do you like sales? Do you like to work with people? Are you good with numbers? Come work in our insurance company. We sell every kind of **insurance policy**: auto, home, life, and medical.

Computer Animation Artist
Are you artistic? Are you good with computers? Do you like to play video and computer games? Then we have the right job for you. Our video game company makes games that are popular with many people, from children to adults of all ages. We are looking for young **creative** people to help us create interesting new characters for our games.

Restaurant Blogger
Do you like good food and eating out in restaurants? Are you a good writer? Then we need you! For this job, you will need to **taste** different kinds of food—even spicy food, such as Thai or Mexican. You also need a good sense of taste. Your **tongue** must be able to taste many different **flavors**, such as sweet or sour, so you can write about the foods you try.

Professional Secret Shopper
Do you like to shop, but you don't like to spend money? Then you have what it takes to **get started** as a **professional** shopper. Go shopping and get paid for it! Our stores hire secret shoppers to make sure the salespeople are doing a good job.

2 Match the words on the left with the definitions on the right.

d	1. concentrate	a.	able to make new things or think of new ideas
____	2. factory	b.	an agreement with an insurance company to be paid money in case of an accident, illness, or death
____	3. insurance policy	c.	to begin doing or working on something
____	4. creative	d.	~~to be careful and pay attention~~
____	5. income	e.	a building where things are made
____	6. taste *(v.)*	f.	the part inside of your mouth that moves and is used for tasting food and speaking
____	7. professional	g.	the particular sweetness, saltiness, sourness, spiciness, or bitterness of a food or drink
____	8. flavor	h.	relating to your job or work
____	9. get started	i.	try food by eating a little bit
____	10. tongue	j.	the money you earn when you work

Go to the **Pearson Practice English App** or **MyEnglishLab** for more vocabulary practice.

PREVIEW

1 People can have many different kinds of jobs. Some are usual and some are offbeat. Look at the picture and listen to the beginning of *What's My Job?* Circle the correct answer to complete each statement.

1. You are listening to a ________________ .
   a. job interview b. game show c. radio show
2. Wayne is a ________________ .
   a. host b. contestant c. guest
3. Rita is a ________________ .
   a. host b. contestant c. guest
4. Peter is going to describe ________________ .
   a. his job b. his company c. himself

2 Make predictions. What will Peter talk about? Check (✓) your guesses.

☐ what he does
☐ how much money he makes
☐ what he likes to do
☐ where he works
☐ what he is like

LISTEN

1 **Listen to the whole game show. Create a chart like the one below to take notes.**

TAKE NOTES What's my job?

Main Ideas	*Details*
Game show about offbeat jobs	*Wayne Williams = host*
	Rita = contestant
	Peter = guest #1

2 **Compare your notes with a partner's. How can you improve your notes?**

Go to MyEnglishLab to view example notes.

MAIN IDEAS

Circle the correct answers. Use your notes to help you.

1. Rita asks Peter ________ questions to guess his job.
   a. two b. three c. four
2. Peter works in a ________ .
   a. restaurant b. factory c. bakery
3. Peter is ________ .
   a. a factory worker b. a chef c. an ice-cream taster
4. Peter has to be careful with ________ .
   a. his taste buds b. the ice cream c. the factory machines
5. Peter thinks his job is ________ .
   a. tiring b. great c. dangerous

DETAILS

1 Listen again and add to your notes. Then read the statements. Write *T* (true) or *F* (false). Correct the false statements. Use your notes to help you.

____ 1. Peter can be creative at work.

____ 2. Peter thinks of new ice-cream flavors.

____ 3. He eats all the ice cream at work.

____ 4. He doesn't eat spicy foods.

____ 5. He doesn't drink alcohol or coffee.

____ 6. He smokes.

____ 7. He has a one-million-dollar insurance policy on his taste buds.

____ 8. He studied ice-cream tasting in school.

2 With a partner, take turns summarizing your notes. Then discuss how your notes and your answers in Preview helped you understand the listening.

Go to **MyEnglishLab** for more listening practice.

MAKE INFERENCES

Inferring the Use of Humor

An inference is a guess about something that is not said directly.

Usually speakers use words to express their true meaning, but sometimes speakers want to be funny or humorous. We often know when people are using humor when they use words we don't expect. Their words may be surprising, or they may express the opposite of what they mean. We also know when people are using humor when they laugh or use a humorous sound in their voice.

Listen to the example. Listen to the words and the tone of voice. Is the host expressing his true meaning, or is he using humor? Choose a or b. What words or tone can you hear that tell you the host's meaning?

Example

PETER: That's right. I work in an ice-cream factory. I make sure the ice cream tastes good. I also think of interesting new flavors to make.

HOST: Gee, sounds like a difficult job, Peter. You taste ice cream all day and you get paid for it!

PETER: Yes, that's right. I'm lucky to have such a great job.

a. true meaning

b. humor

Explanation

In the example, the host uses the word **difficult** to describe Peter's job, but the words he uses in the next sentence show that he really thinks it is easy to be an ice-cream taster. He just says it is difficult in order to be humorous. You can also hear from his tone that he is using humor.

Listen to the excerpts. Is Wayne expressing his true meaning or is he using humor? Circle the correct word.

Excerpt One

Wow! You do have to be careful.

a. true meaning b. humor

What words or tone of voice can you hear that tell you the speaker's meaning?

____

Excerpt Two

1. Gee, you do have an important job, Peter.

   a. true meaning b. humor

   What words or tone of voice can you hear that tell you the speaker's meaning?

   ____

2. Did you go to ice-cream tasting school?

   a. true meaning b. humor

   What words or tone of voice can you hear that tell you the speaker's meaning?

   ____

DISCUSS

USE YOUR NOTES

APPLY Find information in your notes to use in your discussion.

Work in a small group. Read the questions. Discuss your ideas

1. What three questions did Rita ask? Why didn't they help her guess Peter's job? Imagine she could ask another question. What question would help her guess his job?
2. What does Peter need to be able to do his job? Which parts of his job are easy? Which are difficult?
3. How did Peter get started in his job? Imagine you wanted to work as an ice-cream taster. What would you do to get started?

Go to MyEnglishLab to give your opinion about another question.

LISTENING TWO | A Conversation with a Job Counselor

VOCABULARY

1 Read the words in the box aloud. Then read the conversation and circle the correct definition of the boldfaced words.

career	quit	relaxing	stressful	tiring

Henry: Hi! How are you?

Eva: I'm great!

Henry: So, what's new?

Eva: Well, the big news is I have a new job.

Henry: You don't work at the bank anymore?

Eva: No, I **quit** my job at the bank six months ago.

Henry: Why?

Eva: I was working really long hours. It was so **tiring**. And there were so many problems at the bank. I was awake every night worrying about work. It was just too **stressful**. So I made a **career** change.

Henry: Really? What do you do now?

Eva: I'm a yoga teacher.

Henry: No kidding! That sure is a change. From bank manager to yoga teacher! How did you do it?

Eva: Well, I was already doing yoga all the time—to help with the stress—so I decided to take some classes to learn how to teach it. Now I work at a yoga studio, and I love it. Doing yoga is so **relaxing**. I'm not stressed anymore, and the best part is I get to help other people relax, too.

Henry: Good for you!

1. quit
   a. leave a job
   b. continue working at a job
2. tiring
   a. making you feel unhappy
   b. making you feel you want to rest
3. stressful
   a. causing you to feel worried
   b. difficult
4. career
   a. something you study in school
   b. a kind of work you do for a long time
5. relaxing
   a. helping you to rest
   b. helping you to work hard

Go to the **Pearson Practice English App** or **MyEnglishLab** for more vocabulary practice.

NOTE-TAKING SKILL

Taking Notes with Key Words

When you take notes, don't write every word you hear. Instead, write only the key words to help you to remember the ideas.

Write the key words that carry meaning. For example, write the important nouns, verbs, and adjectives. Don't write words that are not important to the meaning, such as pronouns, articles, and helping verbs.

Read and listen to the example below. Read the notes. Notice how they contain the key words.

Example

You hear:	You write:
PETER: At my job, I work with food. My work is very interesting because I can enjoy good food and I can be creative.	*Peter's job* *– work w/* food* *– enjoy good food, be creative*

* *w/* is a common way to shorten the word with in notes

1 **Listen to the sentences. Write the key words.**

a. ______________________________

b. ______________________________

c. ______________________________

d. ______________________________

2 **Review your notes from Listening One. Circle key words. Cross out words that aren't important. Then compare your edits with a partner.**

Go to **MyEnglishLab** for more note-taking practice.

COMPREHENSION

1 **Listen to two people talking with a job counselor about their jobs. A job counselor is someone who helps people find the right job or career. Create a chart like the one below to take notes. Try to write only the key words.**

USE YOUR NOTES

Compare your notes with a partner's. How can you improve your notes next time?

TAKE NOTES A Conversation with a Job Counselor

Main Ideas	*Details*

2 **Look at the statements in the chart below. Circle the key words. Then look for those key words in your notes. Use your notes to help you complete the chart. Put a check (✓) in the correct column for the window washer or the professional shopper. Some statements may be true for both.**

window washer

professional shopper

	WINDOW WASHER	PROFESSIONAL SHOPPER
a. I like my job.		
b. I work outdoors.		
c. I earn a high salary.		
d. My work is dangerous.		
e. I like to work with people.		
f. I'm good with money.		
g. I'm good with my hands.		
h. My work is tiring.		
i. It was difficult to get started in this job.		
j. I have my own business.		
k. I want to quit and find a new job.		
l. I don't want to be the boss.		
m. I like working for myself.		

LISTENING SKILL

1 Look at the sentences below. How can you complete them? Discuss your ideas with a partner.

1. I wanted to become a professional basketball player, but ________________.
2. My sister went to law school. However, ________________.

Think about the ideas you used to complete each sentence. Are they similar to or different from the first idea in each sentence?

Recognizing Contrast

But and *however* are connectors that introduce a clause with an idea, opinion, or action that is different from the first idea. They show a contrast.

Listen to the example.

Example

Notice the contrast word. What do you hear?

Explanation

The speaker is contrasting two ideas:

Idea 1: It was difficult to get started.

Idea 2: He started his own business. He likes working for himself.

He uses **but** to connect the two ideas.

2 Listen to the excerpts. Complete the ideas you hear. Then write the connector the speaker uses to show contrast.

Excerpt One

Idea 1: I love ________________, and I like ________________.

I'm very good ________________.

Idea 2: My job ________________.

I'm ________________, so my work ________________.

What word does she use to show the difference? ________________

Excerpt Two

Idea 1: I ________________ my job, and ________________.

I like ________________.

Idea 2: I have to ________________, and ________________.

What word does she use to show the difference? ________________

Go to **MyEnglishLab** for more skill practice.

CONNECT THE LISTENINGS

ORGANIZE

USE YOUR NOTES

APPLY Review your notes from Listening One and Two. Use the information in your notes to complete the chart.

Read the questions about these three unusual jobs. Then answer the questions with the information from Listening One and Two.

	WINDOW WASHER	PROFESSIONAL SHOPPER	ICE-CREAM TASTER
1. What does the person do?		*A professional shopper goes shopping for people who are busy.*	
2. What are the positive parts of this job?	*It's relaxing.*		
3. What are the negative parts of this job?			*You can't eat the ice cream.* *You have to take care of your taste buds.* *You can't eat spicy food.*
4. What skills do you need to do this job?	*You need to be good with your hands.*		

Compare your answers with a partner's. Discuss any differences.

SYNTHESIZE

Take turns asking each other about offbeat jobs. Use the questions and the information in the chart. Compare two of the offbeat jobs. What is similar? What is different?

Example

A: What does a professional shopper do?

B: A professional shopper goes shopping for people who are busy.

Switch roles and talk about a different job.

Go to **MyEnglishLab** to check what you learned.

3 FOCUS ON SPEAKING

VOCABULARY

REVIEW

Match the statement on the left with the best response on the right.

__b__ 1. My friend went to school to learn to cook. She just got her first job cooking in a French restaurant. She loves her job.

_____ 2. Working for myself isn't easy. I have a lot of work to do.

_____ 3. I don't like my job. I want to get a new job.

_____ 4. I need to work where it's very quiet. I have to pay very close attention so I don't make any mistakes.

_____ 5. I love making up stories. Someday I want to write my own book.

_____ 6. I want to be a doctor. I know I need to be in school for a long time, but being a doctor is my dream.

_____ 7. I worked really hard all week, so last weekend I just stayed home and watched movies.

_____ 8. I think walking dogs for a job is fun. The only problem is that all the walking is a lot of work!

a. It sounds like you want to **quit**!

b. ~~You're so lucky your friend is a **professional** chef! Does she ever cook for you?~~

c. Wow, having your own business sounds **stressful**.

d. You're very **creative**.

e. That sounds **relaxing**!

f. If that's really what you want to do, I think it's a **career** you will enjoy.

g. Yes, it's a **tiring** job.

h. You really need to **concentrate**.

EXPAND

Work with a partner. Read the sentences below. Circle the best definition for each boldfaced word or phrase.

A **workaholic** works long hours.

1. I work 60 hours a week, and I always think about my work. I'm a **workaholic.**

   A **workaholic** is a person who ________________ .

   a. finds it difficult not to work   b. thinks too much

2. I want a career where I can work with money. I am very **good with numbers.**

   Someone who is **good with numbers** ________________ .

   a. likes to count and do math   b. doesn't like doing math

3. I want to be a professional shopper because **I don't want to have a boss.**

   If **I don't want to have a boss**, I want to ________________ .

   a. work for myself   b. work in a big company

4. Some people like office jobs. Not me. I enjoy a job that lets me make things. I'm **good with my hands.**

   A person who is **good with his or her hands** ________________ .

   a. likes to do office work all day   b. is good at fixing or building things

A carpenter is **good with her hands.**

5. I'm good at finding solutions to difficult situations. My friends often ask me to help them. They say I am a good **problem solver.**

   A **problem solver** ________________ .

   a. is good at finding the best way to do something   b. needs a lot of help doing things

6. I think being up high washing windows is exciting, but it's important to be careful so you don't fall or have an accident. If you aren't careful, it can be very **dangerous.**

   A **dangerous** job is not ________________ .

   a. exciting   b. safe

7. I'm good at telling people what I think, and I can explain things well. I'm clear when I speak. I have **good communication skills.**

   A person with **good communication skills** ________________ .

   a. is difficult to understand   b. is easy to understand

8. I always come to work on time and do my work well. Sometimes I stay longer at work to finish my job. My boss says I'm **hardworking**.

   A **hardworking** person ________________ .

   a. works a lot and is not lazy
   b. doesn't do a good job

9. My favorite job was working in a restaurant. There were many people working there, and we worked well together. We were all **team players**.

   A **team player** ________________ .

   a. works alone and doesn't help others
   b. works in a group and helps others

10. I worked in a store last year. The boss let me count the money at the end of the day and take it to the bank. My boss didn't worry because I am **trustworthy**.

   A **trustworthy** person is ________________ .

   a. honest
   b. not honest

11. I love my job as a dog walker. I don't have to sit indoors at a desk. I can work **outdoors** in the fresh air and sunshine.

   A job that is **outdoors** is ________________ .

   a. not a desk job
   b. inside a building

12. I really enjoy working in a store because I like talking to and helping people. I have **good people skills**.

   Someone with **good people skills** ________________ .

   a. can relate well with other people
   b. is usually shy

She has **good people skills**.

CREATE

1 Look at the words in the chart. Add more ideas. Think about your skills and characteristics. Then think about the types of jobs that are related to your skills and characteristics.

SKILLS *Talents or abilities*	CHARACTERISTICS *Your strengths (strong points) and weaknesses (weak points)*	TYPES OF JOBS
be good with numbers	friendly	indoors
be good with my hands	creative	outdoors
have good people skills	hardworking	safe
have good communication skills	trustworthy	dangerous
____________________	a team player	high-paying
____________________	a problem solver	offbeat
____________________	a workaholic	stressful
	____________________	relaxing
	____________________	tiring
	____________________	____________________
		____________________
		____________________

2 APPLY Work with a partner. Student A, you are a job counselor. Ask the questions below. Student B, you want to change jobs. Answer your partner's questions. Use the words from the box above and vocabulary from Review and Expand in your answers.

1. **A:** Tell me about yourself. What do you do now? What's it like?
   B: I'm ____________________.
   It's ____________________.
2. **A:** What are your strengths? Can you give me an example?
   B: I ____________________.
   For example, ____________________.
3. **A:** What are your weaknesses? Could I have an example?
   B: I ____________________.
   For example, ____________________.
4. **A:** What type of job do you want? Why do you want this job?
   B: I'd like a job as ____________________.
   I'd like a job that is ____________________.
   I want this job because ____________________.
5. **A:** What skills do you have?
   B: I ____________________.

Now switch roles.

Go to the **Pearson Practice English App** or **MyEnglishLab** for more vocabulary practice.

GRAMMAR FOR SPEAKING

1 Work with a partner. Read the conversations aloud. Look at the underlined words. Then answer the questions.

1. **A:** What's your job like?
   B: My job is <u>interesting</u>.

2. **A:** What kind of person are you?
   B: I'm a <u>friendly</u> person.

a. Look at the answers to the questions. What is the verb in each sentence?
b. What is the noun in each sentence?
c. Which words describe the nouns? Where do they come in the sentences?

Descriptive Adjectives

ADJECTIVES DESCRIBE NOUNS.	
1. Adjectives can come after the verb ***be***.	*My job* ***is tiring****.*
2. Adjectives can also come before a noun.	*Artists are* ***creative people****.*
3. When a singular noun follows an adjective, use ***a*** before the adjective if the adjective begins with a consonant sound.	*This isn't* ***a high-paying job****.*
4. When a singular noun follows an adjective, use ***an*** before the adjective if the adjective begins with a vowel sound.	*Peter has* ***an offbeat job****.*

2 Some words describe a person, some describe a job, and some describe both. Write the words in the correct box. If the word can describe a person and a job, write it in both boxes.

boring	dangerous	friendly	hardworking	interesting	offbeat	safe	tiring
creative	difficult	happy	high-paying	low-paying	relaxing	stressful	

WORDS ABOUT PEOPLE	WORDS ABOUT JOBS
a(n) ________________ person	a(n) ________________ job

3 Work with a partner. Take turns making statements using the nouns and adjectives provided. React by saying, "I agree" or "I don't agree. / I disagree." If you don't agree with a statement, correct it.

Example

Restaurant blogging / dangerous

A: Restaurant blogging is dangerous.

B: I don't agree. Restaurant blogging isn't dangerous. It's safe.

1. a bike messenger's job / tiring
2. an ice-cream taster / creative person
3. selling insurance / stressful
4. computer animation /offbeat job
5. window washing / interesting job
6. a game show host / hardworking
7. a professional shopper's job / relaxing

4 APPLY Make a list of your top five favorite jobs. Discuss them with a partner. Use descriptive adjectives to describe the jobs on your list.

Go to the **Pearson Practice English App** or **MyEnglishLab** for more grammar practice. Check what you learned in **MyEnglishLab**.

PRONUNCIATION

Using Word Stress

In words with multiple syllables, one syllable is stressed. Stressed syllables sound longer than unstressed syllables. They are also louder and higher in pitch than unstressed syllables.

Listen to the examples.

Example One

careful	creative

A compound noun is formed when two nouns are used together as one noun. In compound nouns, the stress is stronger on the stressed syllable in the first word in the compound.

Example Two

bike messenger	salesperson

When an adjective is followed by a noun, the stress is usually stronger on the noun.

Example Three

A professional shopper	A good salary

1 **Listen to the adjectives. Write the number of syllables you hear in each adjective. Then listen again and underline the stressed syllable. Listen a third time and repeat the words.**

____ 1. dangerous

____ 2. important

____ 3. tiring

____ 4. educated

____ 5. difficult

____ 6. spicy

____ 7. unusual

____ 8. interesting

2 **Read each item and underline the stressed syllable. Next, listen to check your answers. Then work with a partner. Take turns saying each item and listening for the correct stress.**

1. animation artist
2. window washer
3. boring job
4. computer assembler
5. ice cream
6. spicy foods
7. department store

3 **Work with a partner. Student A, ask *Wh-* questions with the phrases on the left. Student B, respond with the correct answer from the phrases on the right. Be sure to use the correct stress. Switch roles after item 4.**

Example

A: What do you call someone who washes windows?

B: A window washer.

__b__ 1. someone who washes windows

____ 2. a frozen dessert

____ 3. someone who sells things

____ 4. someone who makes animated movies or games

____ 5. a large store that sells many different products

____ 6. someone who puts together computers

____ 7. a person who delivers letters and packages by bike

____ 8. someone who helps people find the right job or career

a. bike messenger

b. ~~window washer~~

c. job counselor

d. computer assembler

e. ice cream

f. department store

g. animation artist

h. salesperson

SPEAKING SKILL

Showing Interest

When we speak to others, it is polite to show interest in the other person and in what he or she says. We can show interest with our words and also with body language.

ASKING SOMEONE QUESTIONS	TALKING ABOUT YOURSELF	SHOWING INTEREST	
		WITH WORDS	WITH BODY LANGUAGE
What do you do?	*I'm not working right now.* *I'm a (student / chef / homemaker).* *I'm retired.*[1]	*Oh . . . really?*	Make eye contact. (Look at the person.) Nod your head up and down to show you are listening.
How do you like it?	*It's great.* *It's interesting.*	*Good for you.*	Smile at the person.
	It's all right, but . . . *I don't like it at all.*	*Oh, I see.* *Oh, why not?*	Use a facial expression to show concern.
What do you like to do in your free time?	*I like to (listen to music / play tennis).* *I enjoy (reading / playing computer games).*	*That's interesting.* *That's nice.* *Really? Me, too!* *Oh, yeah?*	Raise your eyebrows to show you are pleasantly surprised and interested.

[1] **retired:** no longer working at a job, usually because of age

Showing concern

Showing pleasant surprise and interest

Work with a partner. Complete the conversation with your own information. Then practice it aloud. Show interest with your words and body language.

A: Hi. My name's ______________________.

B: Hi. I'm ______________________. Nice to meet you.

A: Nice to meet you, too. So what do you do?

B: I'm ______________________.

A: ______________________. How do you like it?

B: ______________________. How about you? What do you do?

A: ______________________.

B: ______________________. So what do you like to do in your free time?

A: ______________________. How about you?

B: ______________________.

Go to MyEnglishLab for more skill practice and to check what you learned.

Using the right body language helps make a good impression during a job interview.

FINAL SPEAKING TASK: A Job Interview APPLY

In this activity, you will take part in a job interview. You will choose a job that you would like to have. Your partner will interview you for the job.

STEP 1

Choose one job from the list below or another job. List the reasons you want to have this job. Then list the strengths and skills you have that will help you to do that job. Use words and phrases from Review and Expand. Give examples of times you used those strengths and skills.

computer animation artist	bike messenger	restaurant blogger
insurance salesperson	computer assembler	game show host
window washer	ice-cream taster	professional shopper
other: ____________		

Example

JOB: COMPUTER ANIMATION ARTIST		
Why do you want this job?	*like to work with computers* *like cartoons* *want to work indoors in an office*	
What are your strengths?	*creative* *hardworking* *team player*	*Examples:* *think of my own characters and cartoons* *finish my school work on time* *work with other students on group projects*
What skills do you have?	*good with computers* *good with my hands* *good at drawing pictures*	*Examples:* *know computer animation programs*

STEP 2

APPLY **Use the vocabulary, grammar, pronunciation, and speaking skills from the unit. Use the checklist to help you.**

- ☐ **Vocabulary:** Read through the list of vocabulary on page 25. Which words can you include in your notes from Step 1 to make it clearer and more interesting? Choose at least three words or phrases to use and add them to your notes.
- ☐ **Grammar:** Scan your notes for descriptive adjectives. Are they in the correct place? Do you need to add *a* or *an* in front of them?
- ☐ **Pronunciation:** Look for examples of compound nouns and adjectives + nouns in your notes. Which syllable should you stress in each? Underline it.
- ☐ **Speaking Skill:** Review ways to show interest in the other person with words and body language.

STEP 3

1 **Work with a partner. Student A, you are the job interviewer. Greet your partner and ask questions to find out if they are the right person for the job. Take notes of your partner's answers. Student B, you are interviewing for a job. Answer the interviewer's questions. Then switch roles.**

2 **Report back to the class. Do you want to hire (choose) your partner for the job? Why or why not?**

ALTERNATIVE SPEAKING TOPIC

APPLY **Discuss the questions. Use the vocabulary, grammar, pronunciation, and speaking skills you learned from the unit.**

1. Why do you think some people like offbeat jobs?
2. How do you think most people get started in their offbeat jobs in the first place?
3. What job skills do you think are the most difficult to learn? Why do you think they are difficult?
4. What skills do you think are most important for students to learn so they can find a job or start a career in the future?

CHECK WHAT YOU'VE LEARNED

Check (✔) the outcomes you've met and vocabulary you've learned. Put an X next to the skills and vocabulary you still need to practice.

Learning Outcomes
- ☐ Infer the use of humor
- ☐ Take notes with key words
- ☐ Recognize contrast
- ☐ Use descriptive adjectives
- ☐ Use word stress
- ☐ Show interest

Vocabulary
- ☐ career
- ☐ concentrate AWL
- ☐ creative AWL
- ☐ factory
- ☐ flavor
- ☐ income AWL
- ☐ insurance policy
- ☐ professional AWL
- ☐ quit
- ☐ relaxing (*adj.*) AWL
- ☐ stressful AWL
- ☐ taste (*v.*)
- ☐ tongue
- ☐ tiring

Multi-word Units
- ☐ get started

Go to **MyEnglishLab** to watch a video about an offbeat job, access the Unit Project, and take the Unit 1 Achievement Test.

LEARNING OUTCOMES

- > Infer the purpose of questions
- > Take notes with questions
- > Identify disagreement
- > Use the simple present
- > Identify stressed and unstressed words
- > Use your voice effectively

Go to **MyEnglishLab** to check what you know.

UNIT 2

Where Does the Time Go?

1 FOCUS ON THE TOPIC

1. Look at the student in the photo. What activities do you think he is doing? Do you ever do any of these activities at the same time? Which ones?
2. *Challenges* are things that are difficult to do. What are some challenges that students face? What are some challenges you face as a student?
3. Read the title of the unit. What do you think this expression means? When do people say this?

2 FOCUS ON LISTENING

LISTENING ONE | Student Success Workshop

VOCABULARY

1 Read and listen to the college website about a student workshop. Notice the boldfaced words. Try to guess their meanings.

City College Counseling Center
Student Success[1] Workshop

- Do you feel like you don't have enough time to finish all of your daily **tasks** and assignments?
- Do you spend a lot of time studying but still get poor grades?
- Do you have trouble concentrating in classes and lectures?
- Do you delay doing your school work and **put off** your assignments until just before they are due?

If you answered "yes" to any of these questions, then this College Success Workshop is for you!

There are many **factors** that lead to student success, such as choosing the right classes, having good study skills, getting help from teachers and counselors, and staying healthy and active. Another important factor is time management. Many students don't know how to **manage** their time well. For example, do you try to multitask or do other activities when you study, such as text messaging friends while you do homework? You may think you are saving time, but in fact multitasking has a **negative** effect on your ability to think and learn. Many **research studies** show that our brains are not able to concentrate on more than one challenging task at a time. Studies also show that students who multitask do worse in school than students who don't. They take more time to finish their work, and they receive lower test scores and grades.

Another big problem for students is **procrastination**. Do you have a hard time getting started on assignments? Do you **avoid** your schoolwork by doing other activities instead? Or maybe you quit working on assignments when you don't know how to finish. Then you are a procrastinator. Procrastinators avoid doing the things they should be doing now, saying they will do them later.

But don't worry. We are here to help. In our one-day workshop, we will give you **strategies** to help you:

- set **goals** and organize the tasks you need to get done
- learn better study habits
- avoid **distractions** that keep you from getting your work done
- stop procrastinating and get things done on time

Don't put it off any longer! Sign up in the counseling office today. College success will be your **reward**!

[1] **success:** being able to do what you tried to do or want to do

2 Match each boldfaced word or phrase in the text with its definition or synonym.

h	1. tasks	a.	things you want to do in the future
____	2. put off	b.	things that make it difficult to think or pay attention
____	3. factors	c.	something that is given for doing good work
____	4. manage	d.	harmful or bad
____	5. negative	e.	to have control of something
____	6. research studies	f.	plans or ways to get something done
____	7. procrastination	g.	to delay something
____	8. avoid	h.	~~jobs or pieces of work that must be done~~
____	9. strategies	i.	things that cause a situation
____	10. goals	j.	careful studies to report new knowledge about something
____	11. distractions	k.	the act of delaying something you must do, usually because you do not want to do it
____	12. reward (*n.*)	l.	to choose not to do something or to stay away from someone or something

Go to the PearsonPracticeEnglishApp and **MyEnglishLab** for more vocabulary practice.

PREVIEW

A college counselor welcomes new students to a workshop on time management for college success.

Listen to the beginning of a student success workshop. What strategies do you think the counselor will suggest to study and manage your time?

1. ______________________________

2. ______________________________

3. ______________________________

LISTEN

1 Listen to the whole workshop. Create a chart like the one below to take notes.

TAKE NOTES Student Success Workshop

Main Ideas	Details
Multitasking → negative effects on success	*Ex: surf web + chat + study* *Goal: avoid*

2 Compare your notes with a partner's. How can you improve your notes?

Go to **MyEnglishLab** to view example notes.

MAIN IDEAS

Check (✓) the strategies that the counselor suggests. Use your notes to help you.

____ 1. Set goals and write down all of the tasks you need to do.

____ 2. Put your list of goals in order.

____ 3. Review your class notes every day.

____ 4. Use a calendar to schedule your time.

____ 5. Divide big assignments into smaller tasks.

____ 6. When school is stressful, take a lot of breaks.

____ 7. Avoid distractions.

____ 8. Join a study group.

____ 9. Reward yourself for finishing your work on time.

DETAILS

1 Listen again and add to your notes. Circle the best answer to complete each statement. Use your notes to help you.

1. ________ of the students in the workshop like to multitask while they study.

   a. A few

   b. A lot

   c. All

2. ________ percent of students procrastinate sometimes.

   a. 20–35

   b. 70–85

   c. 80–95

3. The counselor suggests that you order your goals from ________ .
   a. most important to least important
   b. most difficult to least difficult
   c. biggest to smallest
4. The counselor suggests that you schedule things like ________ .
   a. exercising, taking naps, and seeing movies
   b. exercising, getting enough sleep, and seeing friends
   c. eating, doing homework, and taking breaks
5. The counselor thinks you should ________ to get your work done.
   a. find the strategies that work best for you
   b. always use the "Do Nothing" strategy
   c. do your English paper all at once
6. With the "Do Nothing" strategy, you can ________ .
   a. do your work or do nothing
   b. get distracted or do nothing
   c. turn off your phone or do nothing
7. ________ is NOT a way to remove distractions.
   a. Putting away your video games
   b. Turning off your Internet
   c. Reading but not answering your text messages
8. Piers Steel took ________ to finish his research on procrastination.
   a. 2 years
   b. 10 years
   c. 20 years
9. Piers Steel suggests giving away ________ if you don't get your work done.
   a. some money
   b. your phone
   c. your video games

2 With a partner, take turns summarizing your notes. Then discuss how your notes and your answers in Preview helped you understand the listening.

Go to **MyEnglishLab** for more listening practice.

MAKE INFERENCES

Inferring the Purpose of Questions

An inference is a guess about something that is not said directly.

Speakers often ask questions when they are teaching or presenting information. This is a way to get our attention and involve us in the presentation. Sometimes we need to guess when a speaker wants responses to a question or when a speaker wants us to just listen for the answer. When speakers want us to respond, they may use a signal phrase, for example, *Tell me* or *How many...?* These phrases tell us the speaker wants the audience to answer. Speakers also pause and wait for us to answer the question or raise our hands.

However, sometimes speakers just want us to pay attention and think about the answer to a question. In this case, speakers don't wait long enough for us to respond. Instead, they answer the questions themselves.

Read and listen to the example. How do you know the speaker wants a response?

Example One

COLLEGE COUNSELOR: So, how many of you like to multitask—you know, like surf the web or chat with your friends while you study? . . . OK, I see a lot of you.

Explanation

In this example, the speaker signals that she wants the audience to respond to the question by saying "So how many of you...?" She also pauses and waits for the students to respond.

Read and listen to the example. How do you know the speaker doesn't want a response?

Example Two

COLLEGE COUNSELOR: And be careful with big assignments, like that English paper. You can't do it all at once, right? No, you need to divide it into smaller tasks that you can do one at a time.

Explanation

In this example, the speaker doesn't wait for responses. She just wants us to think about the answer, but then she answers the question herself.

Listen to three excerpts from the workshop. Does the speaker want the students to respond? How do you know? Circle the correct answer.

Excerpt One

1. The speaker ________________.
   a. wants the audience to respond   b. just wants the audience's attention

How do you know?

2. The speaker ________________ to invite a response.
   a. uses signal phrases   b. doesn't use signal phrases
3. The speaker ________________ for a response.
   a. waits   b. doesn't wait

Excerpt Two

1. The speaker ________________ .

   a. wants the audience to respond   b. just wants the audience's attention

How do you know?

2. The speaker ________________ to invite a response.

   a. uses signal phrases   b. doesn't use signal phrases

3. The speaker ________________ for a response.

   a. waits   b. doesn't wait

Excerpt Three

1. The speaker ________________ .

   a. wants the audience to respond   b. just wants the audience's attention

How do you know?

2. The speaker ________________ to invite a response.

   a. uses signal phrases   b. doesn't use signal phrases

3. The speaker ________________ for a response.

   a. waits   b. doesn't wait

USE YOUR NOTES

APPLY Find information in your notes to use in your discussion.

DISCUSS

Work in a small group. Read the questions. Discuss your ideas.

1. How does multitasking affect students' ability to study? Why do you think it has this effect? Why do you think people multitask?
2. How many students procrastinate? What do you think is the main reason that students procrastinate? What reason is given in the text? Is there ever a good reason to procrastinate?
3. Which of the strategies mentioned by the counselor is the most useful for students? Are there any you would never try? Why or why not? What other strategies do you use?

Go to MyEnglishLab to give your opinion about another question.

LISTENING TWO | A Student Discussion

VOCABULARY

Read the words in the box aloud. Then read the statements. Circle the best definition for the boldfaced word or phrase.

achieve	focus	positive attitude	pressure	waste

1. Anita wants to graduate from college. She is a good student, so I'm sure she will **achieve** her goal.

   a. to want to do something

   b. to succeed in doing something you want

2. When you are in class, it's important to **focus** on what the teacher is saying. You should pay attention so you can remember the important points.

   a. to direct your attention or effort

   b. to remember what someone told you

3. This history class is challenging, but I have a **positive attitude**, and I think that I can do well if I work hard.

   a. a hardworking person

   b. a hopeful way of thinking

4. At my school, there is a lot of **pressure** to get good grades. Some parents and teachers even expect you to get straight A's.

   a. getting good grades in school

   b. feeling of stress because people expect you to do something

5. My roommate **wastes** a lot of time talking on the phone when she should be doing her homework. Then she never has enough time to finish.

   a. to use something in a way that is not useful or effective

   b. to do something quickly

Go to the **Pearson Practice English App** or **MyEnglishLab** for more vocabulary practice.

NOTE-TAKING SKILL

Taking Notes with Questions

Speakers ask questions for different reasons. Sometimes they want listeners to answer a question, sometimes they want them to just think about a question, and sometimes they ask questions to introduce the important ideas that they will discuss. Noting questions and answers about the important information can help you to remember and study it later.

Listen to the example and read the notes. Notice how the notes include information about both the question and the answer.

Example One

How often Ss procrastinate?

- *80–95% sometimes*
- *20% often*

Even if a speaker doesn't ask questions about the important ideas, it is helpful to write your own questions that will help you to review and study your notes. Before you listen, leave extra space on the margins of your paper to write questions. After you listen, review your notes and write questions next to the information you want to remember. To study, ask yourself the questions and try to answer them without looking at your notes.

Listen to another example and look at the notes. Notice how the student added a study question to the notes after class.

Example Two

	Factors → student success
	• *choose right classes*
What are some factors in student success?	• *good study skills*
	• *get help from teachers + counselors*
	• *stay healthy + active*
	• *time management*

1 **Listen to the excerpts. Note the questions and answers.**

Excerpt One

____?

1. ____

2. . . .

Excerpt Two

____?

1. ____

2. . . .

2 Listen and take notes. Then write a question that will help you to review the information. Compare your notes and study question with a partner.

____

____

____

3 Review your notes from Listening One. Write questions that you can use to review and study your notes.

Go to **MyEnglishLab** for more note-taking practice.

COMPREHENSION

USE YOUR NOTES

Compare your notes with a partner's. How can you improve your notes next time?

1 Listen to a group of students having a discussion in the college success workshop. Create a chart like the one below to take notes. Try to note questions and answers in your notes.

TAKE NOTES A Student Discussion

Main Ideas	*Details*

2 Who would say these statements? Check (✓) Annie, Sam, and / or Justin. Some statements may be true for more than one student. Use your notes to help you.

	ANNIE	SAM	JUSTIN
a. My grades aren't very good.			
b. I want to go to medical school.			
c. My parents pressure me to get straight A's.			
d. I multitask while I'm studying or in class.			
e. I listen to music and chat with friends while I study.			
f. I surf the web while I'm working on the computer.			
g. Sometimes it's hard for me to focus in class.			
h. I don't think multitasking is so bad for you.			
i. I put off assignments that are hard.			
j. I put off assignments I don't like to do.			
k. It's important to me to achieve my goals.			
l. I want to set goals and schedule my time better.			
m. I plan to put my phone away during class.			
n. I plan to give myself rewards for getting my work done.			

LISTENING SKILL

1 Read the statement below. Imagine you have a different opinion. What would you say to disagree?

I think it's OK to multitask while you study.

Identifying Disagreement

Speakers use different phrases to disagree with each other's opinions. To disagree politely, speakers usually avoid saying "I disagree with you" directly. Instead, they use other phrases to disagree and then give a different opinion.

Read and listen to the excerpt. Notice the boldfaced phrases.

Example

SAM: My counselor said this workshop would help, but **I don't know**. I think we're wasting our time.

ANNIE: **Really? You think so?** I hope it's going to be useful. I want to go to medical school, so it's really important for me to do well in school.

Explanation

In this example, Sam expresses his disagreement with the counselor's opinion by saying "I don't know." This is a polite way to say "I disagree" or "I have a different opinion." Annie disagrees by saying "Really?" After expressing disagreement, both Sam and Annie give a different opinion.

2 Listen to excerpts. Write the phrase the second speaker uses to disagree. Then write the speaker's different opinion.

Excerpt One

Phrase to disagree: ______________________________

Different opinion: ______________________________

Excerpt Two

Phrase to disagree: ______________________________

Different opinion: ______________________________

Go to MyEnglishLab for more skill practice.

USE YOUR NOTES

APPLY Review your notes from Listening One and Two. Use the information in your notes to complete the chart.

CONNECT THE LISTENINGS

ORGANIZE

Complete the chart with the students' statements about their bad study habits in Listening Two. Then write the strategies from Listening One that the students could use to improve their study habits.

Try the "Do Nothing" Strategy
~~Waste time playing video games instead of studying~~
Text friends during class
~~Set goals and put them in order of importance~~
Divide big assignments into smaller tasks
Put off assignments that you don't like to do
Listen to music and chat online while doing homework
Use a calendar to plan your time
Give yourself rewards for finishing your work
Avoid starting difficult assignments
~~Remove distractions, such as phones, games, Internet~~
Surf the web while working online

BAD STUDY HABITS FROM LISTENING TWO	STRATEGIES FROM LISTENING ONE
MULTITASKING	
1.	*Remove distractions, such as phones, games, Internet*
2.	
3.	
PROCRASTINATION	
1. *Waste time playing video games instead of studying*	a. *Set goals and put them in order of importance*
	b.
2.	a.
	b.
3.	

SYNTHESIZE

Work in groups of three. Discuss your study habits and strategies for improving them. Use information from the chart. In your discussion, you can ask these questions:

1. Do you multitask? If so, what do you do?
2. Do you procrastinate? Why or why not?
3. What strategies do you want to try?
4. What other strategies do you suggest for each other?

Example

A: Sam, do you multitask?

B: Yes, I do. I use my phone to text friends in class.

C: How about you, Justin?

Go to **MyEnglishLab** to check what you learned.

3 FOCUS ON SPEAKING

VOCABULARY

REVIEW

Work with a partner. Complete the chart with the words and phrases from the box. Which words can go together? Some words and phrases can be used in more than one column. Then think of at least two more words or phrases to add to the chart. Take turns making sentences using a verb and word or phrase from the chart.

~~distractions~~	negative effects	success	tasks
goals	a positive attitude	strategies	time

ACHIEVE	AVOID	HAVE	MANAGE	PUT OFF	SET
	distractions	*distractions*	*distractions*		

EXPAND

1 Read and listen to the conversation. Notice the boldfaced words and phrases. Try to guess their meanings.

A: Hey, how's it going?

B: Not bad. So what's up?

A: Oh, I'm on my way to the library. I need to **hit the books**. I've got a biology midterm tomorrow.

B: Biology? That should be easy.

A: Yeah, easy for you to say! You **aced** biology, right? My problem is I **cut class** a lot at the beginning of the semester, and I didn't study much because my roommate kept asking me to **hang out** with him. I really **fell behind**. Now I have to try to catch up on everything before tomorrow's test.

B: Ouch. Sounds like you really put it off to **the last minute**.

A: Tell me about it. I think I'm going to have to **pull an all-nighter** tonight.

B: I don't know. If you ask me, that's not such a good idea. I pulled a few all-nighters to study last semester, and I **bombed** the tests because I was too tired. It's just too hard to focus without enough sleep.

A: Yeah, well, I guess I'll learn the hard way. So, how about you? What are you up to?

B: I'm just on my way to my chemistry professor's office. There's a homework problem I can't **figure out**, and I need to get some help.

A: OK, well I'd better get to the library. I need to **cram** for that test!

B: Good luck!

2 Match the phrases on the left with the meanings on the right.

____ 1. hit the books
____ 2. ace
____ 3. cut class
____ 4. hang out
____ 5. fall behind
____ 6. the last minute
____ 7. pull an all-nighter
____ 8. bomb
____ 9. figure out
____ 10. cram

a. to stay up all night working on something
b. the last possible time that something can be done
c. to study
d. to understand or solve by thinking
e. to receive a grade of an "A," or to complete something easily and successfully
f. to fail to do something as quickly as planned or as required
g. to quickly prepare right before a test
h. to skip a class or day of school without an excuse
i. to fail a test
j. to spend time in a certain place or with people

CREATE

APPLY **Work with a partner. Choose one of the situations. Use at least 5–7 words from Review and Expand to write a conversation. Tell the class how many different words you used (but don't tell them which words). Perform your conversation for the class. The other students will listen and answer these questions:**

- Who are the speakers?
- What is the situation?
- Which speaker do you agree with? Why?
- Which vocabulary items did the speakers use? Did they use them correctly?

SITUATION 1: You are a student and a professor discussing an assignment that is due. Student A, you ask the professor for more time to finish the assignment. Student B, you are the professor. You want the student to turn in the assignment on time.

SITUATION 2: You are a student and a counselor. Student A, you need some help managing your time and learning better study habits. Student B, you are the counselor. Give the students some advice.

SITUATION 3: You are a student and a parent talking about school. Student A, you are not doing very well in school. Student B, you are the parent. You are disappointed. Ask your child to explain his or her poor grades.

SITUATION 4: You are roommates in college. Student A, you have a big test tomorrow and want to study. You're nervous. Student B, you want to have a party, but your roommate doesn't want one. You're upset with your roommate.

Go to the **Pearson Practice English App** or **MyEnglishLab** for more vocabulary practice.

GRAMMAR FOR SPEAKING

1 Read the questions and responses. Then answer the questions below.

Questions	Answers
Are you a student?	Yes, I am.
Is she in your class?	No, she isn't.
What is your major?	My major is English.
Do you procrastinate?	Yes, I do.
Does your class meet today?	No, it doesn't.
How often do you go to the library?	I go to the library every evening.
Where does your friend live?	He lives in the dormitory.
Why do they always eat out?	They don't know how to cook.

a. What is the verb in each question or answer? Underline it.

b. Which questions and answers have only one-part (or one-word) verbs? Which ones have two-part verbs (the main verb and an auxiliary verb)? Write *1* or *2* next to them.

c. What form are the verbs? ______________

Simple Present

1. Use the simple present tense to talk about actions that happen again and again, such as habits and routines.	*I usually **go** to sleep at 11:00 pm.*
2. Use the simple present tense to tell facts.	*About 20 percent of students **procrastinate** often.*
3. Use the simple present with non-action, or stative, verbs such as *be, have, know, understand, like, prefer, need,* and *want*.	*I **prefer** to study alone.*
4. In affirmative statements, use the base form of the verb with subjects *I, you, we,* and *they*. Add *–s* or *–es* with *he, she,* or *it*.	*I **hope** to do better on the next test.* *Ruben **likes** to play soccer after class.*
5. In negative statements, use **does not** (*he, she, it*) or **do not** (*I, you, we, they*) before the base form of the verb. Use **doesn't** and **don't** in speaking and informal writing.	*My math professor **doesn't allow** cell phones in class.*
6. For questions in the simple present, use **do** or **does** before the subject. The second part of the verb is always in the base form.	***Do** we **need** to finish this today?* ***Does** your family **call** you often?*
7. Do not use **do** or **does** for questions with **be**.	***Is** she good at multitasking?* *What **are** your goals?*

2 **Work with a partner. Look at the conversation between a college counselor and a student. Complete the questions and answers with the correct forms of the verbs in parentheses. Use contractions when possible. Then Student A, ask one of the questions. Student B, listen to the question and choose the answer and read it aloud. Switch roles after item 4.**

Questions

1. What ________ (be) your professional goals?
2. What ________ (be) your favorite class?
3. ________ your parents ________ (pressure) you to do well in school?
4. How often ________ you ________ (go) to the library?
5. ________ your roommate ever ________ (have) a negative effect on you?
6. When ________ you ________ (hang out) with friends?
7. ________ you ________ (get) enough sleep? You should get at least seven hours every night.
8. We ________ (not have) much time left today. ________ you ________ (have) any questions for me?

Answers

a. After class and on the weekends. We sometimes ________ (cook) dinner together or ________ (watch) a movie.

b. Yes, she ________ (do). She ________ (throw) a lot of parties. She ________ (make) a lot of noise, and she ________ (not clean) the apartment!

c. Not very often. I ________ (prefer) to study in my room.

d. No, not usually. I ________ (be) often really tired during the day because I ________ (stay up) late.

e. Yes, ________ you ________ (know) any good time management strategies?

f. I ________ (want) to become a lawyer. I ________ (think) I can do it.

g. Yes, sometimes they ________ (do). But I ________ (not listen) to them! It's too stressful.

h. It ________ (be) definitely my music class. My professor ________ (create) really interesting lessons.

3 APPLY **Work with a partner. Ask and answer the questions from Exercise Two using your own information.**

Go to the **Pearson Practice English App** or **MyEnglishLab** for more grammar practice. Check what you learned in **MyEnglishLab**.

PRONUNCIATION

1 ▶ Read and listen to the conversation. Notice the underlined syllables and words. How are they different from the other words?

A: Do you have any homework?

B: Yeah, I do. I need to finish my English paper. It's due on Monday. How about you?

A: I'm invited to a party on Saturday. Do you think you can come?

B: Maybe. Give me a call!

Identifying Stressed Words and Unstressed Words

Stressed Words

- In sentences, some words are *stressed* and others are *unstressed.* In a word with more than one syllable, only one syllable in the word is stressed. The stressed syllable is longer, higher, and louder than the other syllables in the word.
- Stressed words are usually *content words.* Content words are words that carry meaning in the sentence, such as nouns, main verbs, adjectives, and adverbs. In addition, we usually stress question words, and negatives, such as *not*, *isn't*, *aren't*, *don't*, *doesn't*, and *can't*.
- Stressed words are easier to hear. Putting stress on the content words helps listeners hear the important words in the sentence. This helps them pay attention to the meaning,

Unstressed Words

- Unstressed words are often *grammar words*:
  – helping verbs, such as *be* and *do*, and modal verbs, such as *can*
  – articles, such as *a* and *the*, and prepositions, such as *to*, *on*, *in*, *at*, *about*
  – pronouns, such as *I*, *you*, *he*, *she*, *it*
- Unstressed words are shorter, lower in pitch, and quieter than stressed words.
- Unstressed words are harder to hear. By not putting stress on unimportant words, we help listeners pay attention to the words in the sentence that carry the meaning.
- One way to make words weak when we are speaking is to use contractions, such as *I'm*, *it's*, *she's*, *he's*, *you're*, *we're*.

2 ▶ Read and listen to the conversation. Underline the stressed words in each sentence.

A: Hey, do you want to go to the beach? It's such a nice day.

B: Well, we don't have much time. Our class starts in two hours.

A: That isn't a problem. We can cut class today!

B: I'm not sure about that. I'd like to go to the beach, but I can't fall behind before the test.

A: OK. I'm not going to twist your arm[1]!

3 ▶ Listen again and check your answers. Then practice saying the conversation out loud with a partner.

---

[1] **twist your arm:** force you to do something

SPEAKING SKILL

Using Your Voice Effectively

During a presentation, it is important to speak clearly and confidently so that your audience will understand you and be interested in what you are saying. To do this, you should do the following:

- Speak loudly enough so that everyone can easily hear you. This will also help you to sound confident.
- Speak slowly and clearly. Practice the pronunciation of difficult words before your presentation.
- Remember to stress important words. This will keep listeners interested in what you are saying and help them identify the important parts of your presentation.
- Practice your presentation many times so you can speak smoothly and avoid using non-words (saying *uh, um* between words).

1 Think about these questions and take notes on your answers. Write only key words, not sentences.

a. What time of day do you usually study?

b. How many hours do you study?

c. Do you usually study alone or with others?

d. How often do you multitask while studying? If you multitask, what do you do?

2 APPLY **Make a short presentation about your study habits to a small group. Use information from Exercise One. Practice using your voice effectively. Look at your notes briefly to remember what to say, but look up at your classmates while you are speaking. Use the checklist to give feedback to your group:**

□ Did he / she speak loudly?

□ Did he / she speak slowly and clearly?

□ Did he / she pronounce words, especially long or difficult ones, correctly?

□ Did he / she stress important words?

□ Did he / she speak smoothly without long pauses or non-words?

Go to MyEnglishLab for more skill practice and to check what you learned.

FINAL SPEAKING TASK: Oral Presentation APPLY

In an oral presentation, a speaker prepares ideas and presents them to the class. In this activity, you will give a two-minute oral presentation to the class on a strategy for school success.

PREPARE

1 Choose a strategy from the list below or choose another strategy that helps you to be a successful student.

- Make to-do lists.
- Use flashcards.
- Join a study group or club.
- See a teacher or counselor to get advice.
- Use a calendar or schedule to plan your time.
- Organize your notes and papers.
- Other: ___________________

2 Prepare your speech. Answer these questions.

a. What strategy do you use?

b. How do you use the strategy? Give details and examples to describe the strategy.

c. How often do you use the strategy?

d. How does it help you to be a successful student?

3 **Make a visual (a poster or a slide presentation) of your strategy. Put the name of your strategy at the top. Include a picture that shows what your strategy looks like. Also make notecards to help you remember what to say during your presentation. Write only one idea on each card. Use only the key words and phrases, not complete sentences.**

4 APPLY **Use the vocabulary, grammar, pronunciation, and speaking skills from the unit. Use the checklist to help you.**

- ☐ **Vocabulary:** Read through the list of vocabulary on page 49. Which words can you include in your presentation to make it clearer and more interesting? Choose at least three words or phrases to use and add them to your notes.
- ☐ **Grammar:** Scan your notes for the simple present tense. Are you forming and using it correctly?
- ☐ **Pronunciation:** Underline the key words to stress when you are speaking. Record yourself practicing. Then listen back. Are you stressing the key words?
- ☐ **Speaking Skill:** Mark the pronunciation of difficult words. Speak slowly, loudly, and clearly. Are you using your voice effectively?

PRACTICE

1 **Practice giving your oral presentation to a partner. Use your notecards to help you remember what to say, but don't read them. Look at your partner when you are speaking. Use your visual to show your partner what your strategy looks like.**

2 **Give feedback to your partner:**

- Did you understand the speaker's ideas?
- Did the speaker use his or her voice effectively? How could the speaker improve?

PRESENT

Take turns giving your presentation to the class.

LISTENING TASK

While your classmates are speaking, listen and take notes.

After the presentations, discuss the questions below.

1. Which strategy is the most helpful?
2. Which strategy is the most unusual?
3. Which strategy do you want to try?

ALTERNATIVE SPEAKING TOPIC

APPLY **Discuss the following questions in a group. Explain your opinions. Use the vocabulary, grammar, pronunciation, and speaking skills you learned in the unit.**

1. What do you think is the most important factor in student success?
2. What is your biggest challenge as a student? What can you do to manage this challenge better?
3. What do you think this quote means? Do you agree or disagree with this quote? Why?

> "Multitasking arises out of distraction itself." — Marilyn vos Savant

CHECK WHAT YOU'VE LEARNED

Check (✔) the outcomes you've met and vocabulary you've learned. Put an X next to the skills and vocabulary you still need to practice.

Learning Outcomes

- ☐ Infer the purpose of questions
- ☐ Take notes with questions
- ☐ Identify disagreement
- ☐ Use the simple present
- ☐ Identify stressed and unstressed words
- ☐ Use your voice effectively

Vocabulary

- ☐ achieve AWL
- ☐ avoid
- ☐ distraction
- ☐ factor AWL
- ☐ focus AWL
- ☐ goal AWL
- ☐ manage
- ☐ negative AWL
- ☐ pressure (*n.*)
- ☐ procrastination
- ☐ research study
- ☐ reward (*n.*)
- ☐ strategy AWL
- ☐ task AWL
- ☐ waste

Multi-word Units

- ☐ positive attitude
- ☐ put off

Go to **MyEnglishLab** to watch a video about study skills, access the Unit Project, and take the Unit 2 Achievement Test.

LEARNING OUTCOMES

- Infer feelings from intonation
- Take notes with symbols
- Recognize and understand emphatic stress
- Use comparative adjectives
- Pronounce numbers and prices
- Make suggestions and come to an agreement

Go to **MyEnglishLab** to check what you know.

UNIT 3

A Penny Saved Is a Penny Earned

1 FOCUS ON THE TOPIC

1. Look at the photo. What do you think it means?
2. How do you usually pay for the things you need? What are some ways that people can save their money? What are some reasons why people have trouble saving money?
3. Read the title of the unit. It is a famous American saying. What do you think it means?

2 FOCUS ON LISTENING

LISTENING ONE | A Barter Network

VOCABULARY

1 Read and listen to the timeline and the article about the history of money and bartering. Notice the boldfaced words. Try to guess their meanings.

MONEY SERIES

PART ONE: The History of Money and Bartering

9000 B.C.E.[1]
farm animals and plants used as money

640 B.C.E.
first metal coins

806 C.E.[2]
first paper money made in China

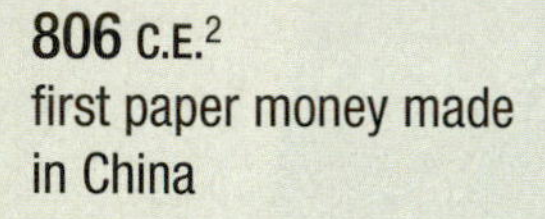

1619
tobacco used as money in Virginia

1762
first printed check used in England

1840
first student loans made at Harvard University

1950
first credit card

1969
first ATM (Automated Teller Machine)

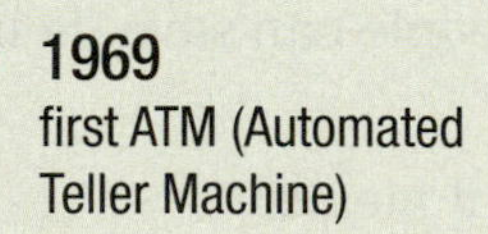

Today
electronic cash

Before people used money, they used other things that were **valuable** to them, such as plants or animals, to pay for things. Over the years, people developed more convenient[3] ways to buy things such as loans, checks, and credit cards. Another convenient type of money is electronic money. Electronic money is used just like real money but can be saved on a computer or on an electronic cash card, such as a debit card or gift card. Electronic money makes it easy to send and receive money with a card, a computer, or a phone app. Today, there are many ways to buy things. But it is also easy to **spend** too much money. People can have problems when they spend more than they **earn**. As a result, many people are often looking for ways to save money.

One way for people to save money is bartering. Bartering means to **exchange** one thing for another without using money. For example, one person might exchange some food for some clothing or other **item** with **equal** value.

Before people used money, they bartered for the things they needed. Today, people, businesses, and governments still barter as a way to save money. For example, a business might barter for goods, such as machines, or **services**, such as **designing** a website, that another business can do for them. Some people use the Internet to find other people who **are interested in** bartering. Other people use community barter **networks**. A barter network is a group of people that trade with each other. A barter network **provides** its **members** with the chance to save money and get to know other people in their community.

---

[1] **B.C.E.:** Before the Common Era
[2] **C.E.:** the Common Era
[3] **convenient:** allowing you to do something easily

2 Circle the best definition for each boldfaced word or phrase.

	a.	b.
1. **valuable**	(a.) useful, important	b. living
2. **item**	a. a thing	b. clothing
3. **spend**	a. get money	b. pay money
4. **earn**	a. get money by working	b. pay money
5. **be interested in**	a. want or care about	b. understand
6. **exchange**	a. buy a new thing	b. trade; give one thing for another
7. **service**	a. something you do for someone	b. a thing you buy someone
8. **provides**	a. gives	b. gets
9. **member**	a. person who barters	b. person who belongs to a group
10. **designing**	a. creating	b. using
11. **equal**	a. different	b. the same
12. **network**	a. a group of people who work together	b. a group of nearby communities

Go to the **Pearson Practice English App** or **MyEnglishLab** for more vocabulary practice.

PREVIEW

1 Listen to the beginning of *A Barter Network.* Then read each question and circle the correct answer.

1. What are you listening to?
   a. a radio announcement
   b. a meeting
   c. a class
2. Who is listening while Carol speaks?
   a. members of the barter network
   b. people who work for the barter network
   c. people who are interested in joining the network

2 **Circle more than one answer to complete each sentence.**

1. Carol is going to discuss . . .
   a. what bartering is
   b. why people like to barter
   c. how to use the barter network
   d. how to join the network
2. Carol will give information about . . .
   a. examples of things people barter
   b. how old the barter network is
   c. how many members belong to the network
   d. names of other members
   e. how to find other members
   f. an example of a barter exchange

LISTEN

1 Listen to the whole discussion about the City Barter Network. Create a chart like the one below to take notes.

TAKE NOTES A Barter Network

Main Ideas	Details
Carol talking about City Barter Network (CBN)	ppl interested in joining
What is bartering?	bartering = exchanging items

2 Compare your notes with a partner's. How can you improve your notes?

Go to MyEnglishLab to view example notes.

MAIN IDEAS

Put a check (✓) next to the things that members do. Use your notes to help you.

- ☐ barter for things and services
- ☐ only barter for services
- ☐ earn money
- ☐ need to provide a service before they can get one
- ☐ earn Time Dollars
- ☐ use Time Dollars to buy services
- ☐ spend money

DETAILS

1 Listen again and add to your notes. Then read each statement. Write *T* (true) or *F* (false). Correct the false statements. Use your notes to help you.

_____ 1. Members can list their services on a website.

_____ 2. Most members provide services like cooking, cleaning, or fixing things.

_____ 3. Members don't provide unusual services like taking photographs or giving music lessons.

_____ 4. Some services are more valuable than others.

_____ 5. Carol spent two hours cleaning another member's house.

_____ 6. A member spent one hour fixing Carol's television.

_____ 7. The man doesn't think he has skills.

_____ 8. Carol needs someone to walk her dog.

2 With a partner, take turns summarizing your notes. Then discuss how your notes and your answers in Preview helped you understand the listening.

Go to MyEnglishLab for more listening practice.

MAKE INFERENCES

Inferring Feelings from Intonation

An inference is a guess about something that is not said directly. To make an inference, use information that you understand from what you hear to try to understand more than the words the speaker says. For example, listening for intonation can help you understand how a speaker is feeling. This can help you understand the speaker's meaning.

Different intonation expresses different feelings. A rising intonation can show that you are surprised. A rising and falling intonation can show that you are happy or interested, and a flat intonation can show that you are not interested.

Read and listen to the example. How does Woman 2 feel?

Example

Carol:	But, ah . . . well, some people provide more unusual services like taking photographs, designing a website, or even giving music lessons.
Woman 2:	Music lessons?! So, do you think I could get piano lessons? I've always wanted to learn how to play the piano.
Carol:	Yeah, sure.
Woman 2:	Wow! That's great!

Explanation

In the example, the second woman's voice rises and falls. This shows that she feels excited about learning to play the piano.

Listen to two excerpts from the meeting of the barter network. After listening to each excerpt, read the questions and circle the correct answers.

Excerpt One

1. How does the man feel about exchanging services?
   a. He feels excited.
   b. He doesn't feel excited.
2. How do you know?
   a. His voice is flat.
   b. His voice rises and falls.

Excerpt Two

1. How does the man feel about the woman's question?
   a. He's surprised.
   b. He isn't surprised.
2. How do you know?
   a. His voice is flat.
   b. His voice rises.

DISCUSS

Work in a small group. Read the questions. Discuss your ideas.

> **USE YOUR NOTES**
>
> APPLY Find information in your notes to use in your discussion.

1. In the City Barter Network, services do not have equal value. What do you think are some services that are expensive to buy? What are some services that are cheap to buy? Why do you think their values are different?
2. How does joining the City Barter Network help people to save money? What are some other reasons people might barter?
3. Imagine you joined the City Barter Network. Which service(s) would you provide? Which services(s) would you want to use?

Go to **MyEnglishLab** to give your opinion about another question.

LISTENING TWO | The Compact

VOCABULARY

Read the words in the box aloud. Then read the statements and circle the correct definition of the boldfaced word or phrase.

borrow	stuff	necessities	used	I bet	That's it

1. When I don't have something I need, I can always **borrow** it from my neighbor. It's easy to give it back when I am done.
   a. give to someone
   b. get from someone temporarily
2. My house is so crowded and full of **stuff** I don't need. I should clean it out.
   a. things, items
   b. full
3. Some things are **necessities**. For example, food is a necessity because you can't live without it.
   a. things you like to have
   b. things you must have
4. I like new clothes, but to save money, sometimes I buy **used** clothes. They are cheaper.
   a. new
   b. not new
5. **I bet** you would like the new computer I bought. It's really fast!
   a. I think I know
   b. I am not sure if something is true
6. I only bought two things today—groceries and gas for my car. **That's it**!
   a. That's great.
   b. That's all.

Go to the **Pearson Practice English App** or **MyEnglishLab** for more vocabulary practice.

NOTE-TAKING SKILL

Taking Notes with Symbols

A symbol is a picture that stands for a word or phrase. Some common symbols are:

Symbol	Meaning	Symbol	Meaning
$	money / dollars	↑	going up
+	and, positive, pro / advantage	↓	going down
–	negative, con / disadvantage	>	more than
/	or	<	less than
=	equals, the same	@	at
#	number		

1 **Listen to the phrases and sentences and take notes using symbols. Compare your notes with a partner's.**

1. ______________________________
2. ______________________________
3. ______________________________
4. ______________________________
5. ______________________________
6. ______________________________

2 **Review your notes from Listening One. Are there any symbols you could use? Add them to your notes.**

Go to MyEnglishLab for more note-taking practice.

COMPREHENSION

1 Listen to the conversation between two members of the City Barter Network. Create a chart like the one below to take notes. Try to use symbols in your notes.

TAKE NOTES The Compact

Main Ideas	*Details*

2 Circle the best answer to complete each sentence. Use your notes to help you.

1. The Compact is a group of people who promised ________ .
   a. to barter for a year
   b. not to buy anything new for a year
2. Members of the Compact can buy new ________ .
   a. food, medicine, and necessities
   b. food, cars, and necessities
3. The members of the Compact think ________ .
   a. clothes, cars, and electronics are too expensive
   b. most people have too much stuff they don't need
4. Members of the Compact ________ to get what they need.
   a. borrow, buy things used, or barter
   b. buy used things and barter for food
5. Mark needed to buy ________ .
   a. new paint
   b. a new house
6. There are ________ of members in the Compact.
   a. hundreds
   b. thousands
7. Natalie likes shopping for ________ .
   a. used clothes
   b. new clothes

USE YOUR NOTES

Compare your notes with a partner's. How can you improve your notes next time?

Used items in a thrift store

LISTENING SKILL

1 Listen to the sentence. Which words are stressed more than the others? Why do you think the speaker stressed those words?

Recognizing and Understanding Emphatic Stress

Emphatic stress means putting extra stress, or emphasis, on certain words in a phrase or sentence. We *emphasize* a word or words that are especially important for understanding the speaker's meaning. When we emphasize a word, the stressed syllable is higher, longer, and louder than a syllable with regular stress.

Example

Read and listen to the conversation.

NATALIE: No kidding! You aren't going to buy ANYTHING new for a whole YEAR?

MARK: Well . . . actually, we CAN buy new necessities, things, you know, that you NEED for your health and safety . . . for example, food and medicine.

Explanation

Natalie says, "You aren't going to buy ANYTHING new for a whole YEAR?" She can't believe people really don't buy anything at all for such a long time, so she stresses the words **anything** and **year**.

In Mark's response, he wants to bring attention to the fact that in the Compact, people can buy some necessities, or things they need. He emphasizes the words **can** and **need**.

2 Listen to the excerpts. What words are the speakers emphasizing? Discuss why with a partner.

Excerpt One

What words does the man emphasize? ______________________

What words does the woman emphasize? ______________________

Why do they emphasize those words? ______________________

Excerpt Two

What word does the man emphasize? ______________________

Why do you think he emphasizes that word? ______________________

Go to **MyEnglishLab** for more skill practice.

CONNECT THE LISTENINGS

ORGANIZE

USE YOUR NOTES

APPLY Review your notes from Listening One and Two. Use the information in your notes to complete the chart.

1 Look at the list of goods (things you can buy) and services (things you pay people to do for you) mentioned in the listenings. Write each item in the correct column in the chart.

car	fix a television	paint someone's house
~~clean someone's house~~	food	walk someone's dog
clothes	give someone piano lessons	
computer	medicine	

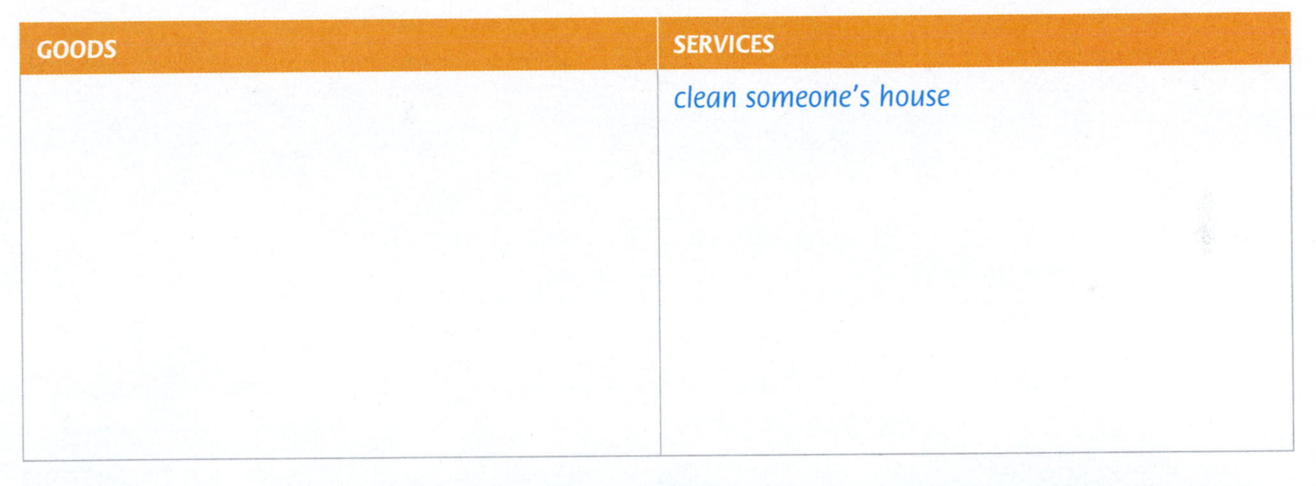

GOODS	SERVICES
	clean someone's house

2 How can members of the Compact get the goods and services they need? Write each good and service from the chart in the correct place on the graphic organizer. Then compare your answers with a classmate's.

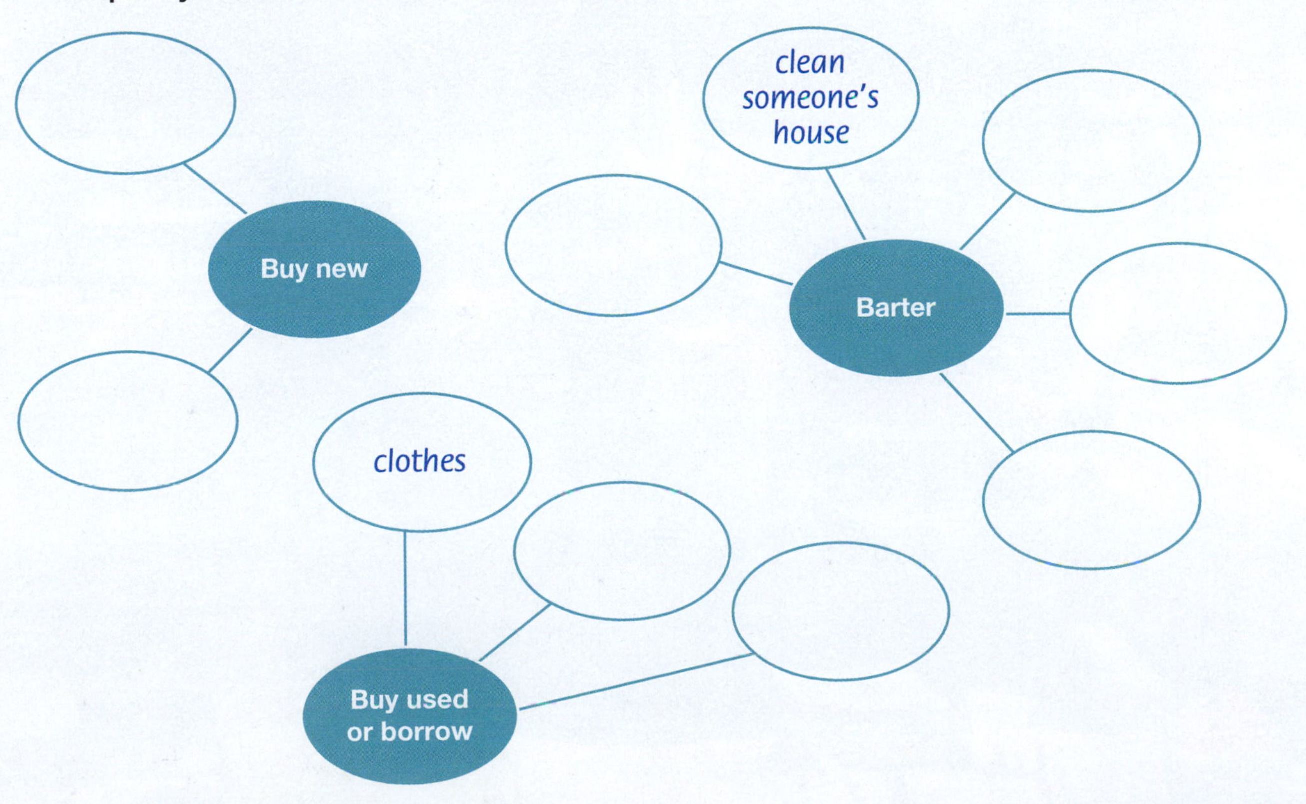

SYNTHESIZE

Work with a partner. Imagine you are in the City Barter Network and the Compact. Student A, say what you need. Student B, suggest a way to get each thing. Use the information from Organize.

Example

A: I want someone to clean my house.

B: You can get that by bartering.

Go to **MyEnglishLab** to check what you learned.

3 FOCUS ON SPEAKING

VOCABULARY

REVIEW

Complete the conversations with words from the box. Use the underlined words to help you. Then work with a partner to practice reading the conversations aloud. Switch roles after item 4.

be interested in	equal	I bet	services	stuff	~~used~~
borrow	exchange	necessity	spend	That's it	valuable

1. **A:** I bought a chair at a thrift store yesterday. It isn't new, but it's very nice.
   B: Do you really like to buy ___used___ things?
2. **A:** This sweater is too big. I need to take it back to the store and trade it for a smaller one.
   B: Does that store let you ________________ things?
3. **A:** Do you want to go shopping? I need to get some things for my apartment.
   B: No, thanks. I already have too much ________________ .
4. **A:** I wish I knew how to do something useful, like fixing cars.
   B: Yeah, you're right. Fixing cars is a ________________ skill.
5. **A:** I need to buy a car.
   B: Really? Is a car a ________________ for you? You can ride your bike or take the bus anywhere you need to go.
6. **A:** I don't want to pay a lot of money for a television.
   B: How much do you want to ________________ ?
7. **A:** That department store does so many things for you. They even have personal shoppers, people who help you choose what to buy.
   B: Yeah, they do offer a lot of ________________ .
8. **A:** Do you think these two cameras cost the same?
   B: Yeah, I think the cost is pretty ________________ .
9. **A:** My car broke down. Can I use yours to get to school today?
   B: Sure, you can ________________ it anytime.
10. **A:** I am thinking about taking a class. I want to learn more about saving money.
    B: That's sounds good. Maybe I will join you. I ________________ that as well.
11. **A:** You mentioned that new movie. I think I know what you want to do tonight!
    B: ________________ you do!
12. **A:** We need some milk and eggs from the store. Anything else?
    B: No. ________________ . We really don't need much.

EXPAND

1 ▶ **Read and listen to the newsletter article about Freecycle. Notice the boldfaced words and phrases. Try to guess their meanings.**

The Barter Network Newsletter — By Carol Murphy

This Week's Money-Saving Tip: FREECYCLE®

1 Last week I wrote about thrift stores, where you can get a good price on used items and save lots of money. But an even better way to save money is *Freecycle*. *Freecycle* is an online group. People give away things they don't need anymore—for free! Other people get things they need, for free, so they don't have to **pay an arm and a leg**.

2 When you join *Freecycle*, you select a group that is near you. There are groups all over the world, in over 100 countries, so there is probably a group near you. After you join, you can see lists of items that people are giving away near your home.

3 People list all kinds of things: furniture, clothes, artwork, electronics, and more. You may need something that you can't **afford** to buy. But on *Freecycle*, it's free! What a great **bargain**!

4 Another way to save money is to go to flea markets where people sell stuff cheap. Some people like **to bargain** with the sellers. I **got a good deal** this weekend at a flea market on a jacket. At first, the seller asked $100 for it, but I bargained with him until he agreed to take only $50. But my friend got an even better deal. She used *Freecycle* and got a jacket for free; no cost. And the jacket was **worth** a lot of money!

5 At *Freecycle* or at a flea market you may have to spend some extra time looking for what you want, but it can be a lot of fun. You can also save a lot of money. It's really **worth it**!

2 **Match the phrases on the left with the definitions on the right.**

____ 1. pay an arm and a leg
____ 2. afford
____ 3. bargain (*n.*)
____ 4. bargain (*v.*)
____ 5. get a good deal
____ 6. cost
____ 7. be worth
____ 8. be worth it

a. to have a particular value
b. to have a particular price
c. to have enough money to pay for something
d. to get a good price on something
e. to spend a lot of money
f. to discuss the price of something you are buying in order to get a better price
g. to be good to do even though you had to make an effort
h. something you buy for less than the usual price

CREATE

APPLY **Work in a small group. Take turns asking and answering the questions. Use the boldfaced words and vocabulary from Review and Expand in your answers.**

1. Do you like **to bargain** with sellers when you shop? Do you bargain when you buy from street vendors? Why or why not?
2. Do you like to buy things **used**? Why or why not? If yes, what are some things that you like to buy used? What are some things you never buy used?
3. Name a store or place to shop that you think has good **bargains**. What kinds of bargains can you get there?
4. Name something you bought that you **got a good deal** on. Where did you get it? Why do you think it was a good deal?
5. Do you have a lot of **stuff** in your house? What do you usually do with stuff that you don't use anymore—do you prefer to keep it, throw it away, or give it to someone else?
6. Name something you own that was **cheap** to buy. How much did it cost? Name something that you **paid an arm and a leg** for.
7. Do you own something that is **worth** more now than when you bought it? How much did you **spend** on it? Was it **worth it**?

GRAMMAR FOR SPEAKING

1 Read the sentences. Then answer the questions below.

The thrift store is cheaper than the department store.

This jacket is more expensive than that one.

a. What is the adjective in the first sentence? What does it describe? What two letters does the adjective end with?

b. What is the adjective in the second sentence? What does it describe? What word comes before *expensive*?

c. What word comes after *cheaper* and *more expensive*?

Comparative Adjectives

1. Use the comparative form of the adjective to compare two people, places, or things. Use ***than*** before the second person, place, or thing. You can leave out ***than*** when it is clear which two things you are comparing.	*Your car is **cheaper than** mine.* *It is **smaller**, too.*
2. Add ***–er*** to form the comparative of short (one-syllable) adjectives. Add ***–r*** if the adjective ends in ***e***.	*cheap* *cheap**er*** *old* *old**er*** *close* *close**r***
3. When a one-syllable adjective ends in a consonant + vowel + consonant, double the last consonant and add ***–er***.	*big* *big**ger*** *hot* *hot**ter***
4. When two-syllable adjectives end in ***–y***, change the ***y*** to ***i*** and add ***–er***	*easy* *eas**ier*** *funny* *funn**ier***
5. Some adjectives have irregular comparative forms.	*good* ***better*** *bad* ***worse***
6. To form the comparative of most adjectives of two or more syllables, add ***more*** before the adjective. ***Less*** is the opposite of ***more***.	*Some services are **more valuable** than others.* *Used clothing is **less expensive** than new clothing.*

This week's special: a used Ecosmart

Condition: Like New
Views: 106
Date Posted: April 25
Asking Price: $4,000

Description: This Ecosmart is almost new, and it runs great! It gets excellent gas mileage, and it's on sale now for only $4,000!

2 Work with a partner. Look at the ads for the cars. Take turns making sentences comparing the two cars. Use the adjectives from the box. Then say which car you would like to buy and why.

bad for the environment	comfortable	good for a big family	safe
big	easy to park	nice	stylish
cheap to drive	expensive	old	

Example

A: The Indulge is bigger than the Ecosmart.

B: The Indulge is more expensive than the Ecosmart.

3 APPLY **Work with a partner. Student A, you want to buy the Indulge. Student B, you want to buy the Ecosmart. You can only buy one car. Have a conversation comparing the two cars. Decide which one you will buy.**

Example

A: I want to buy the Indulge because it's bigger than the Ecosmart.

B: Yeah, but the Ecosmart is cheaper to drive.

Go to the **Pearson Practice English App** or **MyEnglishLab** for more grammar practice. Check what you learned in **MyEnglishLab**.

PRONUNCIATION

Pronouncing Numbers and Prices

When we say the numbers 13 through 19, *-teen* is stressed and the letter *t* in *-teen* sounds like /t/. When we say the numbers 20, 30, 40, 50, 60, 70, 80, and 90, the first syllable is stressed and the letter *t* in *-ty* sounds like a fast /d/.

Listen to the examples.

Example One

13	16	19
/thirteen/	/sixteen/	/nineteen/
30	60	90
/thirdy/	/sixdy/	/ninedy/

There are two ways to say prices.

Read and listen to the examples. Pay attention to what is stressed.

Example Two

$4.29
four dollars and twenty-nine cents
four twenty-nine

$53.99
fifty-three dollars and ninety-nine cents
fifty-three ninety-nine

1 **Read and listen to the numbers. Circle the number you hear.**

1. 13 30
2. 14 40
3. 15 50
4. 16 60
5. 17 70
6. 18 80
7. 19 90

2 **Work with a partner. Look at the numbers in Exercise One. Take turns. Say a number. Remember to stress the correct syllable. Your partner points to the number you say.**

3 **Listen and write the prices you hear. Then practice saying them aloud in two different ways.**

1. $____________________
2. $____________________
3. $____________________
4. $____________________
5. $____________________

4 APPLY **Work with a partner. Take turns asking each other how much you usually spend on the items listed. Write your partner's answers. Share the information with your classmates.**

Example

A: How much do you usually spend on a haircut?

B: I spend eighty dollars. How about you?

A: I spend fifteen dollars.

1. a haircut $____________________
2. a movie ticket $____________________
3. your phone bill $____________________
4. a meal in a restaurant $____________________

SPEAKING SKILL

Making Suggestions and Coming to an Agreement

When two or more people need to make a decision together, they need to negotiate; they need to come to an agreement. When negotiating, you need to make suggestions until each person agrees.

MAKING SUGGESTIONS	AGREEING WITH SUGGESTIONS	DISAGREEING WITH SUGGESTIONS
Let's buy this chair. *Why don't we go to the thrift store?* *How about buying a used car instead of a new one?* *Would you like to sell your computer?*	*OK. / All right.* *That's fine with me.* *That's a good idea.* *Let's do it.* *It's a deal.* *OK. Why not?*	*Well, I don't know. How about . . . ?* *I have another idea. Why don't we . . . ?* *I don't think so.*

1 **Look at the list of things. Imagine you have $2,500 to buy things for your new house or apartment. Make a list of the things you would like to get.**

used couch—$100
new couch—$650
large armchair—$300
new table and chairs—$400
lamp—$25
bookcase—$115
wall art—$175
video game console—$300
plants—$50
pet kitten—$100
pet dog—$130
computer—$800
music system—$250
used piano—$300
small used television—$85
large new television—$700

Your List

______________ ______________ ______________

______________ ______________ ______________

2 APPLY **Now work in a small group. Imagine you are roommates. You need to agree on what things to buy for your new house or apartment. You have $2,500 to spend. Take turns suggesting things to buy. When everyone agrees, write your group's list below.**

Example

A: Let's buy the used couch for $100.

B: Well, I don't know. I don't want a used couch. How about buying the new one?

C: But it costs a lot. Why don't we buy the table and chairs? We can use them for eating or studying.

A: I have another idea. Let's get a free table and chairs from Freecycle. Then we can buy the new couch.

Your List

______________ ______________ ______________

______________ ______________ ______________

3 **Share your group's list with another group. Explain why your group chose each thing. The other group listens and answers. Did you choose the same things? Why or why not?**

Go to **MyEnglishLab** for more skill practice and to check what you learned.

FINAL SPEAKING TASK: Bartering APPLY

In this activity, you will practice bartering for goods and services with your classmates.

STEP 1

1 Get five blank cards. On four of the cards, write the following:

a. name of an item you would like to exchange (and a drawing, if you'd like)

b. how old it is

c. how much money you think it is worth now

Do this for four items. On the fifth card, write a service you can provide, such as "cook dinner."

2 APPLY Use the vocabulary, grammar, pronunciation, and speaking skills from the unit. Use the checklist to help you.

- ☐ **Vocabulary:** Read through the list of vocabulary on page 71. Which words can you use while bartering? Choose at least three words or phrases to use and add them to your note cards.
- ☐ **Grammar:** Choose some adjectives you could use to describe your items. Write the comparative forms on your notecards.
- ☐ **Pronunciation:** Practice the pronunciation of the prices that your items are worth. Use the correct stress.
- ☐ **Speaking Skill:** Review the phrases to use to make, agree, and disagree with suggestions. Plan to use some of them when you barter with your classmates.

STEP 2

Go around the class and barter with your classmates. Compare your items and services and negotiate with each other until you come to an agreement. When you come to an agreement, trade your cards.

Example

A: How about exchanging your television for my computer?

B: But my television is newer than your computer.

A: Yeah, but my computer is more valuable.

B: Thanks, but that's not worth it. I want to keep looking.

or

B: OK. It's a deal.

STEP 3

Report back to the class. Tell them about one of the items or services you received. Answer the questions below.

1. What did you exchange it for?
2. Why did you decide to make this trade?
3. Did you get a good deal?

LISTENING TASK

Listen to your classmates' reports. Who got the best deal?

ALTERNATIVE SPEAKING TOPIC

APPLY **In a small group discuss the questions. Use the vocabulary, grammar, pronunciation, and speaking skills you learned in the unit.**

1. Do you think that most people have too much stuff? Why or why not? What are some problems caused by having a lot of stuff? Give examples.
2. Do you think the Compact is a good idea or a bad idea? Why? Could you keep a promise not to buy anything new for a year? Explain.
3. Do people in your culture buy and sell used stuff? If yes, where? If no, why not?
4. What kinds of things do you only want to buy new? What will you buy used? Why will you buy some things used but others new?

CHECK WHAT YOU'VE LEARNED

Check (✔) the outcomes you've met and vocabulary you've learned. Put an X next to the skills and vocabulary you still need to practice.

Learning Outcomes

- ☐ Infer feelings from intonation
- ☐ Take notes with symbols
- ☐ Recognize and understand emphatic stress
- ☐ Use comparative adjectives
- ☐ Pronounce numbers and prices
- ☐ Make suggestions and come to an agreement

Vocabulary

- ☐ borrow
- ☐ design (*v.*) AWL
- ☐ earn
- ☐ exchange (*v.*)
- ☐ equal (*adj.*)
- ☐ item AWL
- ☐ member
- ☐ necessities
- ☐ network (*n.*) AWL
- ☐ provide
- ☐ service (*n.*)
- ☐ spend
- ☐ stuff (*n.*)
- ☐ used (*adj.*)
- ☐ valuable

Multi-word Units

- ☐ be interested in
- ☐ I bet
- ☐ That's it

Go to **MyEnglishLab** to watch a video about money, access the Unit Project, and take the Unit 3 Achievement Test.

LEARNING OUTCOMES

- Infer contrasting ideas
- Organize your notes
- Recognize and understand summaries and paraphrases
- Use *can*, *could*, and *would*
- Use rising and falling intonation in questions and statements
- Make polite offers and invitations

Go to **MyEnglishLab** to check what you know.

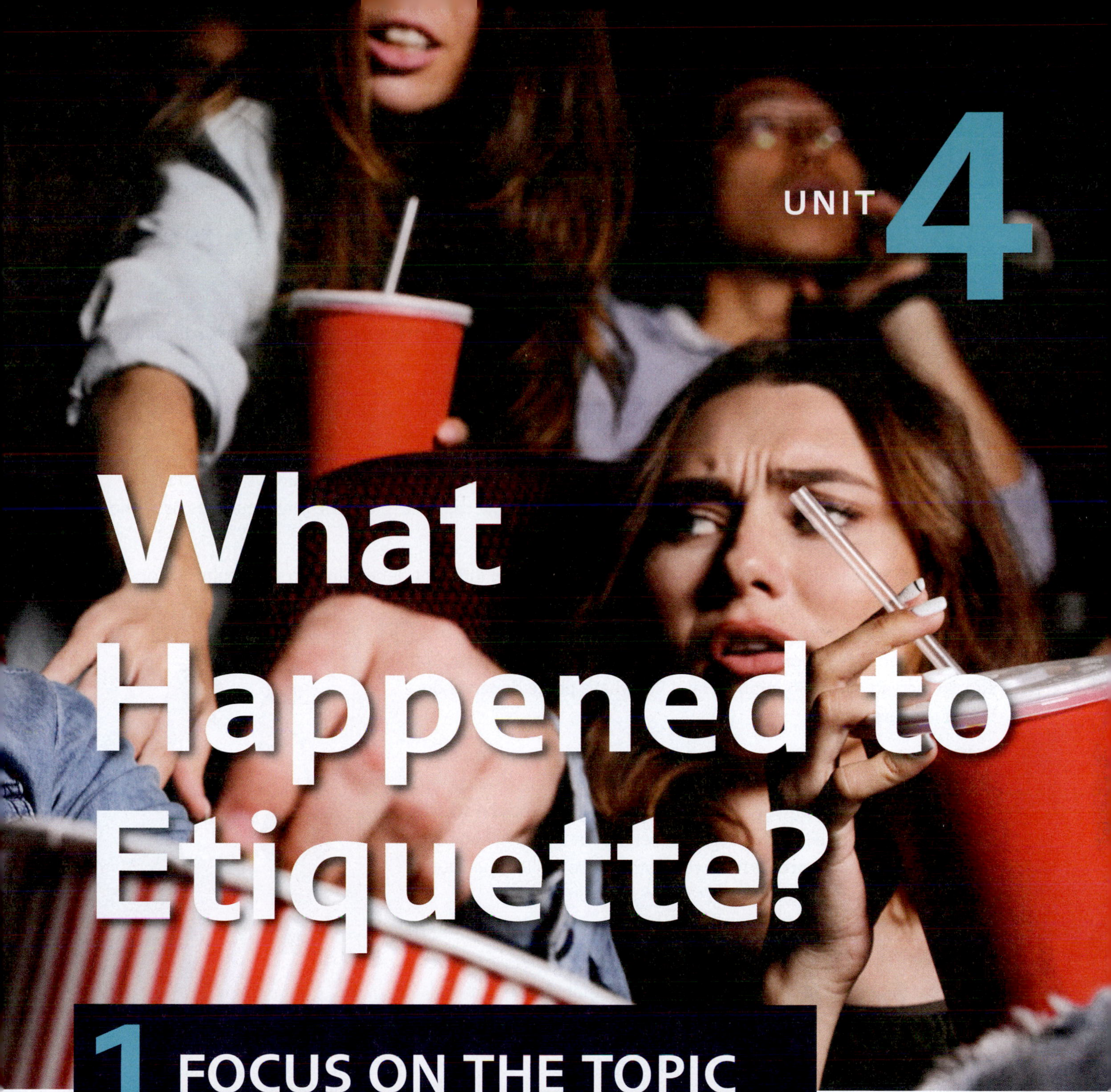

UNIT 4

What Happened to Etiquette?

1 FOCUS ON THE TOPIC

1. Look at the photo. What is the man doing?
2. What are some reasons that people might think this behavior is rude? Are there situations where this behavior is acceptable?
3. *Etiquette* means the rules we follow to behave (act) politely. What are some other actions that people think are polite? What are some that are rude (not polite)? Why are these behaviors considered rude or polite?

2 FOCUS ON LISTENING

LISTENING ONE | What Ever Happened to Manners?

VOCABULARY

1 Read and listen to the beginning of a radio show. Notice the boldfaced words. Try to guess their meanings.

HOST: Thanks for tuning into *Your World*. In today's show, we're going to focus on **manners**.

Maybe, like me, you **were raised** by your parents to be **courteous**. My mother always said, "**Treat** others as you want them to treat you." In other words, show **respect** to others. Many cultures have the same idea. In English, this is called "the golden rule."

However, what is considered to be polite **behavior** will be different depending on your culture. For example, in some countries, when you're invited to dinner at someone's home, you should arrive on time. If not, it's considered **rude**. In other countries, when you're invited to someone's home for dinner, it's rude to arrive *on time*. You should instead arrive 30 minutes late! So, what's polite depends on where you are.

If you drop papers, how likely is it that someone will help you pick them up?

Behavior can be different even in the same culture. For example, imagine you are at work and have a folder of important **documents** to give to your boss. On your way to her office, you drop the whole folder! Will someone stop to help you pick up the papers? Maybe. Maybe not. We all **appreciate** it when others are polite to us, but it seems like many people just aren't polite anymore.

In a recent survey[1] that was **conducted** in the U.S., 76 percent of the people said that manners are changing and people are less courteous now than they were in the past. They believe that, these days, Americans are more **likely** to behave and speak in a rude way than they have in the past. Is this true? Are people becoming less courteous? Let's find out.

[1] **survey:** a set of questions you ask a large number of people to learn their opinions or behavior

2 Match the words on the left with the definitions on the right.

b	1. manners	a. used to show that something will probably happen
____	2. be raised	~~b. polite ways to behave or speak~~
____	3. courteous	c. speaking or acting in a way that will probably offend or annoy people
____	4. treat (*v.*)	d. to act or think toward someone in a particular way
____	5. respect (*n.*)	e. a piece of paper with official information on it
____	6. behavior	f. polite
____	7. rude	g. a feeling that something or someone is important
____	8. document (*n.*)	h. to be grateful or thankful (for something)
____	9. appreciate	i. the way someone acts
____	10. conduct (*v.*)	j. to plan and do something, such as a test or study
____	11. likely	k. be taken care of as a child: be brought up

Go to the **Pearson Practice English App** or **MyEnglishLab** for more vocabulary practice.

PREVIEW

Many people think the general public doesn't have good manners anymore. Discuss this idea with a partner. Then listen to the radio show.

Listen to the beginning of the radio show called *What Ever Happened to Manners?* How do you think Sarah Jones tested the manners of people in different countries? List three possible ways.

1. ______________________________
2. ______________________________
3. ______________________________

LISTEN

1 Listen to the complete interview. Create a chart like the one below to take notes.

TAKE NOTES What Ever Happened to Manners?

Main Ideas	*Details*
SJ (reporter) did int'l study on manners	what happening w/ manners? ppl less polite?

2 Compare your notes with a partner's. How can you improve your notes?

Go to **MyEnglishLab** to view example notes.

MAIN IDEAS

Circle the correct answer to each question. Use your notes to help you.

1. How did the reporters conduct their study?
   a. They asked people for their opinions about manners.
   b. They observed people's language and behavior.
   c. They gave people a written test of polite behaviors.
2. Where did the reporters conduct their study?
   a. in different coffee shops
   b. in different workplaces
   c. in different cities
3. What behaviors were included in the study?
   a. holding the door for someone, helping someone pick up some documents, and letting someone sit down
   b. helping someone pick up some documents, helping someone cross the street, and saying "thank you"
   c. holding the door for someone, helping someone pick up some documents, and saying "thank you"
4. What reason did most people give for being courteous?
   a. They were raised to be courteous.
   b. They want to help others.
   c. They follow "the golden rule."
5. Who did the reporters test?
   a. all kinds of people
   b. students and businesspeople
   c. only cashiers

DETAILS

1 Listen again and add to your notes. Then complete the summary of the survey. Use your notes to help you.

Two reporters went to large cities all around the world. They went to ________ (1.) countries. The reporters did three tests: a ________ (2.) test, a ________ (3.) drop, and a customer ________ (4.) test.

For the door test, they wanted to see if people would ________ ________ ________ ________ (5.) for the reporters. For the second test, they wanted to see if anyone would help them pick up a ________ (6.) of important papers. For the customer service test, they wanted to see if people who work in stores were polite and said ________ ________ (7.).

In the most courteous city, ________ (8.) percent of the people passed the door test, but when the reporters dropped their papers, only ________ (9.) percent helped pick them up. For the customer service test, ________ (10.) out of 20 cashiers passed the test. Men were more ________ (11.) to help than women. In the document test, ________ (12.) percent of the men and ________ (13.) percent of the women helped the reporters. In the study, ________ ________ (14.) was the most courteous city.

2 With a partner, take turns summarizing your notes. Then discuss how your notes and your answers in Preview helped you understand the listening.

Go to **MyEnglishLab** for more listening practice.

MAKE INFERENCES

Inferring Contrasting Ideas

An inference is a guess about something that is not said directly.

We *contrast* two different ideas when we want to show how they are different. To help us understand contrasts, speakers put extra stress on the words in the sentence that show how two ideas are different. This helps listeners to focus on the key words that will help them to understand the contrasting ideas.

Read and listen to the example. Which words does the speaker stress? What are the two ideas the speaker is contrasting?

Example

HOST: You know, what I'm curious about is why some people are courteous and some others aren't.

Explanation

In this example, the speaker stresses the words **some** and **are**, and also the words **others** and **aren't**. The speaker is contrasting two ideas: **some people are courteous, but other people are not.**

Listen to two excerpts from the interview. After listening to each excerpt, write down two pairs of words or numbers that are stressed. What are the two ideas the speaker is contrasting?

Excerpt One

Stressed words: *almost everyone* ______ *door* ______

______ ______

Contrasting ideas: 1. *Almost everyone held the door.*

2. ______

Excerpt Two

Stressed words: ______ ______

______ ______

Contrasting ideas: 1. ______

2. ______

DISCUSS

Work in a small group. Read the questions. Discuss your ideas.

> **USE YOUR NOTES**
>
> APPLY Find information in your notes to use in your discussion.

1. In the survey, how did the reporters test manners in each city? If you could design a test of manners, what would you do? Why?
2. In the survey, which city was the most courteous? Are you surprised by that result? Why or why not? How do you think people in your hometown would do on this manners test?
3. According to the listening, what do people believe is happening to manners? Do you agree? What do you think may be causing that change? Give examples to support your opinion.

Go to MyEnglishLab to give your opinion about another question.

LISTENING TWO | Why Is There a Lack of Manners?

VOCABULARY

Read the words in the box aloud. Then read the blog entry and circle the correct definition of the boldfaced word or phrase.

confusing	face-to-face	text	electronic device	immediate response

I was talking to my grandmother, and I realized how much things have changed in her lifetime. For example, she has a cell phone, but she doesn't like to use it. She says she would rather communicate **face-to-face** instead of using an **electronic device**. On the other hand, I can't imagine life without my cell phone! She also prefers to write letters and send them in the mail. She thinks people don't write very well anymore because we just **text** short messages with incorrect spelling and grammar. She says my messages are **confusing**. Maybe that's true, but I can't imagine having to wait days to hear back when I send a message. I like texting because you can get an **immediate response**. Even so, I see her point. I think I'll try to visit and write letters to her more often.

1. face-to-face
   a. online　　b. in person
2. electronic device
   a. a machine that is fast　　b. a machine or piece of equipment that uses electricity
3. text
   a. send a written message by phone　　b. send an email through your computer
4. confusing
   a. difficult to understand　　b. difficult to say
5. immediate response
   a. a polite answer　　b. a fast answer

Go to the Pearson Practice English App or MyEnglishLab for more vocabulary practice.

NOTE-TAKING SKILL

Organizing Your Notes

When you take notes, it's important that you organize them to show how the ideas are connected. Then, when you go back to review your notes, you will be able to understand what you have written and find the information that you need. One way to organize your notes is to indent details under each topic or important idea. You can write each detail on a different line. You can also use a dash (–) or bullet point (•) to mark each detail.

Topic / Important Idea #1

– Detail 1

– Detail 2

– Detail 3

Topic / Important Idea #2

– Detail 1

– Detail 2

Sometimes a detail will have even more specific information related to it. In those cases, you can indent again in our notes.

Topic / Important Idea #1

– Detail 1

- *More information about Detail 1*
- *More information about Detail 1*

– Detail 2

– Detail 3

- *More information about Detail 3*

After listening and taking notes, it's a good idea to review them to make sure you can read and understand them. Check for missing or unnecessary information and re-write your notes so that they are organized and easy to understand. Rewriting your notes will help you to remember the information and study it later.

1 Listen to the excerpt from Listening One. What three important ideas are discussed?

1. ______________________________

2. ______________________________

3. ______________________________

2 Listen again. Take notes on the important ideas and details on a separate piece of paper. Organize your notes by indenting the details under the important ideas or by putting them in chart.

3 Compare your notes to a partner's. Did you organize them the same way? Can you easily find the different ideas?

4 Review your notes from Listening One with a partner. How could you organize your notes differently to understand them more easily?

Go to **MyEnglishLab** for more note-taking practice.

COMPREHENSION

1 Listen to the second part of the radio show. Listeners were invited to call in with their ideas about why people are rude. Create a chart like the one below to take notes. Try to organize your notes to show how the ideas are connected.

TAKE NOTES Why Is There a Lack of Manners?

Main Ideas	*Details*

2 Look at the list of reasons why people are rude. Check (✓) the reasons the callers give. Use your notes to help you.

There is a lack[1] of manners because . . .

□ parents don't spend enough time teaching their kids manners.

□ people don't know each other well, so they are less polite.

□ children don't learn manners at school anymore.

□ living with people from many different cultures is confusing.

□ because of electronic devices, people give immediate short responses.

□ people follow the behavior they see on TV.

□ people forget how to talk to someone face-to-face.

USE YOUR NOTES

Compare your notes with a partner's. How can you improve your notes next time?

[1] **lack:** not having any or enough of something

LISTENING SKILL

1 Listen to the excerpt. Do you think this is the beginning or the end of the program? How do you know?

Recognizing and Understanding Summaries and Paraphrases

In *summaries*, speakers repeat the main points of what was said in a whole discussion or lecture. When they *summarize*, speakers include only the most important information, and they leave out details.

In *paraphrases*, speakers use their own words to repeat important information that was just said. This shows that the listener was paying attention and understood.

Listening for summary sentences and paraphrases can help you to understand and remember the main ideas of a listening.

Read and listen to the excerpt again.

Example

HOST: Well, we're out of time, but to wrap up: we need more family time, a better understanding of our different cultures, and more face-to-face time . . . certainly some things to think about! That's all for now, until next week.

Explanation

In the example, the host summarized all of the caller's comments at the end of the program in one sentence: *We need good manners at home, a better understanding of our different cultures, and more face-to-face time.*

2 Listen to the following excerpts from Listening Two. Take notes. Then write a sentence that paraphrases what the speaker said. Then listen to how the host paraphrases the callers' opinions. Compare your sentences. Did you include the same information?

Excerpt One

Key words: ______________________________

My paraphrase: ______________________________

The host's paraphrase: ______________________________

Excerpt Two

Key words: ______________________________

My paraphrase: ______________________________

The host's paraphrase: ______________________________

Go to MyEnglishLab for more skill practice.

CONNECT THE LISTENINGS

ORGANIZE

Complete the chart. Look at the list of ideas from Listening One and Two. Each idea belongs to one of the categories in the chart below. Categorize each idea and write it in the correct column. Then compare your completed chart with a partner's.

> **USE YOUR NOTES**
>
> APPLY Review your notes from Listening One and Two. Use the information in your notes to complete the chart.

~~Small things like holding the door are easy to do.~~

~~Parents don't teach manners at home.~~

People communicate using electronic devices, such as cell phones.

You don't know how long to hold the door for someone.

Sometimes your hands are full and you can't help.

It shows respect for others.

People follow "the golden rule."

People from other cultures may seem rude but they have different rules of etiquette.

People are raised to be polite.

REASONS FOR POLITE BEHAVIOR	REASONS FOR IMPOLITE BEHAVIOR
• *Small things like holding the door are easy to do.*	• *Parents don't teach manners at home.*
• ______	• ______
• ______	• ______
• ______	• ______
	• ______

SYNTHESIZE

Work with a partner. Student A, you are conducting a survey about manners. Ask questions to find out examples of and reasons for polite and impolite behavior. Student B, answer Student A's questions. Use the information from Organize. Then switch roles and repeat the conversation.

Example

A: Hello. I'm interviewing people about manners. Can you give me an example of polite behavior?

B: Sure. I think it's polite to hold the door for someone.

A: True. Why do you think people do that?

B: Well, you're opening the door anyway. It's an easy thing to do.

A: But some people aren't polite. Why is that?

B: I think one reason is parents don't spend enough time teaching their children manners anymore.

Go to **MyEnglishLab** to check what you learned.

3 FOCUS ON SPEAKING

VOCABULARY

REVIEW

Read the magazine column about etiquette. Write the correct word in the blank. Use the words from the box.

appreciate	confusing	face-to-face	respect	treat
behavior	courteous	raised	rude	

Ask Miss Manners

Q

Dear Miss Manners,

Thanks for all your great advice. I really ________________ (1.) it. I wish everyone cared about manners. I think people are not as polite now as they used to be. It seems that every day someone gets in front of me in line or starts texting when I'm talking to them. People are just not ________________ (2.). —Clara

A

Dear Clara,

Unfortunately, there does seem to be a lack of manners these days. The question is, what do we do about it? I think the important thing to remember is to ________________ (3.) others in a nice way. If we can all just remember to ________________ (4.) each other, I think we can all get along.

Dear Miss Manners,

I'm really bothered by children who misbehave in public places. I know children are all ______________ (5.) differently, so you see a lot of different ______________ (6.), but I want to do something about it. I was shopping the other day, and one kid was running around and making a mess in the store. It was hard to shop. What should I do in that situation?

—Annoyed Shopper

Q

A

Dear Annoyed Shopper,

Well, one idea is to tell the manager. It's really the manager's job to deal with customers. It's not always best for you to talk to the person ______________ (7.).

Q

Dear Miss Manners,

The neighbors who live in the apartment above me are so ______________ (8.) because they talk so loud and play music late at night. What do you suggest I do?

—Julius K.

A

Dear Julius K.,

When you live in an apartment building, you can find many different kinds of people living in one place. We often don't share the same rules of etiquette with our neighbors. I know it can be ______________ (9.) when we don't understand another person's way of life, but we all have to learn to get along.

EXPAND

1 Read and listen to the conversation. Notice the boldfaced words and phrases. Try to guess their meanings. Then take turns reading the conversation with a partner.

A: I had a terrible day today.

B: Really? What happened?

A: Well, do you remember that girl from my math class that I was telling you about?

B: Yeah . . .

A: Well, I finally got up the courage to text her and ask her to **go out** with me.

B: So what did she say?

A: That's the problem. I asked her out two weeks ago, and she didn't respond at all until yesterday.

B: Oh no. Why did she **leave you hanging** for so long?

A: I don't know, but she finally agreed to go see a movie with me tonight. I was so excited. I was really **looking forward to** it.

B: So, what happened?

A: Well, I waited at the movie theater for almost half an hour. Finally, she texted me to **call off** our date. She gave me an excuse saying she needed to study for a test.

B: Oh, that's too bad. It was really **rude** of her to blow you off like that. I hate to say this, but it sounds like she never wanted to go out with you in the first place. Maybe she was afraid to **turn** you **down** because she didn't want to hurt your feelings.

A: Yeah, you're probably right.

B: Cheer up! She doesn't sound worth it. And hey, what time is the next show? Maybe we could still catch that movie!

A: Thanks, but I think **I'll have to pass**. I don't feel like doing anything now. Can I **take a rain check**?

B: Sure, no problem. Maybe next weekend.

A: OK, **sounds good**. I'll see you later.

2 Match the phrase on the left with its meaning on the right.

_____ 1. go out

_____ 2. leave someone hanging

_____ 3. look forward to

_____ 4. call something off

_____ 5. sounds good

_____ 6. turn down

_____ 7. "I'll have to pass."

_____ 8. take a rain check

a. to cancel or delay an event; to decide that an event will not happen

b. to keep someone waiting for a decision or answer

c. to tell someone that you can't do something with them now, but you would like to do it at another time

d. "I can't accept your invitation."

e. a way to say that you agree with someone's suggestion

f. to say "no" to an invitation

g. go on a date

h. to be excited and pleased about something that is going to happen

CREATE

APPLY **Work in pairs. Look at the list of actions. Take a side: either you think it is polite or impolite. Explain your reasons. After you have finished the list, join with another pair to make a group of four. Repeat the debate, adding ideas and vocabulary. Use the words from Review and Expand in the box.**

appreciate	courteous	raised	treat
behavior	face-to-face	respect	turn down
blow off	go out	rude	
call something off	leave someone hanging	take a rain check	
confusing	look forward to	to pass	

Actions

Taking your shoes off before entering someone's home

Talking on your cell phone while in a restaurant with friends

Not responding to an invitation

Texting while having a conversation with someone

Throwing garbage on the ground (littering)

Example

A: I think taking your shoes off before entering someone's house is very courteous. It shows respect for the other person. I really appreciate it when people take their shoes off when they come to my house. Plus, it helps to keep my house clean.

B: Really? I don't think it's courteous to take them off. I wasn't raised to do that, so I don't think it shows a lack of manners to leave them on.

Go to the **Pearson Practice English App** or **MyEnglishLab** for more vocabulary practice.

GRAMMAR FOR SPEAKING

1 Read the examples. Then answer the questions below.

Can you hand me that pencil?

Could you please hold the door open for me?

Would you help me pick up my papers?

Could you help me, please?

a. What is the first word in each question?

_______________ _______________ _______________ _______________

b. What possible answers do you expect from all of the questions? _______________

c. Look at the main verb in each question. What is the form? _______________

Can, *Could*, and *Would* in Polite Requests

1. ***Can*, *could*, and *would*** are modals. Modals are verbs that are usually used with other verbs to express certain ideas. Use *can*, *could*, and *would* when you want to make a polite request or politely ask someone for something. Use the base form of the verb after *can*, *could* and *would*.	***Can** you **do** me favor?* ***Could** you **hold** the door for me?* ***Would** you **help** me with the dishes?*
2. When your request contains another question, use statement word order in the second question.	*Could you tell me **where the restroom is**?*
3. Use *please* to make the question even more polite.	*Could you **please** hold the door for me?* *Would you help me with the dishes, **please**?*
4. To answer politely, use these typical responses. When we say *no*, it's polite to give a reason.	*Yes, of course.* *Sure.* *Certainly.* *No problem.* *I'd be glad to.* *Sorry, I can't. I have to go to class now.* *I'd be happy to.* *I'd like to, but I'm busy.*

2 Choose the correct words and phrases to complete the conversations. Then practice saying them with a partner.

1. **A:** (*Can you* / *You can*) help me with these bags?

   B: Certainly. I'd (*be glad to* / *like to*).

2. **A:** Could (*please you* / *you please*) repeat that?

   B: (*Yes,* / *Sorry,*) I said, "Open your books."

3. **A:** Could you tell me what time (*is it* / *it is*)?

   B: (*Sure.* / *Yes, please.*) It's 3:00.

4 **A:** (*You'd* / *Would you*) loan me $50?

   B: Sorry, I (*can't* / *wouldn't*). I don't have any cash.

3 **Work with a partner. Student A, use the situations below to make a polite request using *can, could,* and *would.* Student B, respond politely. Then switch roles.**

Example:

A: Could you please close the window?

B: Sure, no problem.

1. Close the window.
2. Help me pick up these papers.
3. Turn off your cell phone.
4. Tell me what time your store closes.
5. Drive me to school tomorrow.
6. Help me move.

4 APPLY **Think of five more situations. Practice making requests and responding politely with *can, could,* and *would.***

Go to the **Pearson Practice English App** or **MyEnglishLab** for more grammar practice. Check what you learned in **MyEnglishLab**.

PRONUNCIATION

1 **Read and listen to the examples in the chart. What do you notice about the intonation?**

Using Rising and Falling Intonation in Questions and Statements

Our intonation can rise or fall at the end of a sentence. Our intonation helps listeners to understand the type of question we are asking and to understand when we have completed a sentence or statement.

***Yes / No* Questions** Your voice falls to a low note and then rises to a high note at the end of the question.	*Do you have the time?* *Could you hold the door for me, please?*
***Wh-* Questions (*who, what, where, when, why, how*)** Your voice rises on the important word at the end of a question, and then it falls to a low note.	*What time is the movie?* *Where do you want to meet?*
Statements Your voice rises on the important word at the end of a statement, and then it falls to a low note.	*I'd be happy to.* *Sorry, I can't.*

2 Read and listen to the questions. Draw lines to show where your voice rises and falls at the end. Then listen again and repeat the questions.

1. Would you help me?
2. Is this seat taken?[1]
3. Can I borrow your book, please?
4. Are you going to the party on Saturday?
5. Do you have the time?
6. How much money do you make?
7. What happened to your date?
8. Where did you learn manners?

3 Read and listen to the statements and repeat them. Make your voice rise and then fall at the end.

1. Certainly.
2. Sorry, but I'm using it.
3. I'd rather not say.[2]
4. From my parents.
5. Yeah, I'm looking forward to it.
6. It's four-thirty.
7. No, go ahead.
8. She called it off.

4 Work with a partner. Practice putting the questions from Exercise Two together with an appropriate response from Exercise Three. Pay attention to your intonation.

[1] You can use this question when there is an empty seat next to someone who is sitting.

[2] You can use this statement to respond to a question that you would prefer not to answer.

SPEAKING SKILL

Making Polite Offers and Invitations

There are different ways to make offers and invitations. There are also different ways to accept (say "yes") and to decline (say "no" or turn down the invitation).

MAKING POLITE OFFERS AND INVITATIONS	ACCEPTING AND DECLINING
1. When making an offer, you can use polite questions with *would you like*: *Would you like something to drink?* *Would you like some help?*	 *Yes, I would.* *No, thank you.* *Yes, please.*
2. We can also make offers in less formal ways: *Help yourself to a drink.* *Do you need any help?*	 *Thanks, I appreciate it.* *No, thanks. I'm good.*
3. We can use polite questions with *would like* to invite someone to do something: *Would you like to go to a movie?*	 *I'd love to.* *Sure. That sounds great.* *I don't know. I need to check my schedule.* *Sorry, but I have to study tonight. Can we take a rain check?*

APPLY Go around the class. Use the following information and your own ideas to make polite offers and invitations to your classmates. When you decline an invitation, be sure to give a reason.

Example

A: Would you like something to drink?

B: No, thanks. I'm good.

Offer your classmates:

1. something to drink
2. some chocolate
3. help on their homework
4. a ride home from school

Invite your classmates to:

1. go to a concert tonight
2. come to your house for dinner on Saturday
3. play soccer after class
4. go mountain climbing this summer

Go to **MyEnglishLab** for more skill practice and to check what you learned.

FINAL SPEAKING TASK: Role-play APPLY

A role-play is a short performance. The actors take on roles, or become characters, and act out a situation. The situations are often similar to experiences that people might have in real life.

In this task, you will discuss a situation, then prepare a 3–5-minute role-play that relates to manners.

STEP 1

1 Work in a group of three. Read each situation aloud in your group. Discuss the situations. What could you say? Use *can, could,* and *would.*

a. You are in a restaurant having dinner with a friend. A person is sitting alone at a table near you, talking loudly on a cell phone. You can't hear your friend or enjoy your meal.

b. You are at a party with your friend. Another person comes over and enters the conversation and makes small talk with you. Your friend gets bored and starts texting.

c. You go to your friend's house for dinner. Your friend is from another culture. During dinner, your friend's mother offers you different kinds of food that you've never had before. After trying them, you realize that there is one kind of food that you don't like. Your friend's mother keeps offering more of it to you.

d. You bought expensive tickets to see a concert. You invite your friend to go with you. Your friend turns you down, but you don't believe the reason.

2 Choose one situation and prepare a role-play. Assign roles. Make notes to plan what you will say.

3 APPLY Use the vocabulary, grammar, pronunciation, and speaking skills from the unit. Use the checklist to help you.

☐ **Vocabulary:** Read through the list of vocabulary on page 93. Which words can you include in your role-play to make it clearer and more interesting? Choose at least three words or phrases to use and add them to your notes.

☐ **Grammar:** Think of some polite requests with *can, could,* and *would* to use in your role-play.

☐ **Pronunciation:** Mark your questions and statements with the correct intonation.

☐ **Speaking Skill:** Think of a polite offer or invitation you can use in your role-play.

STEP 2

1 Practice your role-play with your group.

2 Give feedback to your group.

- Did they use the vocabulary correctly?
- Did they use *can, could,* and *would* correctly?
- Did they use appropriate language for polite offers and invitations, accepting and declining?
- Did they use the correct intonation on questions and statements?

STEP 3

Role-play your situation for the class.

LISTENING TASK

Listen to each group's role-play. For each role-play, take notes on the questions below. Then discuss your responses with the class.

1. What situation did the group choose?
2. How did the characters respond?
3. Do you agree with the response? Why or why not?
4. Can you suggest a better way to handle the situation?

ALTERNATIVE SPEAKING TOPIC

APPLY **Work in a small group. Read and discuss the quote below. What do they mean to you? Explain each quote in your own words. Do you agree or disagree with the quote? Explain. Use the vocabulary, grammar, and pronunciation skills you learned in the unit.**

> Treat everyone with politeness, even those who are rude to you—not because they are nice, but because you are.
>
> Author Unknown

> Consideration for others is the basis of a good life, a good society.
>
> Confucius

> Visitors should behave in such a way that the host and hostess feel at home.
>
> J.S. Farynski

CHECK WHAT YOU'VE LEARNED

Check (✔) the outcomes you've met and vocabulary you've learned. Put an X next to the skills and vocabulary you still need to practice.

Learning Outcomes

- ☐ Infer contrasting ideas
- ☐ Organize your notes
- ☐ Recognize and understand summaries and paraphrases
- ☐ Use *can, could,* and *would*
- ☐ Use rising and falling intonation in questions and statements
- ☐ Make polite offers and invitations

Vocabulary

- ☐ appreciate AWL
- ☐ behavior
- ☐ conduct (*v.*) AWL
- ☐ confusing (*adj.*)
- ☐ courteous
- ☐ document (*n.*) AWL
- ☐ electronic device
- ☐ likely
- ☐ manners
- ☐ respect (*n.*)
- ☐ rude
- ☐ text (*v.*)
- ☐ treat (*v.*)

Multi-word Units

- ☐ be raised
- ☐ face-to-face
- ☐ immediate response

Go to **MyEnglishLab** to watch a video about etiquette, access the Unit Project, and take the Unit 4 Achievement Test.

LEARNING OUTCOMES

- Infer meaning from context
- Take notes on cause and effect
- Recognize incomplete and complete ideas
- Distinguish between the simple present and the present progressive
- Link sounds
- Show confidence

Go to **MyEnglishLab** to check what you know.

UNIT 5

The Sounds of Our Lives

1 FOCUS ON THE TOPIC

1. One meaning of *perception* is "the way you notice things with your senses (touch, taste, smell, sight, and hearing)." What kinds of things do we notice from hearing? Give some examples.
2. Imagine you are standing on the city street pictured above. What sounds might you hear? What effect would these sounds have on you? In other words, how would they make you feel? What are some other sounds that affect your *emotions* (your feelings)? How do they make you feel?

2 FOCUS ON LISTENING

LISTENING ONE | Sound Experience

VOCABULARY

1 Read and listen to the beginning of a podcast. Notice the boldfaced words. Try to guess their meanings.

Sound Experience: **Episode 16**

HOST: Hello. This is Sound Experience. I'm Oliver Lee, and today we're talking about noise – a topic that **reminds** me of how my day started yesterday. Guess what time I woke up? 3:00! In the morning! Why? No, I did *not* set my alarm clock for 3 a.m. A car alarm outside my apartment woke me up. There's nothing like the **sudden** sound of a car alarm to make your heart **beat** a little faster at 3 a.m.! Finally, the alarm stopped and I went back to sleep. Then guess what? A fire truck! It came racing down the street with its **high-pitched** siren screaming. Now, I know it's important for alarms and sirens to get our attention and act as a **warning** to people, but how's a guy supposed to sleep?

Noise is a big problem, and it doesn't just **affect** our sleep. Loud noises in our **environment** can make us feel stressed and **anxious**, develop health problems, and lose our hearing. Actually, the number one cause of hearing loss isn't old age. It's noise. Babies and young children are especially **sensitive to** sounds in their environment. Studies show a strong **association between** noisy home environments and learning and memory problems in babies and young children.

Noise causes problems at work and school, too. And sounds don't have to be loud to create "noise" in our environment. Have you ever tried to get some work done while other people are hanging out and talking nearby? It's **annoying**, right? That's because it's hard to concentrate when there is noise around, and human voices are a big distraction. A noisy classroom can keep you from hearing 50% of what is being taught!

So what can we do about all this noise? Well, unless you live on top of a mountain, it isn't easy to find a peaceful environment anymore. But, you can help others around you by limiting the noise *you* make. If you're trying to work, study, or sleep in a noisy environment, try putting in some ear plugs. I know that's what *I'll* be doing tonight.

2 Match the words on the left with the definitions on the right.

f	1. remind	a. making someone feel a little angry or uncomfortable
____	2. sudden	b. the people and things around you
____	3. beat (*v.*)	c. making a sound that is high in pitch (intonation)
____	4. high-pitched	d. something that tells you that something bad or dangerous is going to happen so that you can be ready or avoid it
____	5. warning (*n.*)	e. to do something that makes a change happen in someone or something
____	6. affect (*v.*)	~~f. to make someone remember something~~
____	7. environment	g. to make a regular movement or sound
____	8. anxious	h. a connection or relationship between things
____	9. sensitive to	i. feeling afraid or nervous
____	10. association between	j. easily changed, upset, or hurt by something
____	11. annoying	k. happening quickly when you are not expecting it

Go to the **Pearson Practice English App** or **MyEnglishLab** for more vocabulary practice.

PREVIEW

Listen to the beginning of a podcast on sound. Read and answer each question.

1. Who is the guest?
   a. a musician
   b. a medical doctor
   c. a scientist
2. What is the topic?
   a. how sounds in our environment affect us
   b. sounds in our environment that we enjoy
   c. sounds we hear when we're sleeping
3. What else do you think the speakers will talk about? Make three predictions.
   a. ____________________
   b. ____________________
   c. ____________________

LISTEN

1 Listen to the whole podcast. Create a chart like the one below to take notes.

TAKE NOTES Sound Effects

Main Ideas	*Details*
How sounds affect us	• *always hear, even when asleep* • *brains check for sounds in environment -> know what's happening* • *big effect on body, mind, emotions*

2 Compare your notes with a partner's. How can you improve your notes?

Go to **MyEnglishLab** to view example notes.

MAIN IDEAS

Read each statement. Write *T* (true) or *F* (false). Correct the false statements. Use your notes to help you.

_____ 1. Sudden loud sounds make our hearts beat faster.

_____ 2. Our ears are most sensitive to sounds that are low in pitch.

_____ 3. As we get older, we are better able to hear high-pitched sounds.

_____ 4. Loud, low-pitched sounds can make us feel scared.

_____ 5. There is a strong association between sounds and emotions.

DETAILS

1 Listen again and add to your notes. Then use your notes to circle the best answer to complete each statement.

1. Dr. Amari suggests waking up to _________ .
   a. an alarm clock b. light c. nature sounds

2. The sound of the bicycle brakes is an example of a sound that is very _________ .
   a. loud b. sudden c. high-pitched

3. "The Mosquito" is an electronic device that creates very _________ sounds.
   a. high-pitched b. scary c. relaxing

an alarm clock

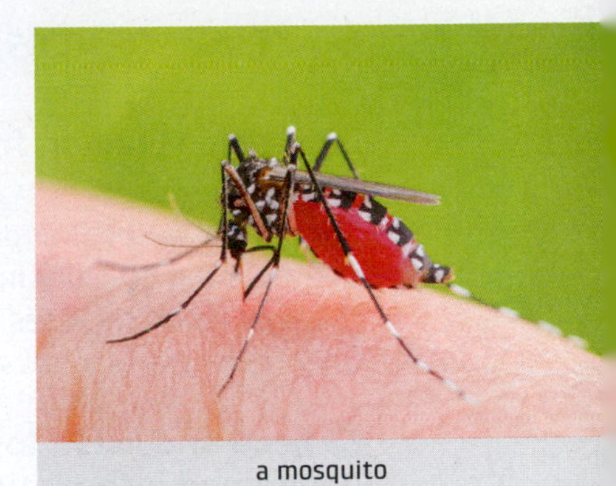
a mosquito

4. The Mosquito can be heard by people around _________ years old

   a. 3–5 b. 13–25 c. 15–35

5. Shopkeepers use the Mosquito to _________ their stores.

   a. keep young people away from b. bring young people into c. bring old people into

6. Loud, low-pitched sounds can cause a "fight or flight" response in which your body gets ready to fight or _________ from danger.

   a. get help b. hide c. run away

7. Loud sounds in our environment such as airplane noise can make us feel _________ .

   a. sad b. anxious c. excited

8. Dr. Amari played a sound of a mosquito as an example of the association between _________ .

   a. high-pitched sounds and insects b. nature sounds and feelings c. sounds and emotion

the peaceful sound of running water

9. Listening to peaceful nature sounds can cause you to stop focusing on _________ .

   a. your thoughts and worries b. your heartbeat c. noise in your environment

2 With a partner, take turns summarizing your notes. Then discuss how your notes and your answers in Preview helped you understand the listening.

Go to **MyEnglishLab** for more listening practice.

MAKE INFERENCES

Inferring Meaning from Context

Sometimes a speaker does not directly say what he or she means. The listener can infer, or guess, the meaning by thinking about the context (situation), the other words that the speaker says, and the way he or she uses intonation and emphatic stress. Inferring a speaker's meaning will help you to fully understand what a speaker is trying to say.

Read and listen to this example. What does the host mean when he says the underlined information?

Example

DR. AMARI: Actually, a study done by the National Institute of Health in Japan showed that if you wake up to the sound of an alarm clock it may be bad for your heart. You may want to wake up to light instead.

HOST: What do you know? Well, you should tell **that** to the people who make car alarms!

Explanation

When the host says, "You should tell **that** to the people who make car alarms!" his intonation tells us that he has a negative feeling about car alarms. We can infer that the host thinks that car alarms are bad for people, too.

Listen to the excerpts. Take notes of the key words, intonation and stress that you hear. Then read each question and choose the implied meaning.

Excerpt One

What does the host mean when he says, "So, I guess there's one good thing about getting older"?

a. It's good that older people are using the Mosquito.

b. There aren't many good things about getting older.

What words and intonation helped you infer the meaning? ____________________

Excerpt Two

What does the host mean when he says, "Now that's more like it"?

a. That sound is like the other sounds we heard.

b. I enjoy that sound more than the other sounds.

What words and intonation helped you infer the meaning? ____________________

DISCUSS

USE YOUR NOTES

APPLY Find information in your notes to use in your discussion.

Work in a small group. Read the questions. Discuss your ideas.

1. What are the negative effects of loud, sudden sounds or sounds that are very high or low in pitch? What are some examples of sounds that you hear in everyday life that may have negative effects on you?
2. How does the Mosquito work to keep young people from hanging out near shops? What do you think about the Mosquito? Should shopkeepers in your city use it? Why or why not?
3. What are some examples of nature sounds that can help people to relax? Do you ever listen to nature sounds to relax? Do you think that listening to recorded nature sounds has the same benefits as listening to sounds while in nature? Explain your answer.

Go to **MyEnglishLab** to give your opinion about another question.

LISTENING TWO | Music With A Purpose

VOCABULARY

1 Read the interview with a musician. Notice the boldfaced words. Try to guess their meanings.

HOST: So, let's talk about your new song. It's a real hit!

MUSICIAN: Yeah, people seem to love it. Whenever we perform it live[1], people are clapping to the beat or out on the dance floor.

HOST: Yeah, it has a great energy to it, and the **rhythm** makes it perfect for dancing. So, tell us about how you wrote it. What was your creative process?

MUSICIAN: Well, I woke up one day, and I was in a great **mood**. I was feeling happy and **energetic**, and excited about writing a new song. I decided I wanted to write an **upbeat** tune, you know, something to make people feel good.

HOST: So tell us about the **lyrics**. Do they have any special meaning?

MUSICIAN: No, not really. I just wanted to describe how I feel when I'm with my friends and we're having a great time together.

2 Write the boldfaced words next to the correct definitions.

a. ____________ having or showing a lot of energy

b. ____________ happy and positive; making you think good things will happen

c. ____________ the way sounds are repeated over time

d. ____________ the words of a song

e. ____________ the way someone feels at a particular time

Go to the **Pearson Practice English App** or **MyEnglishLab** for more vocabulary practice.

[1] **live:** in front of an audience

NOTE-TAKING SKILL

Taking Notes on Cause and Effect

Causes are the reasons that events or actions happen. *Effects* are the results of events or actions. Speakers use different words and phrases to signal causes and effects. Listening for these words and phrases can help you to identify causes and effects and write them in your notes.

PHRASES THAT INTRODUCE CAUSES AND EFFECTS	
(Cause) causes (effect)	*Loud noises **cause** us to feel stressed and anxious*
(Cause) make(s) someone or something (effect)	*Car alarms can **make you** lose sleep.*
(Cause) help(s) someone or something (effect)	*Nature sounds can **help you** to relax.*
When (cause), (effect)	***When** you hear an alarm, your heart beats faster.*
If (cause), (effect)	***If** you listen to loud music, you can damage your hearing.*
(cause), so (effect)	*The teenagers heard an annoying, high-pitched sound, **so** they left.*

One way you can note causes and effects is by using arrows. Draw the arrow from the cause to the effect to show the relationship between the two ideas. Look at the example below.

Example

You hear:	You write:
Sounds help us know what's happening in our environment.	sounds → know what's happening in envir.

Sometimes a cause can have multiple effects. You can show this in your notes in a few different ways. You can create a list of arrows after the cause; you can separate multiple effects with commas; or you can connect the effects with the plus sign. Look at these three different ways to write such notes:

Hear lion's roar → heart beats faster → breathe quickly → "fight / flight" response	Hear lion's roar → heart beats faster, breathe quickly, "fight / flight" response	Hear lion's roar → heart beats faster + breathe quickly + "fight / flight" response

Sometimes, the effect of something can be the cause of something else. Look at this example:

Example

You hear:	You write:
The Mosquito causes young people to feel annoyed, so they stay away from public places	The Mosquito → young people annoyed → stay away public places

1 Listen to the excerpts and note the causes and the effects. Note the causes before the arrows and the effects after the arrows.

Excerpt One

________________ → ________________

Excerpt Two

________________ → ________________

Excerpt Three

________________ → ________________

Excerpt Four

________________ → ________________ → ________________

2 Compare your notes with a partner's. Use your notes to retell the causes and effects in the excerpts you heard.

Go to **MyEnglishLab** for more note-taking practice.

COMPREHENSION

1 Listen to the speaker talk about the effects of music. Create a chart like the one below to take notes. Try to use arrows to note the causes and effects.

TAKE NOTES Music with a Purpose

Main Ideas	*Details*

Listening to music while studying

Listening to music during exercise

2 Read each question and circle the correct answer. Use your notes to help you.

> **USE YOUR NOTES**
>
> Compare your notes with a partner's. How can you improve your notes next time?

1. How can listening to music before and during exercise make you feel?
   a. more excited b. more energetic
2. Which parts of the brain are connected to hearing a rhythm?
   a. the same parts that help us think b. the same parts that help us move
3. Why does listening to upbeat music help you to exercise longer?
   a. because it improves your mood b. because it plays without stopping
4. What kind of music should you avoid when you work or study?
   a. music with a regular rhythm b. music with lyrics
5. In one study, what helped people to remember information better?
   a. listening to upbeat music b. listening to quiet music
6. In another study, what helped the students to remember new vocabulary words better?
   a. saying the words b. singing the words
7. What is the best music to listen to before you sleep?
   a. music that is not too loud or high in pitch b. music that is not too loud or upbeat
8. What rhythm is the best for helping you to sleep better?
   a. about 16 beats per minute b. about 60 beats per minute

LISTENING SKILL

1 Read and listen to an excerpt from the podcast about sounds. Notice the speaker's intonation at the end of the boldfaced words. Does the intonation change slightly (a little bit), or fall to a low note?

HOST: **Next**, I'd like to welcome today's **guest**, neuroscientist Leila **Amari**. She's here to talk to us about **sounds** and how they affect **us**.

Recognizing Incomplete and Complete Ideas

In speaking, intonation that rises or falls slightly signals that an idea is incomplete. The small change in intonation signals that there is more information to come. Speakers signal incomplete ideas at the ends of phrases or items in a list to show that their statement is not finished, and they are going to say more. Intonation that falls to a low note shows that a speaker's idea is complete. Speakers signal complete ideas at the ends of statements to show that they are finished. Listening for incomplete and complete ideas can help you to follow a speaker's ideas.

Read and listen to another excerpt from Listening One.

Example

HOST: So, we all know that the world's full of sounds. Some we want to hear, and some we don't.

Explanation

In the example, the speaker's intonation changes slightly on **so** and **hear** to show that his thought is incomplete and he is going to say more. His intonation falls to a low note on **sounds** and **don't** to show that his ideas are complete.

2 Read and listen to the following excerpts. Write *I* (incomplete) or *C* (complete) for the final idea in each sentence.

_____ 1. That sound is high-pitched

_____ 2. The sudden sound surprises you

_____ 3. You felt surprised

_____ 4. They get your attention

_____ 5. Your heart beats faster

_____ 6. You breathe more quickly

_____ 7. Your body gets ready to fight or run

_____ 8. We call this the "fight or flight" response

Go to **MyEnglishLab** for more skill practice.

CONNECT THE LISTENINGS

ORGANIZE

Work with a partner. Sort the types of sounds or music and their effects in the chart.

USE YOUR NOTES

APPLY Review your notes from Listening One and Two. Use the information in your notes to complete the chart.

happy music

high-pitched (e.g. bicycle brakes, the Mosquito)

It surprises us and makes our heart beat faster.

music with a strong rhythm

Our mood improves, and we can exercise longer.

quiet, slow, peaceful (e.g. nature sounds, relaxing music)

We feel anxious – "fight or flight" response.

We feel more energetic.

TYPES OF SOUNDS OR MUSIC	EFFECTS
1. loud, sudden (e.g. alarm clock)	
2.	We feel annoyed.
3. loud, low-pitched (e.g. lion, airplanes)	
4.	We feel relaxed.
5.	
6. favorite upbeat music	
7.	It may help us remember information.

SYNTHESIZE

Work with the same partner. Student A, you are an interviewer. Ask Student B questions about the different types of sounds or music and their effects. Student B, you are a neuroscientist who studies the effects of sound and music. Answer Student A's questions. Use the information from Organize. Then switch roles.

Example

A: What is one type of sound or music that affects us?

B: One type of sound is a loud, sudden sound.

A: How does it affect us?

B: It surprises us, and it makes our heart beat faster.

Go to **MyEnglishLab** to check what you learned.

3 FOCUS ON SPEAKING

VOCABULARY

REVIEW

Words can have a positive, negative, or neutral (not positive or negative) meaning.

1 Complete the chart with the words from the box. Think about how the words are used in the listenings.

~~affect~~	beat	lyrics	relaxed / relaxing	stressed
~~annoyed / annoying~~	~~energetic~~	mood	remind	upbeat
anxious	environment	peaceful	rhythm	warning
association between	high-pitched	pleasant	sensitive to	

POSITIVE	NEGATIVE	NEUTRAL
energetic	*annoyed / annoying*	*affect*

2 Work with a partner. Compare your charts and discuss the reasons for your choices. Then take turns making sentences using two different words from the chart.

Example

Music with a strong <u>rhythm</u> can make you more <u>energetic</u>.

EXPAND

1 Read the conversation. Notice the boldfaced words. Try to guess their meanings.

A: Hey, did you listen to that new **album** that I sent you?

B: Yeah, I love it! That's my favorite group!

A: I thought you'd like it. So, what's your favorite **track**?

B: Well, they're all great, but I especially like the first song. It's such a **catchy** tune, I was singing it all day. And the **vocals** are beautiful. The singer has such a lovely voice. How about you? What did you think?

A: I like that song, too, but I think I prefer the second track on the album.

B: Remind me – which one is that?

A: It's the only one that's **instrumental**. There's no singing, but I love it because it has a great beat. It's definitely danceable. You need to **turn up** the **volume** when you listen to that one!

2 Write each boldfaced word in the conversation next to its definition.

1. ________________ easy to remember
2. ________________ a group of songs or pieces of music on a record, CD, download, etc.
3. ________________ music made by instruments playing, not people singing
4. ________________ to make a machine produce more sound by using the controls
5. ________________ one of the songs or pieces of music on a recording
6. ________________ the amount of sound produced by a person or a machine
7. ________________ the part of a piece of music that is sung and not played on an instrument

CREATE

APPLY **Work in a small group. Take turns asking and answering the questions. Use the boldfaced words and at least one other vocabulary word from the box in each of your answers.**

affect	beat	environment	pitch	rhythm	upbeat
association with	energetic	instrumental	remind	sensitive to	vocals

1. Name a sound that you think is **annoying**. Why does this sound annoy you?
2. What sounds put you in a good **mood**? Which sounds put you in a bad mood?
3. What sounds causes you to feel **anxious**? Which sounds cause you to feel relaxed?
4. Do you ever read song **lyrics** as a way to learn new English words? If so, give an example of a song in English that you like. Does listening to music help you to learn the **rhythm** of English? How?

Go to the **Pearson Practice English App** or **MyEnglishLab** for more vocabulary practice.

GRAMMAR FOR SPEAKING

1 Read the sentences. Then answer the questions below.

A: What are you doing right now?

B: I'm listening to a new song. It sounds great!

a. What time period are the people talking about? How do you know?

____

b. What are the verbs? Underline them.

c. What form are the verbs? ______________________________

d. Are all the verbs formed in the same way? ______________________________

Simple Present vs. Present Progressive

1. Use the simple present to talk about habits, customs, routines, or facts.	*My alarm clock **wakes** me up at 7:00 every morning.*
2. Use the present progressive to talk about activities that are happening right now or these days.	***I'm doing** my homework right now.*
3. To form the present progressive, use ***be*** + verb ***-ing***	*Hector **is taking** three classes this semester.*
4. The simple present uses ***do*** and ***does*** as helping verbs in questions and negative statements.	**A:** *Where **do** you usually **study**?* **B:** *I usually study in the library. I **don't like** to study at home. It's too noisy.*
5. The present progressive uses ***am***, ***is***, and ***are*** as helping verbs in questions and statements (both affirmative and negative).	**A:** *What **are** you **doing** right now?* **B:** ***I'm singing** my vocabulary words.* **A:** *Then **I'm not coming** to your house to study!*
6. We don't usually use non-action verbs in the present progressive. Instead, we use the simple present, even if the verb expresses something happening right now. Non-action verbs can be used to: a. express a state of being b. express a need or preference c. describe a thought d. express an emotion e. show possession f. describe sense or appearance Sometimes verbs have an action and a non-action meaning. For example, ***have*** is a non-action verb when it shows possession. It is an action verb when it means to experience something. ***Hear*** is a non-action verb. It is an unplanned action. ***Listen*** to is an action verb. It happens for a purpose.	*I am late for class.* *NOT: I am being late for class.* *I **am** late for class.* *She **prefers** this song.* *Jake **knows** this band.* *I **feel** anxious about the test.* *We **have** a big music collection.* *That song **sounds** upbeat. / You **look** annoyed.* *I **have** one hour to eat lunch.* *I'm **having** a great time at the concert!* *I am trying to study, but I **hear** my classmates talking. It's a distraction.* *I'm studying right now, and I'**m listening to** some music at the same time. It helps me to relax and concentrate.*

2 **Complete the conversation with the simple present or the present progressive form of the verbs in parentheses.**

Anila: What ____________ you ____________ (1. listen to)? I ____________ (2. hear) the music through your earbuds.

Ji-Woo: It ____________ (3. be) my favorite band. Actually, I ____________ (4. watch) a video. They ____________ (5. play) the song "Energetic." I ____________ (6. love) it! It ____________ (7. have) a beautiful piano melody at the beginning. Now, the beat ____________ (8. get) faster and they ____________ (9. dance).

Anila: Now what ____________ they ____________ (10. do)?

Ji-Woo: Oh, they ____________ (11. sing), ____________ (12. hang out) and ____________ (13. have) a good time together!

Anila: It ____________ (14. look) like a fun video. But maybe you should turn down the volume. ____________ you ____________ (15. know) listening to loud music can damage your hearing?

3 APPLY **Work in small groups. Take turns asking acting out an activities and emotions without saying anything. Your group members will guess what you're doing. Use action and non-action verbs.**

Example

A: You hear a fire alarm!

B: No.

C: You're watching fireworks.

B: No.

D: I know. You hear the Mosquito.

B: That's right!

Go to the **Pearson Practice English App** or **MyEnglishLab** for more grammar practice. Check what you learned in **MyEnglishLab**.

PRONUNCIATION

1 Linking means joining words together. When you speak, link the final sound of a word to the next word in the phrase. This will help you move smoothly from one word to the next and sound more fluent. Read and listen to the examples and notice how the final sound in each word is linked to the next word. Then repeat the sentences.

HOST: I'd like to welcome today's guest.

HOST: You should tell that to the people who make car alarms.

2 Read the rules for linking sounds. Then read and listen to the examples in the chart.

Linking Sounds

Final Consonant + Beginning Vowel Join a final consonant sound to the beginning vowel sound of the next word. Pronounce the consonant clearly.	effect on wake up help us car alarms
Final Consonant + Different Beginning Consonant When the final consonant sound is a /p/, /b/, /t/, /d/, /k/, or /g/, hold the final consonant, and say the next word. Don't add a vowel sound between the two consonants.	I'd like like to start with stop focusing
Final Consonant + Same Beginning Consonant When the same consonant sounds come together, say them as one consonant. Don't say the consonant twice.	that to take care one night regular rhythm notice sounds
Final Vowel + Beginning Vowel When two vowel sounds come together, use /y/ or /w/ to link them.	say it see it go away How often?

3 Listen and repeat the sentences. Link the words in each phrase or sentence together.

1. Play it again.
2. I had a hard day. I need to relax.
3. High-pitched sounds are annoying.
4. That sound makes him anxious.

5. Most music has a regular rhythm.
6. How about watching a movie?
7. I'm excited about tonight's show.

4 Work with a partner. Take turns saying sentences using a verb from the box on the left with a word or phrase from the box on the right. Link the words when appropriate.

Examples

A: I'm in a good mood.

B: I'm sensitive to the sound of alarm clocks.

be	listen to
be sensitive to	make
feel	perform
have	play
hear	sing

an alarm clock	fun
an association	in a good mood / in a bad mood
an effect	pitch
annoyed	relaxed
anxious	sounds
a melody	upbeat
a song	

SPEAKING SKILL

Showing Confidence

When you present, you can show confidence and make a connection with your audience by using effective body language. To show confidence:

- Use a confident body posture. Stand up straight, but relax your body. Keep your arms open and stand firmly on both feet.
- Face your audience when you are speaking.
- Make eye contact with your audience. Don't read your notes or look away from your audience when you are speaking.
- Smile and look interested in your topic.

This presenter is showing confidence. He is making a connection with his audience.

This presenter is not showing confidence. He is not making a connection with his audience.

1 **Take notes to answer the question: What is your favorite kind of music? Why do you like it?**

2 **Practice showing confidence. Present to a partner. Tell your partner about your favorite kind of music. Follow the tips listed above.**

3 APPLY **Practice showing confidence again. This time, present the same information to a small group.**

- The group members should sit in a semi-circle in front of you.
- Practice looking at everyone in the group while you speak. Look at one part of the group to make one point; then move your eyes to another part of the group to make your next point.
- Listen, watch, and give feedback to the other members of your group about how they could improve upon showing confidence while presenting information.

Go to **MyEnglishLab** for more skill practice and to check what you learned.

FINAL SPEAKING TASK: Oral Presentation APPLY

In this activity, you will prepare a 2–3-minute oral presentation about a song or piece of music that you enjoy and listen to in your everyday life.

PREPARE

1 Think of a song or piece of instrumental music that you enjoy and listen to often, or that you play yourself. It could be something you listen to when you exercise, work, study, relax, or go to sleep. It could also be music that puts you in a good mood or reminds you of a special time in your life. If possible, find an audio or video recording of the music that you can share with your classmates. Plan to play a short (10–30 second) excerpt of the music during your presentation.

2 Plan your presentation. Complete the chart by taking notes about the music.

1. What is the name of the song or piece of music?	
2. Who is performing the music in your recording? Are different people singing or playing instruments?	
3. Describe the music. What does it sound like? Consider the tune, the beat, and the instruments. If there is singing, consider the vocals.	
4. If there are lyrics, what are they about?	
5. When do you usually listen to it? What do you usually do while you listen?	
6. How does it make you feel?	
7. Why do you like it? Does it help you to exercise, work, relax, or sleep?	

3 APPLY **Prepare what you will say in your presentation. Use the vocabulary, grammar, pronunciation, and speaking skills from the unit. Use the checklist to help you.**

- □ **Vocabulary:** Read through the list of vocabulary on page 117. Which words can you include in your presentation to make it clearer and more interesting? Choose at least three words or phrases to use and add them to your notes.
- □ **Grammar:** Scan your notes for the present progressive tense and non-action verbs in the simple present tense. Did you form the verbs correctly?
- □ **Pronunciation:** Record yourself practicing. Then listen back. Did you link words together?
- □ **Speaking Skill:** Think about how you can show confidence while speaking. Make notecards with only the key words from your presentation so that you can make more eye contact with the audience.

PRACTICE

1 **Practice your presentation with a partner. Start with the name of the piece and the performers. Next, play 10–30 seconds of it. Then continue with your presentation about the music. Use your notecards and make sure to look up at your partner when you are speaking.**

2 **Give feedback to your partner.**

- Did you understand your partner's ideas?
- Did your partner show confidence and make eye contact with you?
- What did your partner do well? How can he or she improve the presentation?

PRESENT

Take turns delivering your 2–3-minute presentation. Your classmates will listen, take notes, and ask you questions when you are finished.

LISTENING TASK

Listen to the other students' presentations. Take notes. When you are finished, discuss these questions:

1. Which song or piece of music is the most upbeat? Relaxing? Emotional?
2. Which song or piece of music do you like the most? Why?

ALTERNATIVE SPEAKING TOPIC

APPLY **Work in a small group. Discuss the questions. Use the vocabulary, grammar, pronunciation, and speaking skills you learned in the unit.**

1. How could your school create a better sound environment for students? Give examples to support your ideas.
2. What are some things that people can do to make less noise in public places, such as workplaces, restaurants, and city streets?
3. Listening to loud music or noises can cause people to lose their hearing. What are some ways that people can protect their ears and avoid losing their hearing?
4. Do you usually prefer a loud, energetic environment or a quiet, calm environment? Give some examples.
5. How is the sound of English like music? Think of the intonation, rhythm, and volume. Give some examples.

CHECK WHAT YOU'VE LEARNED

Check (✓) the outcomes you've met and vocabulary you've learned. Put an X next to the skills and vocabulary you still need to practice.

Learning Outcomes

- ☐ Infer meaning from context
- ☐ Take notes on cause and effect
- ☐ Recognize incomplete and complete ideas
- ☐ Distinguish between the simple present and the present progressive
- ☐ Link sounds
- ☐ Show confidence

Vocabulary

- ☐ affect (*v.*) AWL
- ☐ annoying (*adj.*)
- ☐ anxious
- ☐ beat (*v.*)
- ☐ energetic AWL
- ☐ environment AWL
- ☐ high-pitched
- ☐ lyrics
- ☐ mood
- ☐ remind
- ☐ rhythm
- ☐ sudden
- ☐ upbeat
- ☐ warning (*n.*)

Multi-word Units

- ☐ association between
- ☐ sensitive to

Go to **MyEnglishLab** to watch a video about color psychology, access the Unit Project, and take the Unit 5 Achievement Test.

LEARNING OUTCOMES

- > Infer feelings from tone and word choice
- > Organize your notes with numbers
- > Recognize and understand definitions
- > Use the simple past
- > Pronounce *-ed* endings
- > Use signal phrases in presentations

Go to **MyEnglishLab** to check what you know.

UNIT 6

Everyday Heroes

1 FOCUS ON THE TOPIC

1. Look at the photo. How do you think the people feel? How is the man helping the child?
2. What are some reasons that people help others in need? What are some reasons that people don't help others?
3. What does the word *hero* mean to you? What is an "everyday hero"? What are some ways that people can be heroes in everyday life?

2 FOCUS ON LISTENING

LISTENING ONE | The Subway Hero

VOCABULARY

1 ▶ **Read and listen to the column from a student newspaper about heroes. Notice the boldfaced words and phrases. Try to guess their meanings.**

What Does It Take to Be a Hero?

By Courtney Smith

We can all think of heroes in our lives. But, did you ever think about what it really takes to be a hero? What does someone have to do to become a hero? Well, in my opinion, there are four characteristics of a hero.

First of all, heroes help others in need. For example, a hero may help someone in a dangerous situation. Or, a hero may provide a service to people who live in their **community** who need help.

In addition, heroes make the choice to help out because they want to, not because it is required or because someone told them to do it.

Third, heroes help others even when there are **risks**. This means that heroes will help even in situations where there is a chance that they will get hurt or something bad will happen to them as a result of their actions.

Finally, heroes help others even when there is no reward for their actions. They don't do good things because they want to get something for themselves in return. They just help because they believe it is **the right thing** to do.

For example, take the story of Laurie Eldridge. One day, Ms. Eldridge was outside in her garden, when she looked up and saw a car stuck on some nearby train tracks. Inside the car was an 81-year-old woman who didn't notice there was a train coming toward her. Ms. Eldridge **reacted** quickly. She ran to the car and pulled the woman out of it just before the train arrived. The car was destroyed, but it **turned out** that the woman, Angeline Pascucci, was OK.

Laurie Eldridge didn't think her actions were **brave**. She said she just did what any **ordinary** person would do. However, the people in her community disagreed. They **praised** her actions and gave her an award to thank her for her **courage**.

To me, Laurie Eldridge is a hero because she risked her own life to help someone else in need. In the end, she didn't expect anything for herself. Just knowing she helped another person was reward enough for her.

2 Write each boldfaced word or phrase from the text next to its definition or synonym.

1. ________________ the willingness to do something you know is difficult or dangerous
2. ________________ behaved in a particular way when something happened
3. ________________ to have a particular (and sometimes unexpected) result
4. ________________ a group of people who live in the same area
5. ________________ possibilities that something bad will happen
6. ________________ the correct or acceptable thing
7. ________________ feeling or showing no fear; not afraid
8. ________________ not unusual or special
9. ________________ said good things about

Go to the **Pearson Practice English App** or **MyEnglishLab** for more vocabulary practice.

PREVIEW

A news reporter is telling the story of an everyday hero.

Listen to the beginning of the news program. What happened? What do you think will happen next? List three possible events.

1. ____
2. ____
3. ____

subway platform and tracks

LISTEN

1 Listen to the whole program. Create a chart like the one below to take notes.

TAKE NOTES The Subway Hero

Main Ideas	Details
Meaning of "hero"	• *Superheroes* • *Famous ppl who do great things* • *Everyday ppl who help others?*

2 Compare your notes with a partner's. How can you improve your notes?

Go to **MyEnglishLab** to view example notes.

MAIN IDEAS

All of the statements contain some FALSE information. Use your notes to help you correct the statements. Cross out the parts that are false and write the correct information. Some statements can be corrected in more than one way.

Example

Subway riders were waiting ~~on the train~~. *on the platform*

1. A young woman named Cameron Hollopeter fell on the subway tracks.
2. Wesley Autrey jumped onto the tracks and pulled Cameron Hollopeter back onto the platform.
3. The two men got hurt by the subway train.
4. Wesley Autrey thinks he is a hero.

Wesley Autrey and his two daughters

DETAILS

1 Listen again and add to your notes. Choose the best answer to complete each statement. Use your notes to help you.

1. Cameron Hollopeter is a ________ .
   a. high school student
   b. college student
   c. college teacher

2. Wesley Autrey is a ________ construction worker.

a. 20-year-old

b. 50-year-old

c. 55-year-old

3. Wesley Autrey left his two daughters ____________ on the platform.

a. alone

b. with a woman

c. with his family

4. The train arrived ____________ after Wesley Autrey jumped on to the tracks.

a. two seconds

b. six seconds

c. six minutes

5. The subway train passed ____________ above Mr. Autrey's head.

a. less than an inch

b. less than two inches

c. less than a foot

6. Richard thinks that jumping on to the subway tracks was ____________ .

a. brave

b. crazy

c. exciting

7. Emily thought about ____________ .

a. Cameron Hollopeter

b. Wesley Autrey

c. Wesley Autrey's daughters

8. Wesley Autrey didn't worry about ________ .

a. his daughters

b. being late for work

c. getting hurt

9. Wesley Autrey said his ________ raised him to help people.

a. mother

b. father

c. family

2 With a partner, take turns summarizing your notes. Then discuss how your notes and your answers in Preview helped you understand the listening.

Go to MyEnglishLab for more listening practice.

MAKE INFERENCES

Inferring Feelings from Tone and Word Choice

An inference is a guess about something that is not said directly.

We can often guess speakers' feelings by the tone, or sound, of their voice. For example, tone of voice shows if a speaker is happy, sad, angry, surprised, or worried. We can also guess feelings by the words that speakers use.

Listen to the example. How did the speaker feel? What word best describes the speaker's tone of voice? Was she *surprised* or *worried*? What words does the speaker use to show this feeling?

Example

WOMAN 1: So, this guy was just lying there on the tracks, and he couldn't get up. And then I saw that a train was coming! . . . And then this man—I couldn't believe it—he just jumped down, right onto the tracks!

Explanation

In this example, the speaker uses a *surprised* tone of voice. She also uses the words *I couldn't believe it* to show that the action surprised her.

Listen to three excerpts from the report. After each one, check the adjective that describes the speaker's tone of voice and write down words that show how the speaker was feeling.

Excerpt One

Tone of voice: ☐ surprised ☐ worried

Words to show feelings: ____________________

Excerpt Two

Tone of voice: ☐ surprised ☐ worried

Words to show feelings: ____________________

Excerpt Three

Tone of voice: ☐ surprised ☐ worried

Words to show feelings: ____________________

DISCUSS

Work in a small group. Read the questions. Discuss your ideas.

1. What risks did Wesley Autrey take to save Cameron Hollopeter's life? Would you do it? Why or why not?
2. How did the subway riders Richard and Emily feel about Mr. Autrey's actions? Which person do you most agree with? Why?
3. What reasons did Wesley Autrey give for risking his life to help another person? Do you think most people would do the same? Why or why not?

USE YOUR NOTES

APPLY Find information in your notes to use in your discussion.

Go to MyEnglishLab to give your opinion about another question.

LISTENING TWO | Psychology Lecture—Altruism

VOCABULARY

1 Read the message Mei wrote to her friend Linh. Notice the boldfaced words. Try to guess their meanings.

L: Hey, Mei! How's your summer going?

M: Hi Linh! It's going great! I found an awesome summer job at a camp for kids called "Hero Camp." No, we don't climb buildings or fight criminals!

L: Haha! So what do you do?

M: The goal is to teach kids to **show concern for** others. I'm **responsible for** a group of nine- and ten-year-olds. Every day, we **volunteer** to help out in the community. Yesterday, we cleaned up trash in the park, and tomorrow we are going to help some elderly[1] people with housework. Next week, we're going to an animal shelter[2]. Here is a photo of the kids cleaning up the park.

L: Wow! That's so cool!

M: Yeah, the kids are so excited to go to the animal shelter! They are learning the value of being kind and **unselfish**, and I'm learning that I love working with kids. I think it's in my **genes** since my parents are teachers, too.

L: I'm not surprised. 🙂

M: How about you? How's your summer going?

L: . . .

---

[1] **elderly:** used as a polite way of saying that someone is old or becoming old

[2] **animal shelter:** a place that provides food and care for animals, such as cats and dogs, that have nowhere to go

2 Write the bolfaced word next to the correct definition.

1. _______________ small parts of cells that come from our parents and affect our characteristics
2. _______________ having the job or duty to take care of someone or something
3. _______________ caring about other people and putting their needs before your own
4. _______________ to offer to do something without getting paid or being told you must do it
5. _______________ to demonstrate a feeling of worry

Go to the **Pearson Practice English App** or **MyEnglishLab** for more vocabulary practice.

NOTE-TAKING SKILL

Organizing Your Notes with Numbers

When speakers tell a story or talk about past events, they talk about the events in the order that they happened. Using numbers (*1*, *2*, *3*, etc.) to organize your notes can help you to write down and remember the events in the correct order.

Words that introduce the time order of events:

First . . .

Second . . .

Third . . .

Next . . .

Then . . . .

Later . . .

When . . .

Before . . .

After . . .

Finally . . .

In lectures, speakers often list items. Using numbers can help you to organize all of the items in your notes in the correct order.

Phrases that introduce a list or items in a list:

There are (four) things . . .

The first / One (thing) is . . .

The second / Another (thing) is . . .

In addition, . . .

The third (thing) is . . .

Finally . . . / The final (thing) is . . .

1 **Listen to an excerpt of a presentation and list the characteristics in the correct order. Then compare your notes with a partner's.**

Characteristics of ______________________________

____

____

____

____

2 **Listen to a conversation. Note the events in the story in the correct order. Then compare your notes with a partner's.**

____

____

____

____

Go to **MyEnglishLab** for more note-taking practice.

COMPREHENSION

1 Listen to a psychology lecture on altruism. Create a chart like the one below to take notes. Try to use numbers to note events or lists.

TAKE NOTES **Psychology Lecture—Altruism**

Main Ideas	Details

2 Identify if the statements below are true or false. Use your notes to help you. Write *T* (true) or *F* (false). Correct the false statements.

_____ 1. Altruism means showing concern for ourselves and others.

_____ 2. Holding the door for someone or giving money to a homeless person are examples of altruism.

_____ 3. Only about 40 percent of people take risks to help others.

_____ 4. We are more likely to help strangers than we are to help people we know.

_____ 5. We are more likely to help those in need when we are in a crowd of people.

_____ 6. A study in Germany found that people who are born with a certain gene are more likely to give money to help others.

_____ 7. People who have positive attitudes are less likely to help others.

_____ 8. The way people are raised may be a factor in altruistic behavior.

USE YOUR NOTES

Compare your notes with a partner's. How can you improve your notes next time?

Volunteers helping to feed the homeless

LISTENING SKILL

1 Listen to the excerpt. What word is the speaker defining? What does it mean? What phrase introduces the definition?

Word: ___________

Definition: ___________

Phrase that introduces definition: ___________

Recognizing and Understanding Definitions

In lectures, speakers often define new terms. Listening for definitions can help you to understand and note new terms as you listen.

Listen to the definition again.

Example

How does the speaker emphasize the new word? How does the speaker signal the definition?

Explanation

In the example, the speaker defined the word *risks*. The phrase "this means" introduces the meaning—situations where there is a chance of getting hurt or having something bad happen.

Speakers will emphasize new terms in different ways:

- by saying the term slowly and carefully
- by repeating the term
- by pausing and then defining the term

Speakers sometimes use certain words or phrases to signal a definition:

That is / That means . . .

"Hero" means . . .

A hero is . . .

In other words, a hero is . . .

"Hero" is defined as . . .

2 Listen to the following excerpts from Psychology Lecture: Altruism. Write the word that the speaker is defining, and then write the definition.

Excerpt One

New Term: ___________

Definition: ___________

Excerpt Two

New Term: ___________

Definition: ___________

Excerpt Three

New Term: ______________

Definition: ______________

Go to **MyEnglishLab** for more skill practice.

CONNECT THE LISTENINGS

ORGANIZE

Sort the general ideas from the lecture in Listening Two and the specific examples from Listening One to complete the chart.

USE YOUR NOTES

APPLY Review your notes from Listening One and Two. Use the information in your notes to complete the chart.

- ~~Wesley Autrey risked his life to save a man from being hit by a train.~~
- People with positive attitudes are more likely to help others.
- Wesley Autrey chose to jump onto the tracks to save the man.
- People are less likely to help when they are in a crowd.
- Wesley Autrey's mother raised him to help people when he could.

GENERAL IDEAS ON ALTRUISM FROM THE LECTURE	SPECIFIC EXAMPLES FROM WESLEY AUTREY'S STORY
What does altruism mean? 1. People show unselfish concern for others.	1. *Wesley Autrey risked his life to save a man from being hit by a train.*
2. People volunteer to help others	2. ______________
Why do some people help others? 1. ______________	1. The other people on the platform didn't try to save the man.
2. Some people are raised to help others.	2. ______________
3. ______________	3. Wesley Autrey didn't worry about getting hit by the train.

SYNTHESIZE

Work with a partner. Student A, you are a reporter interviewing a psychology professor about altruism. Ask your partner the questions in the chart. Ask follow-up questions to get more information. Student B, you are a psychology professor. Answer the reporter's questions using the information from Organize.

Example

A: What does altruism mean?

B: Well, altruism is when people show unselfish concern for others.

A: OK. Can you give me an example?

B: Sure. Wesley Autrey showed unselfish concern when he risked his life to save a man from being hit by a train.

A: I see. So, what else can you tell us about altruism?

Switch roles and repeat the conversation.

Go to **MyEnglishLab** to check what you learned.

3 FOCUS ON SPEAKING

VOCABULARY

REVIEW

Complete the magazine article with the words in the box.

community	praised	risks	turned out
courage	reacted	show concern for	volunteer

ALTRUISM IN ANIMALS

Most discussions of altruism focus on people, but what about animals? Does altruism happen in the animal world? Actually, research shows that, in fact, animals also ____________________ (1.) others.

For example, in one study, researchers found that female chimpanzees prefer to share their food rather than keep it for themselves. In the study, one chimp had three choices: feed a piece of banana to herself, feed herself and another chimp, or do nothing. It ____________________ (2.) that almost always, the chimps chose to share the bananas. Other studies with chimpanzees show that they often take ____________________ (3.) to help each other in dangerous situations. Scientists believe this shows that chimpanzees, like people, will choose to help others in their ____________________ (4.), even when they don't get a reward for their actions.

Another study at the University of Chicago found examples of unselfish behavior in rats. In this study, one rat was locked inside a small trap with a door. Another rat showed ____________________ (5.) by approaching the trap and learning how to open the door to free the rat inside. In another test, the free rat was given some chocolate, but rather than eat the chocolate itself, it freed the other rat and shared the chocolate.

These studies show that animals will ____________________ (6.) to help their own kind, but animals can also show concern for different kinds of animals or people. One famous example is Binti the gorilla. One day, a three-year-old boy fell down into the area where Binti lived with the other gorillas at the Brookfield Zoo. The boy was badly hurt and couldn't move. Binti ____________________ (7.) by helping the boy. She carefully picked him up and carried him over to the door where a person could reach him and take him away. Many people were surprised and ____________________ (8.) Binti as a hero.

EXPAND

1 Read and listen to the interview with a real-life superhero. Notice the boldfaced words and phrases. Try to guess their meanings.

Q **So, tell me, what is a real-life superhero?**

A Well, real-life superheroes are ordinary people like me who **do good deeds** in our communities.

Q **So there are others like you?**

A Oh yeah, there are many of us all around the world. We help people in need, and we try to stop crimes from happening.

Q **But that sounds like work for the police. Why don't you just get a job as a police officer?**

A Well, I already have a job. I decided to volunteer as a real-life superhero in my free time because I saw too much crime in my community. I wanted **to get involved** and take action to stop it.

Q **So you walk the streets trying to stop crime? Sounds dangerous. Aren't there safer ways to help out?**

A Well, sure. Many real-life superheroes prefer to help the poor or sick or work with volunteer groups. There are many ways to get involved and **make a difference** in our communities.

Q **Stopping crime, helping others . . . all of these are generous things to do. It sounds like you have a good heart. But, I wonder, why do you wear a superhero costume? Why don't you just wear regular clothing?**

A That's a good question. For me, there are a few reasons. First of all, my costume helps people to **recognize** me. When people see me on the street, they know who I am and they come to me for help, and they often come up to thank me for the work I do. Kids especially love my costume. They are always so excited to see a real superhero.

Q **OK, I see . . .**

A But more important, I want people to notice me because I want to **inspire** others to get involved in their communities, too. Too many people these days just don't show concern for each other, or they don't know how they can help. I want to be a **role model** for others and encourage them to get out and **contribute** in any way they can. I often hear from people who say they **admire** me for being so brave and helping to make our community a better place to live. That's the best reward of all.

2 Match the words and phrases on the left with their meanings on the right.

e	1. contribute	a.	to encourage someone to do something by making them feel confident and eager
____	2. do good deeds	b.	happy to give to or help others
____	3. get involved	c.	a person whose behavior and attitudes others try to copy because they respect them
____	4. generous	d.	to know and remember; to give special attention or notice to
____	5. have a good heart	e.	~~to give something—such as money, time, or goods—to a person or group~~
____	6. recognize	f.	do something kind or helpful
____	7. inspire	g.	have a positive effect on someone or something
____	8. role model	h.	to feel respect or approval for someone or something
____	9. admire	i.	to be kind
____	10. make a difference	j.	to participate in an activity or event

CREATE

APPLY Work in a small group. Take turns asking and answering the questions. Use the boldfaced words and vocabulary from Review and Expand in your answers.

1. Do you think it is a good idea for real-life superheroes to **get involved** in their communities to stop crime? Do you think they take too many **risks**? Explain your answer.
2. Do you think we are **responsible** for caring for others in our community? Do you think one person can **make a difference** in other people's lives? Why or Why not?
3. Do you **volunteer** in your **community**? What kind of volunteer work do you think your community needs the most?
4. Name a person you know who is **altruistic**. Why do you think this person likes to help others? Give an example of something this person did that was **generous** or shows he or she **has a good heart**.
5. Name a person you know who has **courage**. Why do you think this person is **brave**?
6. Name a person you think is a good **role model** for others. What does this person do to **inspire** others?

Go to the **Pearson Practice English App** or **MyEnglishLab** for more vocabulary practice.

GRAMMAR FOR SPEAKING

1 Read the paragraph. Underline the verbs that talk about the past. Then answer the questions.

Last month, I decided to start volunteering in my community. Yesterday, I started my volunteer job at a homeless shelter, where I helped to prepare meals for the people staying there. At the end of the day, I was happy knowing I made a difference in their lives.

a. Notice the form and spelling of the past tense verbs. What do many of them have in common? (Hint: Look at the last couple of letters.)

b. Which past tense verbs don't fit that pattern? How are they spelled?

Simple Past

1. We use the simple past tense to talk about actions that finished at a specific time.	*Yesterday I started my volunteer job.*	
2. To form the simple past tense for **regular** verbs, add ***-ed*** to the base form of the verb.	**Base Form**	**Simple Past**
	start	*started*
If the verb ends in -*e*, add only *d*.	*decide*	*decided*
If the verb ends in a consonant + ***y***, change the ***y*** to ***i*** and then add ***-ed***.	*try*	*tried*
3. Many verbs have **irregular** past tense forms. Here are some of the irregular verbs.	**Base Form**	**Simple Past**
	be	*was / were*
	choose	*chose*
	come	*came*
	do	*did*
	fall	*fell*
	find	*found*
	go	*went*
	have	*had*
	hold	*held*
	get	*got*
	give	*gave*
	make	*made*
	meet	*met*
	see	*saw*
	take	*took*
	win	*won*
4. In negative statements, use ***did not*** + *base form*.		
Use ***didn't*** in speaking and informal writing.	*The woman **didn't see** the train coming.*	

(continued on next page)

5. Time markers, or phrases that indicate different times, usually come at the beginning or end of a sentence.	
• Use ***ago*** after a length of time, such as *two weeks*, *three months*, or *five years*.	*I started volunteering* ***a month ago****.* ***A month ago****, I started volunteering.*
• Use ***last*** before words like *night*, *week*, or *year*.	*I saw an accident* ***last night****.*
• Use ***in*** with names of months (*November*), seasons (*spring*, *summer*, *winter*, *fall*), and years (*1963*, *2018*).	***In 2011****, he became a real-life superhero.*
• Use ***on*** with days (*Monday*) and dates (*July 4th*), and ***at*** with times (*3 p.m.*, *five o'clock*).	*The crime happened* ***on*** *May 23* ***at*** *11:00 p.m.*
6. Questions in the simple past have the same form for regular and irregular verbs.	
• *Yes / No* questions follow the form: ***Did*** **+ subject + base verb**	***Did he save*** *the man? Yes, he did.* ***Did you see*** *him jump? No, I didn't.*
• Most *Wh-* questions in the past begin with the question word followed by ***did*** **+ subject + base verb**.	*What* ***did you do****? I covered my eyes.*
• Questions with *be* are formed by putting ***was*** or ***were*** before the subject.	***Were*** *you surprised? Yes, I was.*

2 Complete the conversation with the past tense form of the verbs in parentheses.

OSCAR: Hi. How ______ (1. be) your weekend?

DIEGO: It ______ (2. be) pretty good. I ______ (3. study) most of the weekend. I'm writing a research paper for my psychology class, so I ______ (4. go) to the library to do some research.

OSCAR: So, what's your topic?

DIEGO: I'm writing about altruism—why some people are altruistic, you know, and want to help others, but other people don't.

OSCAR: That's interesting. What ______ you ______ (5. find out)?

DIEGO: I ______ (6. learn) about some research studies that ______ (7. compare) the brain activity of different people. In one study, they ______ (8. use) machines to look at pictures of people's brains. They ______ (9. find) that the brains of people who ______ (10. choose) to give money to help strangers ______ (11. be) more active in certain areas compared to the brains of people who ______ (12. want) to keep the money for themselves.

3 APPLY **Work with a partner. Look at the timeline of events in Wesley Autrey's life. Take turns asking and answering questions about the events.**

Example

A: When was Wesley Autrey born?

B: He was born on February 6, 1956.

February 6, 1956
- is born in Florida

1968
- moves to New York

1973
- joins the U.S. Navy

1977
- leaves the Navy
- becomes a construction worker

January 2, 2007 – 12:45
- sees Cameron Hollopeter fall on the train tracks
- makes a quick decision to jump down
- holds him down under the train
- hears people cheering from the platform

January 3, 2007
- gets many invitations to speak in interviews and on TV

January 4, 2007
- New York City mayor gives him the city's highest award

January 23, 2007
- goes to Washington D.C.
- meets the president of the United States

December 2007
- wins the "Everyday Hero" Award

2012
- does another interview
- still doesn't think of himself as a hero

Go to the Pearson Practice English App or MyEnglishLab for more grammar practice. Check what you learned in MyEnglishLab.

PRONUNCIATION

1 **Sometimes adding the *–ed* ending to a verb also adds a syllable to the word. Sometimes it does not. Listen to the underlined words in the text.**

Super Hero trained as a police officer and then worked as a professional wrestler. He wanted to make a difference in his community, so he decided to join the Real-Life Hero Project. He helped to start Team Justice, Inc., a group that helps people in the community.

Write the verbs from the text on the correct lines.

The *–ed* ending adds a syllable:

____

The *–ed* ending does not add a syllable:

____

Pronouncing *-ed* Endings

PRONUNCIATION RULES		
The ***–ed*** ending adds a syllable when the verb ends in a /t/ or /d/ sound. The ***–ed*** ending is pronounced /ɪd/ or /ed/.	decide–decid*ed* want–want*ed*	
The ***–ed*** ending does not add a syllable but makes a final /t/ sound when the verb ends in a voiceless sound (a sound that doesn't use the vocal chords).	work—work*ed* /k/ /kt/ miss—miss*ed* /s/ /st/	help—help*ed* /p/ /pt/ laugh—laugh*ed* /f/ /ft/
The ***–ed*** ending does not add a syllable but makes a final /d/ sound when the verb ends in a vowel sound or a voiced sound (a sound that uses the vocal chords).	try—tri*ed* /ai/ /d/	train—train*ed* /n/ /nd/

2 Listen to the past tense verbs. Write the verbs in the correct column. Check your answers with a partner's and practice saying the verbs aloud.

arrived	covered	passed	reacted	thanked	visited
carried	inspired	praised	saved	turned out	waited
contributed	jumped	pushed	showed		

–ed = /ɪd/ or /ed/	*–ed* = /t/	*–ed* =/d/
________	________	________
________	________	________
________	________	________
________	________	________
		________
		________
		________
		________

3 Work with a partner. Complete the sentences with the correct past tense verbs from the box in Exercise One. Not all of the words will be used. Then put the sentences in the correct order to tell Wesley Autrey's story. Practice telling the story to your partner. Remember to use *–ed* endings with correct pronunciation.

_____ Luckily, everything _______________ OK.

_____ It _______________ over the top of the two men.

_____ Then he _______________ Mr. Hollopeter into the space between the tracks.

__1__ Wesley Autrey _______________ quickly when he saw Cameron Hollopeter fall onto the subway tracks.

_____ He _______________ for the train.

_____ The train _______________ six seconds later.

_____ Later that day, Cameron Hollopeter's parents _______________ him for saving their son's life.

_____ Two days later, the mayor of New York City _______________ Wesley Autrey for his brave actions.

_____ First, he _______________ down on to the tracks.

_____ He _______________ Cameron Hollopeter's body and held him down.

SPEAKING SKILL

Using Signal Phrases in Presentations

We use signal phrases in presentations to introduce the topic and to signal a new idea or supporting detail. Signal phrases help the audience to understand your organization and follow your ideas.

INTRODUCING YOUR PRESENTATION	
At the beginning of your presentation, you can get your audience's attention by	
• asking a question	*How many of you have a hero?* *What do you think the word hero means?*
or	
• making a general statement.	*Every year, many crimes happen in our city.* *There are many ways to define a hero.*
• Then you can introduce your topic.	*Today, I'd like to talk about . . .* *My topic today is . . .*
MAKING TRANSITIONS	
There are different kinds of signal phrases you can use to introduce points, transition from one point to another, or give examples.	
• Introduce points	*Let me start with . . .* *First, I'd like to tell you . . .* *First of all,*
• Transition to a new point	*Next, I want to tell you . . .* *Now,* *Why is she my hero?*
• List points	*One reason / factor is . . .* *Another reason is . . .* *A final reason is . . .*
• Give examples	*For example, . . .* *Let me give you an example . . .*
CONCLUDING YOUR PRESENTATION	
You can end your presentation by using a concluding phrase. A good concluding phrase helps your audience to remember your presentation.	*So, now you can see . . .* *This is why I think . . .* *I hope that you . . .*

Look at the presentation introduction and outline. Fill in the blanks with appropriate signal words and phrases. Practice giving the presentation with a partner.

My Hero: Pushpa Basnet

I. Introduction: The person I admire

- Pushpa Basnet
- Young woman from Nepal
- Attention-getter: ______________________________
- Introduction: ______________________________

  ____

Transition to Part II: ______________________________

II. Background of Pushpa

- Born in Kathmandu, Nepal
- Studied social work in college
- 2005: 21 years old; started a daycare for children living in prison with their parents
- 2007: opened a home for children
- 2009: began a program to help parents in prison earn money for their children
- 2012: Won CNN Hero of the Year award
- 2016: Won CNN Superhero Award

Transition to Part III. ______________________________

III. Why I admire her

Transition to Reason A ______________________________

A. Has a good heart

- Gives the children a good home, food, clothing, and education
- Treats the prisoner's children like her own (e.g., lives with the children and they call her "Mommy")

Transition to Reason B ______________________________

B. Brave

- People said she couldn't do it (too young, not enough money)
- Had courage to do it; encouraged people to contribute money

Transition to Reason C ______________________________

C. Hardworking

- Works hard to get money for her programs
- Started programs by herself
- Manages the programs
- Takes care of the children

IV. Concluding statement

____

Go to **MyEnglishLab** for more skill practice and to check what you learned.

FINAL SPEAKING TASK: Oral Presentation APPLY

In this activity, you will prepare a 2–3-minute oral presentation about someone you think is an everyday hero and present it to the class. You will introduce the person and explain why you think he or she is an everyday hero.

PREPARE

1 Think of a topic. Think of someone that you consider to be an everyday hero. It can be someone you know, or it can be someone you have read or heard about.

2 Plan your presentation. Complete the chart by researching and taking notes about the person. Be sure to list at least three reasons you think this person is an everyday hero and include details and examples. See the outline in Speaking Skill as an example.

WHO DO YOU THINK IS AN EVERYDAY HERO?	NAME:
What is this person's background? Describe the person. Include information about things like the person's: • family background • job • volunteer work	Background: ______
Why do you think this person is a hero? List at least three reasons and give details and examples.	Reason 1: ______ Details / Example(s): ______ Reason 2: ______ Details / Example(s): ______ Reason 3: ______ Details / Example(s): ______
If you share a heroic story, describe the events in the order they happened.	Event 1: ______ Event 2: ______ Event 3: ______

3 Make an outline. Write your outline on a separate piece of paper.

4 APPLY **Use the vocabulary, grammar, pronunciation, and speaking skills from the unit. Use the checklist to help you.**

- □ **Vocabulary:** Read through the list of vocabulary on page 143. Which words can you include in your presentation to make it clearer and more interesting? Choose at least three words or phrases to use and add them to your notes.
- □ **Grammar:** Scan your notes for simple past verbs. Did you form the regular and irregular verbs correctly?
- □ **Pronunciation:** Record yourself practicing. Then listen to your recording. Are you pronouncing the *–ed* endings of simple past verbs correctly?
- □ **Speaking Skill:** On your outline, make a note of the signal words and phrases that you will use to introduce your presentation, make transitions between each point, and conclude your presentation. Then use your outline to make notecards to use during your presentation.

PRACTICE

1 **Practice your presentation with a partner. Use your note cards. Include signal phrases to introduce your topic, make transitions, and make a concluding statement.**

2 **Give feedback to your partner.**

- Did you understand the speaker's ideas?
- Did the speaker use signal phrases to help you understand his or her ideas?
- What did the speaker do well? How can the speaker improve the presentation?

PRESENT

In small groups, take turns delivering a 2–3-minute presentation. Your group will listen, take notes, and ask you questions when you are finished.

LISTENING TASK

Listen to the other students' presentations. Take notes. When you are finished, discuss these questions:

Which person is especially generous?

Which person is especially brave?

Which person is a good role model?

What actions made each person an everyday hero?

ALTERNATIVE SPEAKING TOPIC

APPLY **Work in small groups. Read and discuss the quotes. What does each mean to you? Explain each quote in your own words. Do you agree or disagree with the quote? Explain. Use the vocabulary, grammar, pronunciation, and speaking skills you learned in the unit.**

1. You must be the change you want to see in the world. — Mahatma Gandhi

   Mahatma Gandhi (October 2, 1869–January 30, 1948) was an Indian leader who led the Indian people to independence from Britain.

2. From what we get in life, we make a living. From what we give, we make a life. — Arthur Ashe

   Arthur Ashe (July 10, 1943–February 6, 1993) was the first African American to become the world's number one tennis player.

3. The world is a dangerous place, not because of those who do bad things, but because of those who look on and do nothing. — Albert Einstein

   Albert Einstein (March 14, 1879–April 18, 1955) was a German-born theoretical physicist.

4. Work for something because it is good, not just because it stands a chance to succeed. — Václav Havel

   Václav Havel (October 5, 1936–December 18, 2011) was a Czech writer and politician.

5. And the trouble is, if you don't risk anything, you risk even more. — Erica Jong

   Erica Jong (born March 26, 1942) is an American author and teacher.

CHECK WHAT YOU'VE LEARNED

Check (✔) the outcomes you've met and vocabulary you've learned. Put an X next to the skills and vocabulary you still need to practice.

Learning Outcomes

- ☐ Infer feelings from tone and word choice
- ☐ Organize your notes with numbers
- ☐ Recognize and understand definitions
- ☐ Use the simple past
- ☐ Pronounce *-ed* endings
- ☐ Use signal phrases in presentations

Vocabulary

- ☐ altruistic
- ☐ brave
- ☐ community AWL
- ☐ courage
- ☐ genes
- ☐ ordinary
- ☐ praise (*v.*)
- ☐ react AWL
- ☐ risk (*n.*)
- ☐ unselfish
- ☐ volunteer (*v.*) AWL

Multi-word Units

- ☐ responsible for
- ☐ the right thing
- ☐ show concern for
- ☐ turned out

Go to **MyEnglishLab** to watch a video about heroes, access the Unit Project, and take the Unit 6 Achievement Test.

LEARNING OUTCOMES

- > Infer a speaker's assumptions
- > Take notes with abbreviations
- > Recognize and understand clarification
- > Use *should, ought to,* and *have to*
- > Use reductions
- > Ask for and express opinions

Go to **MyEnglishLab** to check what you know.

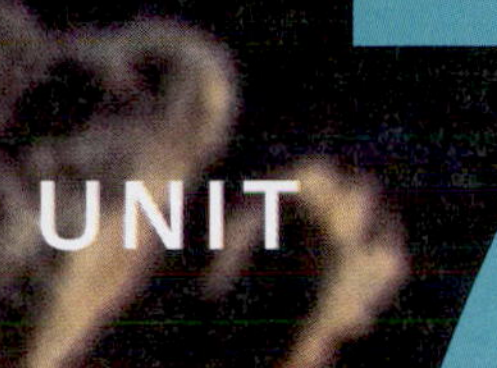

Take Care of Yourself

1 FOCUS ON THE TOPIC

1. Look at the photo of the woman checking her wearable device. What kind of information do you think she is checking? What do you think she will do with the information?
2. Read the title of the unit. What do you think it means? What are some ways that people can take care of their health?
3. *Technology* means new kinds of machines or ways of doing things using science and knowledge. What are some ways that technology can help us to stay healthy? Are there any ways that technology can be bad for our health?

2 FOCUS ON LISTENING

LISTENING ONE | Self-Care

VOCABULARY

1 Read and listen to information from the website about a serious disease: diabetes. Notice the boldfaced words. Try to guess their meanings.

SOME FREQUENTLY ASKED QUESTIONS (FAQS) ABOUT DIABETES

Diabetes is a very serious public health problem in the world today. Here are some important facts about this **chronic** disease.

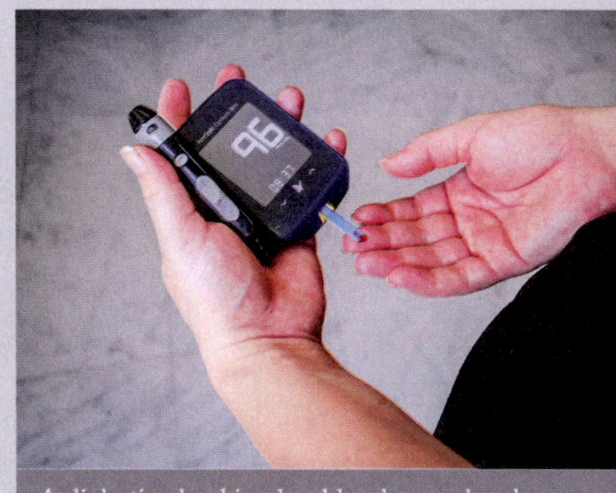

A diabetic checking her blood sugar levels

What is diabetes?

In diabetics, too much sugar collects in the blood. This can lead to very serious health problems.

How serious is the problem?

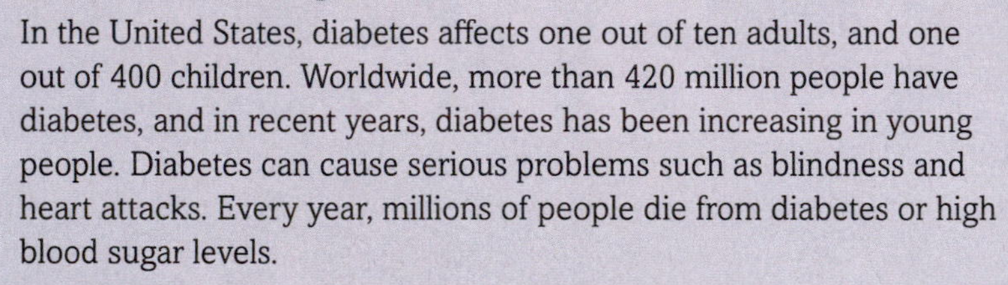

In the United States, diabetes affects one out of ten adults, and one out of 400 children. Worldwide, more than 420 million people have diabetes, and in recent years, diabetes has been increasing in young people. Diabetes can cause serious problems such as blindness and heart attacks. Every year, millions of people die from diabetes or high blood sugar levels.

What are the symptoms of diabetes?

The symptoms of diabetes include feeling more tired, hungry, or thirsty than usual. Diabetes can also cause itchy skin or trouble seeing. If you experience these symptoms, you should see a doctor. To **diagnose** diabetes, your doctor will test your blood sugar levels to see if they are too high.

What are the risk factors for diabetes?

Risk factors can increase your chance of getting diabetes. Some of the risk factors for diabetes include being overweight, not exercising, or having a family history of diabetes.

How can people manage diabetes?

It's important that patients work with their doctors to develop a **treatment** plan that includes developing healthy **habits** and regular doctor check-ups.

- Blood sugar level tests: To **monitor** their blood sugar levels, diabetics must test their blood several times a day or wear a blood sugar monitor.
- Careful control of sugar: Diabetics have to carefully control how much sugar they eat. This is an important part of the treatment for diabetes. Eating a healthy diet and keeping a normal body weight is important in avoiding and treating diabetes.
- Exercise: Exercise is also important in managing diabetes. Most doctors suggest at least 30 minutes of exercise five days a week.
- Medication: Diabetics also treat their diabetes by taking **medication** on a daily basis.

It's important that doctors **motivate** diabetic **patients** to follow their **advice** and take care of their health. Today, more doctors and patients **turn to** technology, such as blood sugar monitors, to help manage diabetes.

2 Match the words on the left with the definitions on the right.

____	1. chronic	a. to find out what health problem a person has
____	2. symptoms	b. to check a situation to see how it changes over a period of time
____	3. diagnose	c. to start to do or use something new, especially as a way to solve a problem
____	4. treatment	d. something that shows you are sick
____	5. habits	e. suggestions about what someone should do
____	6. monitor	f. something that is done to help someone who is injured or sick
____	7. medication	g. drugs that are given to people that are sick
____	8. motivate (someone)	h. continuing or happening again and again for a long time
____	9. patients	i. people who are getting help from a doctor or who are in a hospital
____	10. advice	j. to make someone want to do something, especially by making them want to work harder
____	11. turn to	k. things you do regularly or usually

Go to the **Pearson Practice English App** or **MyEnglishLab** for more vocabulary practice.

PREVIEW

A talk show host is interviewing two guests about self-care.

Listen to excerpts from the beginning of the show. Circle the letter of the correct answer to each question.

1. What does "self-care" mean?
   a. learning to be a medical doctor by yourself
   b. taking medication to treat a health problem
   c. doing things to take care of your own health

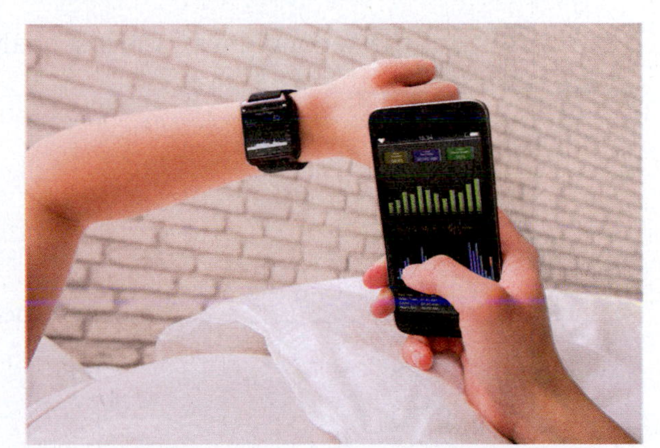

2. Who is the host talking to?
   a. a doctor and a patient
   b. a doctor and a business owner
   c. a business owner and a nurse
3. The guests will talk about "digiceuticals," a new word that combines the words *digital* and *pharmaceuticals* (medication). What do you think *digiceuticals* are? Discuss with a partner.
4. What else do you think the guests will say about the topic? List three ideas.
   a. ______________________________
   b. ______________________________
   c. ______________________________

LISTEN

1 **Listen to the whole interview. Create a chart like the one below to take notes.**

TAKE NOTES Self-care

Main Ideas	*Details*
Self-care	= doing things to take care of own health

2 **Compare your notes with a partner's. How can you improve your notes?**

Go to MyEnglishLab to view example notes.

MAIN IDEAS

Circle the correct answers. Use your notes to help you.

1. One reason that self-care is so popular is that ________ .
   a. people don't like visiting doctors
   b. visiting doctors is expensive
   c. there aren't enough doctors
2. The guests are discussing how people can use ________ to care for their health.
   a. exercise and weight-loss programs
   b. websites and phone apps
   c. computer programs and games
3. According to the second guest, Carlos, health websites and symptom checkers are often ________ .
   a. incorrect
   b. expensive
   c. confusing
4. Digiceuticals are ________ used to treat health problems.
   a. medications
   b. websites
   c. phone apps
5. Carlos thinks that people should see a doctor to get advice and to avoid ________ .
   a. getting hurt or sick
   b. spending too much money
   c. taking too much medication

DETAILS

1 Listen again and add to your notes. Then use your notes to help you decide if each statement is *T* (true) or *F* (false). Correct the false statements.

_____ 1. Americans spend ten million dollars a year on self-care products.

_____ 2. More than 97 million Americans use health websites for advice when they get sick

_____ 3. Online symptom checkers diagnose health problems correctly about 24 percent of the time.

_____ 4. Digiceuticals are apps used by patients to manage their health problems without a doctor.

_____ 5. Digiceuticals monitor patients to get information.

_____ 6. Digiceuticals give patients and doctors advice to treat health problems.

_____ 7. Sometimes digiceuticals can be used instead of medication.

_____ 8. Anita thinks only people with chronic health problems should use health apps.

_____ 9. Carlos thinks that making big changes to diet or exercise can be bad for your health.

_____ 10. Carlos thinks health apps can be used to motivate people to improve their health.

2 With a partner, take turns summarizing your notes. Then discuss how your notes and your answers in Preview helped you understand the listening.

Go to **MyEnglishLab** for more listening practice.

MAKE INFERENCES

Inferring a Speaker's Assumptions

An inference is a guess about something that is not said directly.

When we speak, we often make assumptions about people, things, or situations without saying them explicitly. An **assumption** is something that you think is true even though you don't have proof. Inferring a speaker's assumptions can help you understand his or her point of view.

Read and listen to the example.

Example

CARLOS: Well, of course it's a good thing if people want to educate themselves and take care of their health, but it's important that they get the right information. There are a lot of websites and blogs that give out bad health advice. And websites that diagnose health problems are often wrong.

What assumption is Carlos making?

a. Patients find too much medical information on the internet.

b. Patients believe bad medical information on the internet.

Explanation

Carlos doesn't say that patients find too much information. He says that patients don't always get "the right information." He makes an assumption that most patients (who aren't trained medical professionals) may believe advice that is bad. They may have trouble deciding which advice is good and which advice is bad.

Listen to the excerpts. What assumption does each speaker make?

Excerpt One

Carlos's assumption:

a. Symptom checkers will never improve.

b. Doctors and nurses are more reliable than online symptom checkers.

Excerpt Two

Anita's assumption:

a. Everyone will have access to apps.

b. The advice on the apps will be good.

DISCUSS

Work in a small group. Read the questions. Discuss your ideas.

1. Why does Carlos think that using health websites to diagnose health problems is a bad idea? What do you think? Do you think health websites can be helpful? Give examples to support your opinion.
2. How can digiceuticals help people to stay healthier? What might be some problems with this technology?
3. What are some other ways that people can use technology for their health? Do you use any apps or other technology for your health? How do apps or other technology help to motivate people?

USE YOUR NOTES

APPLY Find information in your notes to use in your discussion.

Go to **MyEnglishLab** to give your opinion about another question.

LISTENING TWO | Let's Hear from Our Listeners

VOCABULARY

1 Read the blog post from a family medicine practice. Notice the boldfaced words. Try to guess their meanings.

cure	convince	deal with	prevent	suffer from

Tri-County Family Medicine

The Health of Our Youth

16 hours ago

Today, I want to talk about health problems in children and young adults. Now it's true that older adults are more likely to **suffer from** health problems, but some health problems are increasing in young people.

One chronic health problem in young people is asthma. Asthma is a disease of the lungs that makes it difficult to breath. It also causes coughing, and tightness in the chest. It can affect both children and adults, but it is more common in children. One in twelve school-aged children has asthma, and it's the main reason for missed school days. There is no **cure** for asthma, but asthma can be treated with medications that are taken using an inhaler.

Cancer is a serious and deadly disease that usually affects older adults, but some types of cancer are increasing in young people. One of these is skin cancer, or melanoma. The best way to **prevent** skin cancer is to wear sunscreen or clothing to protect your skin from the sun.

Unfortunately, depression is also increasing in teens and young adults. The symptoms of depression include a sad or anxious mood that doesn't go away, difficulty concentrating, low energy, and sleep problems. Doctors often need to **convince** young people and their parents that they should get help, but there are effective treatments for depression. It's important that young people see a mental health professional who can help them to **deal with** their illness. Counseling and medication are both effective against depression.

2 Write the boldfaced words or phrases next to their definitions.

1. _____ stop something from happening
2. _____ to make someone feel certain that something is true
3. _____ to have a particular disease or medical condition, especially for a long time
4. _____ a medicine or treatment that makes an illness go away
5. _____ do what you need to do, especially in order to solve a problem

Go to the **Pearson Practice English App** or **MyEnglishLab** for more vocabulary practice.

NOTE-TAKING SKILL

Taking Notes with Abbreviations

Writing abbreviations when you take notes helps you to write information more quickly. Like symbols, abbreviations can help you to save time and write more information in your notes.

An abbreviation is a short form of a word or phrase. There are a few ways to abbreviate a word or phrase:

1. Use the first few letters:

info.	*information*
med.	*medication*
pro	*professional*
tech.	*technology*
EX.	*example*

2. Use the first letter of each word or name:

sc	*self-care*
CP	*Carlos Perez*
w/	*with*

3. Leave out some letters (usually vowels):

Dr.	*doctor*
hlth	*health*
ppl	*people*
mng	*manage*
w/o	*without*

Remember: Make sure to use abbreviations that you will understand when you read your notes later. If you want to use a new abbreviation, it's a good idea to write out the full word or phrase the first time it appears in your notes and put the abbreviation in parentheses after it: *self-care(sc)*. Then you can use only the abbreviation later in your notes.

1 Listen to the phrases and sentences and take notes using abbreviations. Compare your abbreviations with a partner's.

1. ______________________________

2. ______________________________

3. ______________________________

4. ______________________________

5. ______________________________

2 Review your notes from Listening One. Are there any words you could abbreviate?

Go to **MyEnglishLab** for more note-taking practice.

COMPREHENSION

1 Listen to the second part of the radio interview. Listeners were invited to call in with their opinions about self-care. Create a chart like the one below to take notes. Try to use abbreviations in your notes.

TAKE NOTES Let's Hear from Our Listeners

Main Ideas	Details

2 **Check the statements that are true for each caller. Some are true for more than one caller. Use your notes to help you.**

	Caller 1	Caller 2	Caller 3
1. I diagnosed my health problem using a website.			
2. An app helps me to monitor and manage my health problem.			
3. I see a doctor face-to-face to get help.			
4. An app helps me to use less medication.			
5. My app creates reports that help me and my doctor.			
6. Technology helps me to feel better.			
7. My app motivates me to deal with my problem.			
8. I think using an app is convenient.			

USE YOUR NOTES

Compare your notes with a partner's. How can you improve your notes next time?

LISTENING SKILL

1 **Listen to an excerpt from the interview about self-care. What does the host say when he doesn't understand the guest? Why did he say this? How does the guest respond?**

Recognizing and Understanding Clarification

People sometimes need to ask for clarification—that is, they ask the speaker to repeat or explain what was said. To ask for clarification, speakers sometimes repeat the information they heard with rising intonation, and sometimes they use expressions to ask for clarification. Listening for clarification can help you know that the speaker will confirm what he or she said, repeat it, or explain more. If you didn't understand the speaker's point the first time, you get a second chance to understand.

Listen to the excerpt again.

Example

Anita: But even then, technology can help patients and doctors work together to manage their health problems. Digiceuticals, for instance.

Host: Digi-what?

Anita: Digiceuticals. Digiceuticals are phone apps that doctors and patients can use together to manage health problems.

Explanations

In the example, the host asks Anita to clarify the meaning of the word digiceutical. He repeats back the part that he understands but uses a question word —what—with a rising intonation to show that he didn't understand the rest of the word. The speaker knows to repeat the word and explain what it means.

Other expressions that speakers use to clarify:

So, are you saying/You're saying . . . ?

(Do) you mean that . . . ?

In other words, . . . ?

So, . . . ?

2 Listen to the excerpts. Write what the speaker says to clarify. Then write the information that is given in the response.

Excerpt One

a. What does the host say to ask for clarification?

____

b. What information does Carlos give in his response?

____

Excerpt Two

a. What does the host say to ask for clarification?

____

b. What information does Anita give in her response?

____

Go to **MyEnglishLab** for more skill practice.

CONNECT THE LISTENINGS

ORGANIZE

Complete the chart with the advantages and disadvantages of self-care from the listenings using the words in the box.

> **USE YOUR NOTES**
>
> APPLY Review your notes from Listening One and Two. Use the information in your notes to complete the chart.

asthma	chronic	create	habits	mood	treatments
cancer	~~convenient~~	doctor	manage	patients	
changes	counseling	face-to-face	monitor	symptom	

ADVANTAGES OF SELF-CARE	DISADVANTAGES OF SELF-CARE
Self-care is cheap and *convenient* – Look online rather than pay doctor – Online ________ more convenient than in person	Health websites often give bad advice – ________ – checkers correct only 34% of the time – Dangerous for people with serious or ________ health problems – Patient incorrectly diagnosed ________ and became worried
Apps help people ________ health problems – Make changes to sleep ________ – ________ breathing and remind to take asthma medication – ________ reports – Ask questions about ________ and give advice for depression Apps help ________ use less medication	Seeing a medical professional is better and safer than self-care alone – ________ counselling more personal – Asthma patients must discuss reports with ________ – Doctors and nurses know best ________ – Doctors can help make safe and healthy ________ to diet and exercise habits

SYNTHESIZE

Work with a partner. Student A, you are a business owner that makes self-care technology. You want to persuade people to use technology to manage their health. Student B, you are a doctor or nurse. You want to persuade people to be careful about using technology to diagnose health problems or monitor their health. Use the information from Organize to help you.

Example

A: Using technology is cheaper than seeing a doctor. For example, people can self-diagnose and get advice using websites for free!

B: I agree that self-care is cheap and can be convenient—when it works. However, the information on websites is often wrong and . . .

Go to MyEnglishLab to check what you learned.

3 FOCUS ON SPEAKING

VOCABULARY

REVIEW

Use the words and expressions in the box to complete the conversation below.

advice	diagnosed	habits	medication	suffered from

A: Hi! How are you?

B: Well, I'm better now.

A: What do you mean? What happened?

B: Well, a few months ago I got so busy taking care of all of my responsibilities—work, school, family—that I wasn't taking care of myself. I wasn't getting enough sleep or exercise, and I was eating a lot of junk food.[1]

A: Oh, no.

B: Yeah, I felt terrible. And then I got sick.

A: I'm sorry to hear that. Are you OK now?

B: Yeah, My doctor ________________ (1.) my problem and I got some ________________ (2.), so I'm better now.

A: Well, that's good.

B: Yeah, but my illness was a wake-up call.[2] I needed to start paying attention to my health. My doctor gave me some great ________________ (3.) that helped me to become a healthier person.

A: Oh yeah? What did she suggest?

B: Well, first, she helped me to change my sleep ________________ (4.). Before, I used to stay up late working on my computer, and I ________________ (5.) insomnia – I couldn't get to sleep. I would lie awake, and then I had to get up early in the morning. I felt awful! She told me that the bright light from my computer was probably keeping me awake.

---

[1] **junk food:** food that is not healthy because it contains a lot of fat or sugar

[2] **wake-up call:** an experience or event that surprises you and makes you realize you must do something to change a situation

convinced	motivate	prevent

A: Oh really? I didn't know that. It's good I just read a book before bed! Did you make any other changes?

B: Yeah, I also started exercising five days a week and eating healthier foods: more fruits and vegetables. My doctor also ________ (6.) me to quit smoking. I can't believe how much better I feel! It isn't easy, but I use a couple of apps that help me to set goals and ________ (7.) me to keep going. I have a lot more energy, my mood is better, and my doctor says taking better care of myself is helping to ________ (8.) future health problems.

A: That's great!

EXPAND

1 Read the website. Notice the boldfaced words. Try to guess their meanings.

4 APPS TO A HEALTHIER YOU

Download these apps on your smartphone, and start getting healthy today!

1. Sworkit

Sworkit is short for Simply Work It. It's an app that that can help you to achieve your exercise goals to get and **stay fit**. Instead of following set exercises, users can create their own **workouts** and plans to improve **physical** fitness. Each workout is different, so you don't get bored. You can choose from a variety of workouts: yoga, stretching, cardio[1], or strength-building exercises.

2. MyFitnessPal

This app allows you to easily **keep track of** everything you eat and shows you the **calories** you are eating to help you lose weight. You can also keep track of or find recipes for healthy meals and monitor your weight loss. This app connects to other fitness apps and wearable devices, and it also connects you to a community of people who use the app.

3. Calm

Calm is a popular app that helps people take care of their **mental** health. It can help you to manage anxiety, insomnia, depression, or just the stress of everyday life. It contains daily meditations[2], breathing exercises, sleep stories, nature sounds, videos, and classes that **encourage** people to bring peace and relaxation into their daily lives.

4. Sleep Cycle

This app tracks you while you sleep. It then teaches you about your sleep patterns. You can then use the information to change your **patterns** if necessary, so that you can sleep better. Here's how it works. You place your phone on your bed, near your pillow. Then just go to sleep—your phone monitors your movement and breathing during the night. It records this information in an easy-to-read graph that shows you how much you move and how often and when you wake up during the night. It also monitors signals from your body, and chooses the best time to wake you up, so that you have a peaceful start to your day.

---

[1] **cardio:** exercise that causes the heart to beat faster and harder

[2] **meditation:** the act of emptying your mind of thoughts in order to relax

2 Write the boldfaced word or phrase from the webpage on the previous page next to the correct definition.

1. ________________ relating to the mind
2. ________________ the regular and repeated ways things happen or are done
3. ________________ to be healthy and strong especially because you exercise regularly
4. ________________ relating to the body
5. ________________ to persuade someone or give someone the confidence to do something
6. ________________ units that measure the amount of energy food produces
7. ________________ a period of exercise to make your body stronger
8. ________________ to pay attention to something so you know how it is changing

CREATE

APPLY Work in a small group. Take turns asking and answering the questions. Use the boldfaced words and vocabulary from Review and Expand in your answers.

1. What do you think is the best way to **motivate** people to take care of their health? How can doctors **encourage** their **patients** to be healthy?
2. Do you have a favorite **workout?** If not, do you do any other sports or activities to **stay fit**?
3. Do you keep a regular sleep **pattern**, or do you sleep at different times during the week?
4. What are your eating **habits** like? Do you **keep track of** the food you eat or count **calories**?
5. Do you think there is a **connection** between your **mental** health and your **physical** health? Give an example.

Go to the **Pearson Practice English App** or **MyEnglishLab** for more vocabulary practice.

GRAMMAR FOR SPEAKING

1 Read the conversation. Notice the modals that appear in bold. What kind of information comes after them?

A: I **should** go for a walk after dinner to help me stay fit. Do you want to come with me?

B: Great idea! My doctor said I **ought to** get more exercise for my health.

A: My too-tight pants are telling me I **have to** get more exercise or they won't fit soon!

Modals of Advice and Necessity: *Should / Ought to / Have to*

<table>
<tr>
<td>1. Use should to talk about what is right to do for ourselves and to give advice to other people. Use should + the base form of the verb.

Use should not for the negative.

Use the contraction shouldn't in speaking and informal writing.</td>
<td>She should follow her doctor's instructions.

NOT: She should to follow her doctor's instructions.

NOT: She should follows her doctor's instructions.

Diabetics should not eat too much sugar.

Diabetics shouldn't eat too much sugar.</td>
</tr>
<tr>
<td>2. We use should to talk about the present or future.</td>
<td>You should call the doctor now.

You should go to the doctor tomorrow.</td>
</tr>
<tr>
<td>3. Ought to means the same as should, but should is used more often.

Ought to is not usually used in questions or negatives. We use should instead.</td>
<td>We ought to exercise more.

Should I join a health club?

NOT: ~~Ought I to join~~ a health club?

NOT: I ~~ought not to~~ play so many video games.

I think you should exercise more.

Maybe you ought to spend less time playing video games.</td>
</tr>
<tr>
<td>4. When we give advice to someone else, it's polite to use maybe with should or ought to.</td>
<td>Maybe you should see a doctor.</td>
</tr>
<tr>
<td>5. Use have to or has to to talk about things that are necessary. Have to or has to has a stronger feeling than should. Use have / has to + the base form of the verb.

Use don't or doesn't have to to talk about things that are not necessary.</td>
<td>I have to take medicine every day.

She has to lose weight.

I don't have to go to the doctor today.

He doesn't have to lose weight.</td>
</tr>
<tr>
<td>6. We use have / has to to talk about the present or future.</td>
<td>I have to check my blood sugar right now.

He has to go to the doctor tomorrow.</td>
</tr>
<tr>
<td>7. To make questions with have to, use do / does + subject + have to + the base form of the verb.</td>
<td>Do you have to go to the doctor today?

Does he have to keep track of what he eats?</td>
</tr>
</table>

2 Complete the conversation with the correct modal verbs. Use *should / shouldn't, ought to,* or *have / has to*. In some cases, more than one modal verb might be correct.

A: Hi. How are you?

B: Oh, not great. I'm so tired. I was up all night studying, and now I have soccer practice.

A: Oh, that's too bad. Maybe you ________________ (1.) go to practice today.

B: That's a good idea, but I ________________ (2.) go because we have a game tomorrow. Everyone needs me there.

A: I know! You ________________ (3.) try one of those energy drinks.[1] I hear they can really wake you up.

B: Really? ________________ (4.) I really have an energy drink before I exercise? I'm not sure that's a good idea.

A: Why not? Energy drinks are full of vitamins. And I heard that they can help you play better. A lot of athletes use them these days.

B: Well, I heard a news report about those energy drinks. It said that many of them are unhealthy. They have a lot of caffeine and sugar, and you really ________________ (5.) drink them before you exercise.

A: Wow, I didn't know that. Then maybe you ________________ (6.) try the most natural thing.

B: Really? What ________________ (7.) I do?

A: Sleep!

[1]**energy drink:** a drink that gives you the ability to be active and do a lot without feeling tired

3 Listen to the conversation and check your answers. Then perform the conversation with a partner.

4 APPLY **Work in a group of three. Think about a health or food problem that you (or a friend) have. Tell the group the problem. The other members of your group will give you advice. Use *should / ought to* and *have to*.**

Example

A: I fall asleep right away, but then I wake up an hour later and can't get back to sleep. Should I get sleeping pills?

B: No way! Maybe you should exercise every day—but early in the day. That way you'll be more tired at night.

C: I think you ought to listen to relaxing music before bed. That usually works for me.

Go to the **Pearson Practice English App** or **MyEnglishLab** for more grammar practice. Check what you learned in **MyEnglishLab**.

PRONUNCIATION

Using Reductions

In speaking, the modal verbs *ought to, have to,* and *has to* are often reduced. That is, they are pronounced as one word, not two words, and they are not stressed. Usually, the main verb is stressed.

Have to *Have to* is pronounced as one word, /hæftə/. The letter *v* is pronounced /f/. The vowel in *to* is usually pronounced /ə/.	*Do you have to /hæftə/ take your medicine?* *I have to /hæftə/ sleep more.*
Has to *Has to* is pronounced as one word, /hæstə/. The vowel in *to* is usually pronounced /ə/.	*He has to /hæstə/ quit smoking.*
Ought to *Ought to* is pronounced as one word, /ɒdə/.* The vowel in *ought to* sounds like the vowel in *father*. The vowel in *to* is usually pronounced /ə/. The consonant *t* is usually changed to a fast "d" sound: /ɒdə/. *In some dialects of English, the vowel in *ought* is pronounced /ɔ/. This vowel is like the vowel in *saw*.	*He ought to /ɒdə/ exercise.*

1 Listen to the conversations and fill in the missing words. Use *have to, has to, should, shouldn't,* or *ought to*. You might need to write more than one word in the blank.

Conversation 1

A: I'm worried about you. You ______________ (1.) play so many video games. You really ______________ (2.) spend more time outdoors.

B: Yeah, I know I ______________ (3.) exercise more too, but I'm so stressed out from my job. Video games help me relax.

A: You sound anxious. You ______________ (4.) get one of those meditation apps. You know, for your phone?

B: How much do I ______________ (5.) pay for that?

A: You ______________ (6.) pay a cent. It's free.

B: Really? That sounds great.

A: Yeah, you ______________ (7.) go online and check it out.

Conversation 2

A: What do you think? ______________ (1.) I buy a smartphone for my son?

B: Yes! You ______________ (2.) get him one! I know you're worried about his health—a smartphone is a great idea.

A: I'm sorry, but I'm afraid I don't see the connection between cell phones and health.

B: Well . . . there are so many great apps he can download that will motivate him to exercise and eat right.

A: That's crazy! Are you telling me he ______________ (3.) have a cell phone to get healthy?

B: No, he ______________ (4.) have one, but it really can help.

A: How?

B: Well, for example, there's an app called MyFitnessPal. He can use it to record what he eats every day. It gives information about things like nutrition and calories.

A: Oh, come on! He can keep track of his calories now. I ______________ (5.) buy him a cell phone for that.

B: You know, you ______________ (6.) at least check it out. Maybe it will help.

2 Listen to the conversations again. Listen carefully to the reductions. Then practice the conversations with a partner. Try to use reductions.

SPEAKING SKILL

Asking for and Expressing Opinions

In pair or group discussions, it's important that everyone shares his or her ideas. Sometimes we share facts, and sometimes we share opinions. A **fact** is information that is true and correct. An **opinion** is information that tells how you feel. People often have different opinions. That is, sometimes we disagree about opinions.

In a discussion, you can participate by expressing your opinion, asking for other people's opinions, and agreeing or disagreeing with others.

Asking for an Opinion	
What do you think (about) . . . ?	***What do you think about** using self-care apps?*
Do you think (that) . . . ?	***Do you think that** using self-care apps is a good idea?*
Expressing Opinions	
I think . . . / I don't think . . .	***I think** self-care apps are helpful for staying healthy. For example, I use an app that helps to motivate me to exercise.*
In my opinion, . . .	***In my opinion,** people don't need to use an app to stay healthy. I exercise every day without using an app.*
For me, . . .	***For me,** using a fitness app is really helpful. It keeps track of how well I'm doing and gives me advice.*
Expressing Agreement There are different ways to agree with someone. Sometimes we want to express a strong agreement, and sometimes we want to express a weak agreement.	Strong ***I agree** (with you / Maria / Yan).* ***I think so, too.*** ***Maybe.*** ***I guess so.*** Weak
Expressing Disagreement We can also disagree with other's opinions. Sometimes we want to express a strong disagreement, and sometimes we want to express a weak disagreement. A strong disagreement can be less polite.	Strong ***I disagree.*** ***I don't think so.*** ***I'm not sure about that.*** ***I don't know.*** Weak

1 **Read the discussion. Which statements are facts, and which statements are opinions? Which opinions are stronger? Which are weaker and more polite?**

A: I think phone apps are a great way to track your diet. I use an app to keep track of everything I eat and count my calories. It motivates me to eat healthy.

B: I think apps are great, too. For me, I like using my phone to keep track of my diet. My app connects me to other people, too. I like that.

C: I disagree. I don't think people need an app to keep track of what they eat. I think you can do it yourself.

A: What do you think, Tony?

D: I don't know. I don't use an app now, but maybe I should. I eat a lot of junk food. Maybe an app can help me to lose weight.

2 APPLY **Work in a group. Read the following suggestions for taking care of your health. Take turns expressing your opinions and agreeing or disagreeing with each other about the statements. Explain your opinions.**

1. Use phone apps or a wearable device to track your exercise habits.
2. Go to the gym to work out.
3. Walk or ride your bike instead of driving or taking public transportation.
4. Always take the stairs instead of an elevator.
5. Meditate every day.
7. See a doctor every year for a check-up.
8. Drink eight glasses of water every day.
9. Never eat junk food.
10. Get eight hours of sleep every night.

Go to **MyEnglishLab** for more skill practice and to check what you learned.

FINAL SPEAKING TASK: Group Discussion APPLY

In this activity, you will participate in a group discussion. You will ask for and express your opinions about different situations. You will give advice to the people in the situations about ways to improve their health.

STEP 1

1 Work in a group of three. Read each situation and ask for clarification if there is anything you don't understand.

Situation 1 Discussion Leader: ______________

Magda is very busy. She gets up at 6:00 AM and goes to school during the day. After school she works in a fast-food restaurant. To save time, she usually just eats hamburgers and french fries for dinner while she's at work. She gets home from work around 9:00 PM, but she is so tired she sits on the couch and watches TV. At about 11:00 PM she does her homework, and then she goes to bed at about 1:00 AM. On the weekends, she sometimes hangs out with friends, but they just stay in and watch TV. She wants to feel healthier and have more energy.

Situation 2 Discussion Leader: ______________

Patrick is overweight. He knows he should lose weight, but he likes to eat sweets, especially ice cream. He doesn't like to exercise. Lately, he has been feeling tired. He is often hungry and thirsty, even when he isn't active. He started his own diet and exercise plan to lose weight, but his weight and energy levels aren't any better than when he started.

Situation 3 Discussion Leader: ______________

Chen is a student living far from his hometown. He studies English full-time and lives alone. After school, he usually goes back to his room and plays video games until late at night. Lately, he is feeling very sad because he misses his family and friends back home. Some nights he can't sleep, so he feels too tired to go to school. Instead, he stays in his room.

Situation 4 Discussion Leader: ______________

Ella's 10-year-old son Jack has asthma. He loves to run and play sports, but he often has asthma attacks, especially when he is active. Sometimes his attacks are serious, and he has a lot of trouble breathing. Sometimes he forgets to take his medication, and Ella is worried about his health. She wants Jack to stop playing sports.

2 Choose a different person to be the discussion leader for each situation.

STEP 2

1 Take notes on your opinion about each situation and advice you would give the person.

2 APPLY Use the vocabulary, grammar, pronunciation, and speaking skills from the unit. Use the checklist to help you.

- ☐ **Vocabulary:** Read through the list of vocabulary on page 169. Which words can you include in your discussion to make it clearer and more interesting? Choose at least three words or phrases to use and add them to your notes.
- ☐ **Grammar:** Scan your notes for advice and necessities. Which modals can you use? Write them down.
- ☐ **Pronunciation:** Remind yourself how to reduce the modals in your notes. Add pronunciation notes to help you remember.
- ☐ **Speaking Skill:** Think about how you can ask other people in the group for their opinions and express agreement or disagreement with their ideas. Add a few expressions to your notes to help you remember.

STEP 3

Discuss each situation. Follow these roles:

Group Leader:

- Read the situation aloud to the group.
- Ask the group members for their opinions on the question: What should the person do to be healthier?
- Make sure everyone participates in the discussion.
- Take notes on everyone's answers and be prepared to report back to the class.

All Group Members:

- Listen and show interest in what the other group members are saying.
- Express your opinion. Provide details to support your opinions.
- Agree or disagree with other group member's opinions.
- Use *should*, *ought to*, and *have to*.

STEP 4

Group leaders take turns reporting their group's opinions. The class should listen and decide: Which group has the best advice? Why?

ALTERNATIVE SPEAKING TOPIC

APPLY Work in a small group. Read the quotes below. What does each mean to you? Explain them in your own words. Do you agree or disagree with each quote? Explain. Use the vocabulary, grammar, pronunciation, and speaking skills you learned in the unit.

Every human being is the author of his own health or disease.
Siddhartha Gautama

An apple a day keeps the doctor away.
Author unknown

To lengthen thy life, lessen thy meals.
Benjamin Franklin

True silence is the rest of the mind and is to the spirit what sleep is to the body, nourishment and refreshment.
William Penn

Those who think they have not time for bodily exercise will sooner or later have to find time for illness
Edward Stanley

A wise man should consider that health is the greatest of human blessings and learn how by his own thought to derive benefit from his illnesses.
Hippocrates

CHECK WHAT YOU'VE LEARNED

Check (✔) the outcomes you've met and vocabulary you've learned. Put an X next to the skills and vocabulary you still need to practice.

Learning Outcomes
- ☐ Infer a speaker's assumptions
- ☐ Take notes with abbreviations
- ☐ Recognize and understand clarification
- ☐ Use *should, ought to,* and *have to*
- ☐ Use reductions
- ☐ Ask for and express opinions

Vocabulary
- ☐ advice
- ☐ chronic
- ☐ convince AWL
- ☐ cure (*n.*)
- ☐ diagnose
- ☐ habit
- ☐ medication
- ☐ monitor (*v.*) AWL
- ☐ motivate (someone) AWL
- ☐ patient
- ☐ prevent
- ☐ symptom
- ☐ treatment

Multi-word Units
- ☐ deal with
- ☐ suffer from
- ☐ turn to

Go to **MyEnglishLab** to watch a video about health problems, access the Unit Project, and take the Unit 7 Achievement Test.

LEARNING OUTCOMES

- Infer a speaker's viewpoint
- Take notes on reasons and examples
- Recognize and understand pronoun reference
- Use modals of possibility: *Will / May / Might*
- Use contractions of *will*
- Use pauses effectively

Go to **MyEnglishLab** to check what you know.

UNIT 8

Endangered Languages

1 FOCUS ON THE TOPIC

1. Look at the photo of the Rosetta Stone. What do you know about this ancient language tool? Is studying and preserving ancient languages important? Why or why not?
2. Do you speak the same language as your parents? As your grandparents? Why or why not?
3. What do you think an endangered language is? Why might people stop speaking a language?

2 FOCUS ON LISTENING

LISTENING ONE | Language Loss

VOCABULARY

1 Read and listen to an excerpt from a textbook about endangered languages. Notice the boldfaced words. Try to guess their meanings.

LANGUAGE TODAY

DISAPPEARING LANGUAGES

1 There are more than 6,000 languages in the world today. Unfortunately, many of these languages are **endangered**. An endangered language is a language that few people are learning to speak.

2 When an endangered language loses all of its speakers, it becomes **extinct**. Sometimes a language **disappears** when the language of a more powerful or **dominant** community **replaces** it. For example, this happened when English replaced many native languages in North America. Today, many Native Americans only speak English instead of the native language of their culture.

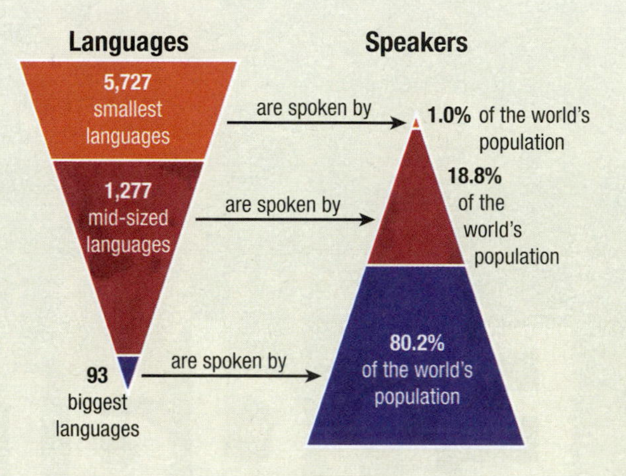

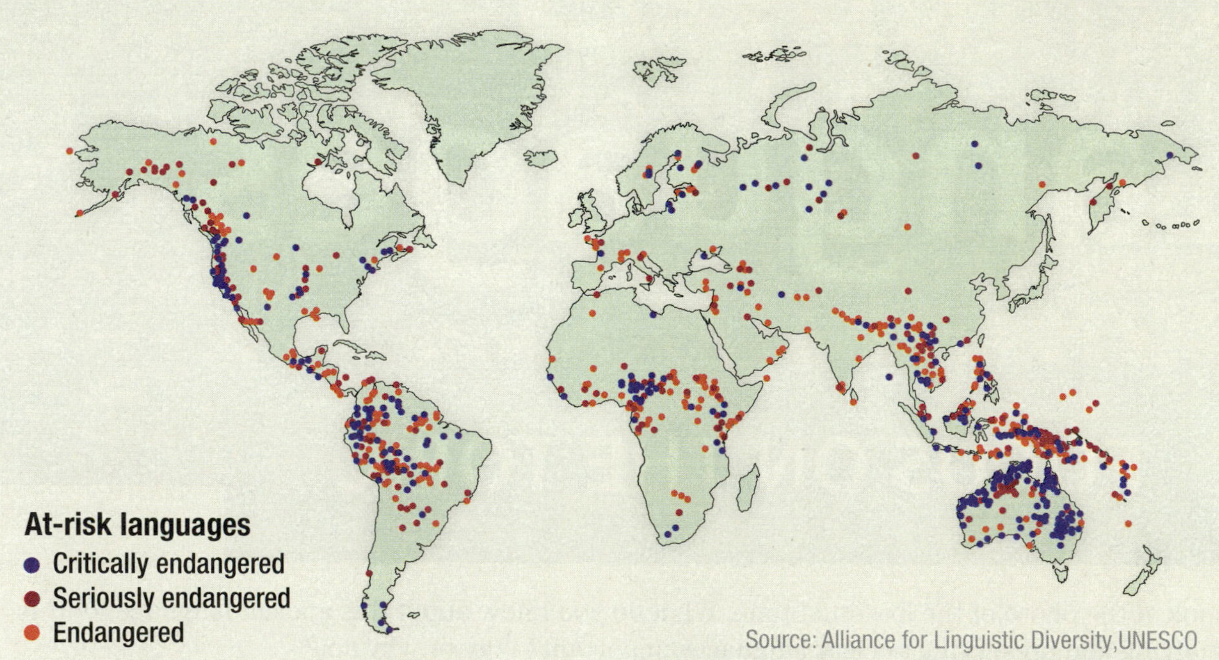

3 Many **linguists** study endangered languages and work to **preserve** them. A number of speakers of these languages also work hard to save them for future **generations**. In many communities, there are special programs that teach children their **native language**. These programs are important for children to **acquire** their native language. The children in these programs grow up to be **bilingual**—they can speak two languages: the language of the more powerful community, as well as their native language.

2 Circle the best answer to complete each statement.

1. An **endangered** language ________________ .
   a. might die soon
   b. is already dead
2. An **extinct** language is ________________ .
   a. very old
   b. no longer used
3. When a language **disappears**, it ________________ .
   a. becomes powerful
   b. stops being used
4. A **dominant** community is ________________ .
   a. strong
   b. large
5. When a language **replaces** another, it is used ________________ the other language
   a. instead of
   b. in addition to
6. **Linguists** are people who ________________ .
   a. speak the same language
   b. study the science of language
7. When people **preserve** a language, they ________________ it.
   a. save
   b. lose
8. A **native language** is a language ________________ .
   a. only old people speak
   b. that belongs to the place of one's birth
9. A **generation** is ________________ .
   a. all the people who are about the same age
   b. all the people who live in the same place
10. A person who is **bilingual** ________________ .
    a. speaks one language
    b. speaks two languages
11. When you **acquire** something, you ________________ it.
    a. learn
    b. teach

Go to the **Pearson Practice English App** or **MyEnglishLab** for more vocabulary practice.

PREVIEW

Listen to the beginning of a lecture on language loss. Read and answer each question.

1. Where is the speaker?
   a. in a class
   b. on TV
   c. on the radio
2. What is the topic?
   a. endangered languages
   b. endangered languages and cultures
   c. endangered and dead languages
3. What do you think the speaker will talk about? Make three predictions.

____

____

____

LISTEN

1 Listen to the whole lecture. Create a chart like the one below to take notes.

TAKE NOTES Language Loss

Main Ideas	Details
Many languages = endangered / dead	*dead lang.= no one speaks it* *endangered = may die soon*

2 Compare your notes with a partner's. How can you improve your notes?

Go to **MyEnglishLab** to view example notes.

MAIN IDEAS

Read each statement. Write *T* (true) or *F* (false). Use your notes to help you.

_____ 1. Linguists care about endangered languages because when a language dies, a culture can die, too.

_____ 2. Languages become endangered when children don't go to school.

_____ 3. Sometimes the government makes it illegal to speak a language.

_____ 4. Dominant communities usually learn the language of the less powerful community.

DETAILS

1 Listen again and add to your notes. Then circle the best answer to complete each statement. Use your notes to help you.

1. By the year 2100, ________ of the world's languages could be extinct.
   a. 50 percent
   b. 40 percent
   c. 20 percent
2. The Manx people lost their native ________ .
   a. culture
   b. traditions
   c. language
3. Before 1987, it was ________ to teach Hawaiian in public schools.
   a. illegal
   b. required
   c. difficult
4. Today, more than ________ students are enrolled in Hawaiian language programs.
   a. 1,000
   b. 2,000
   c. 12,000
5. Once there were ________ Native American languages, but now many have become extinct.
   a. several
   b. hundreds of
   c. thousands of
6. In Greenland, students learn ________ .
   a. Kalaallisut and Danish
   b. only Danish
   c. only Kalaallisut
7. Linguists help create ________ programs where people can study endangered languages.
   a. interesting
   b. community
   c. unusual
8. Linguists preserve languages by ________ .
   a. recording them, studying them, and writing story books
   b. studying them, learning them, and writing history books
   c. recording them, studying them, and writing grammar books

2 With a partner, take turns summarizing your notes. Then discuss how your notes and your answers in Preview helped you understand the listening.

Go to **MyEnglishLab** for more listening practice.

MAKE INFERENCES

Inferring a Speaker's Viewpoint

An inference is a guess about something that is not said directly.

A speaker's viewpoint is the speaker's opinion on a subject. Understanding a speaker's viewpoint will help you understand the full meaning of what a speaker is trying to say. The speaker's viewpoint is not always said clearly. You may need to guess or infer the viewpoint through the words they use and also through stress and intonation.

Listen to the example. Then read the statement. What is the speaker's viewpoint?

Example

PROFESSOR: Good morning, everybody. Today, I'd like to talk about endangered and dead languages. So, who did the reading for today? Hmm, I see. Some of you did. Then who can tell me what a dead language is?

Explanation

In this example, the professor emphasizes the word **some** to express that not all of the students did the reading. The professor wants all the students to do the reading and be prepared to discuss. You can infer that he probably would agree that many students are not prepared for class.

Listen to two excerpts from the lecture and read the statements. Check (✓) *agree* or *disagree*. Write the clues that helped you infer the speaker's viewpoint. Discuss your answers with the class.

Excerpt One

Do you think the professor would agree or disagree with the statement: "Language programs are a good way to preserve languages"?

☐ agree ☐ disagree

Clues: ______________________________

Excerpt Two

Do you think the student would agree or disagree with the following statement: "I'm not sure it's worth it to preserve languages"?

☐ agree ☐ disagree

Clues: ______________________________

DISCUSS

Work in a small group. Read the questions. Discuss your ideas.

1. How many languages do linguists predict will be extinct by 2100? What languages are replacing them? Do you know any endangered languages in your country? If so, who speaks them?
2. What happens when languages are lost? Give some examples.
3. What are some ways that people are trying to save endangered languages? What are the benefits of saving these languages?

USE YOUR NOTES

APPLY Find information in your notes to use in your discussion.

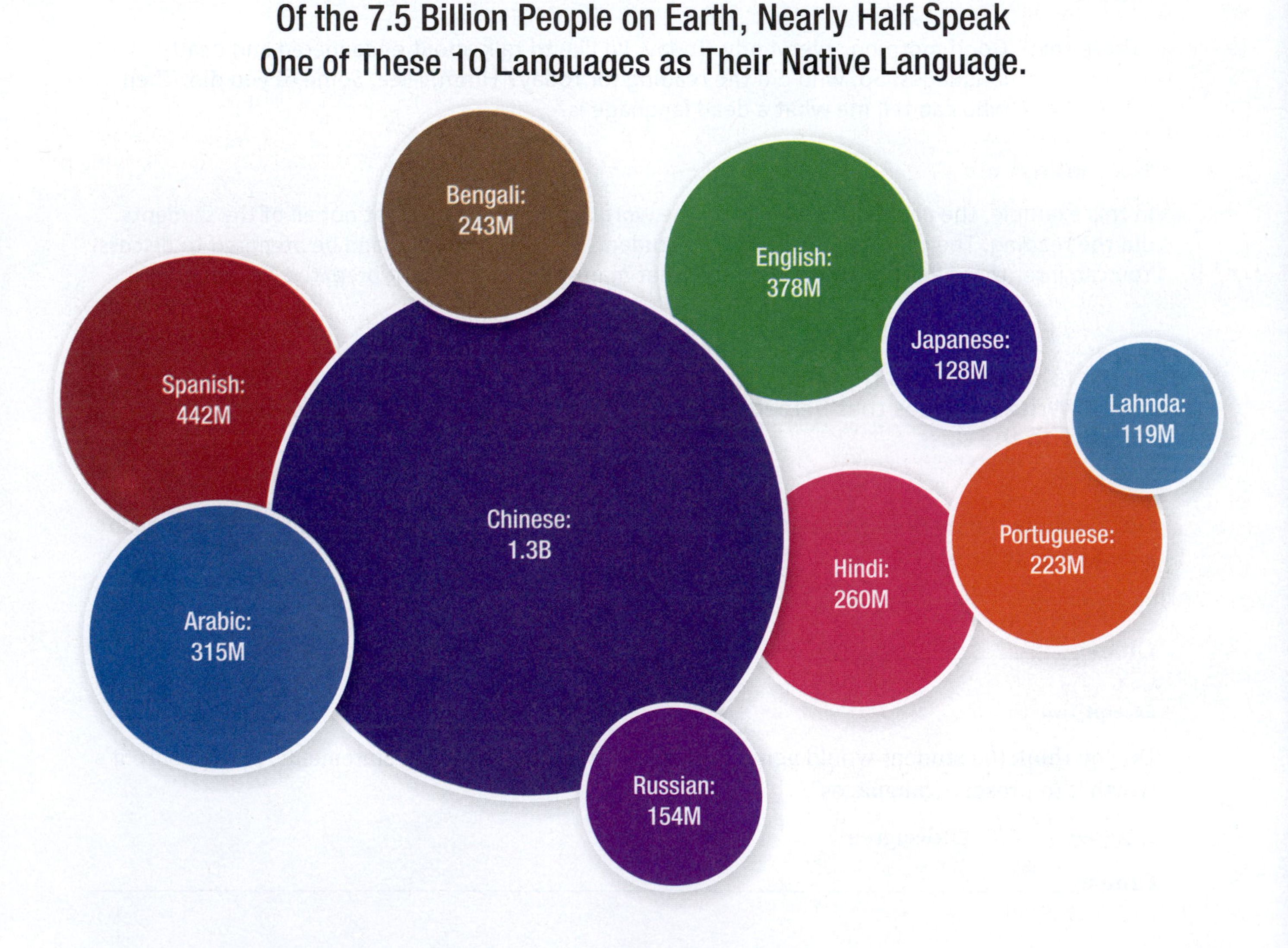

Go to **MyEnglishLab** to give your opinion about another question.

LISTENING TWO | My Life, My Language

VOCABULARY

1 **Read the blog entry. Notice the boldfaced words. Try to guess their meanings.**

My Weekly Blog

SAVING LANGUAGES

3 days ago

1 If you follow my blog, you know I travel all over the world studying endangered languages. Along the way, I have met so many interesting people and learned about their languages and cultures. On my recent trip, I (1) **got together** with several different communities of people to talk about how to preserve their languages. Together we (2) **came up with** some great ideas of how to help slow the loss of their languages. In many situations, language loss occurs when a dominant language becomes the (3) **official language** of a country and replaces other languages. When this happens, people stop using the language or learning it in school, and it can become extinct. In these situations, people have to work with the government to create new language (4) **policy** and rules about language teaching. Without people working together like this, languages will (5) **eventually** become extinct.

Discussing ways we can preserve languages

2 I have posted some stories of people I met. I hope you'll find them interesting and inspiring!

2 **Match the boldfaced words with their definitions. Write the number of the words.**

_____ a. an official way of doing something that was decided by a government or organization

_____ b. at some later time; in the end

_____ c. created, thought of (something)

_____ d. met and spent time together

_____ e. a language approved by the government of a country and taught in schools

Go to the **Pearson Practice English App** or **MyEnglishLab** for more vocabulary practice.

NOTE-TAKING SKILL

Taking Notes on Reasons and Examples

Speakers often support their ideas with reasons or examples. Identifying and noting the reasons and examples can help you to better understand the main ideas. When noting reasons and examples, it's important to connect them with the main ideas they support in your notes.

Phrases that introduce reasons:

The / One reason . . .

There are (several) reasons . . .

(This is) because . . .

Sometimes a speaker states the reason for something first, followed by the result.

Phrases that follow reasons:

. . . That's why . . .

. . . As a result, . . .

. . . So, . . .

Phrases that signal examples:

For example, . . .

An example of this is . . .

For instance, . . .

. . . such as . . .

You can indicate examples in your notes with the abbreviations *ex.* or *e.g.*

Example

You hear:

One reason that a language disappears is that a more powerful language replaces it. For example, English replaced many Native American languages in North America.

You write:

Main Ideas	Details
Language disappears	*1. dominant lang. replaces*
	e.g. English replaced Native Amer. langs in N. Amer.

1 Listen to the excerpts and note the main ideas and the reasons or examples that support them.

Excerpt One

Main Ideas	Details
Reasons to save endangered langs.	1. ________________
	• *Not always, ex* ________________

Excerpt Two

Main Ideas	Details
________	1. ________
	e.g. ________

2 **Work with a partner. Take turns retelling the information in the excerpts using your notes. Say the main idea and give details and examples.**

Go to MyEnglishLab for more note-taking practice.

COMPREHENSION

1 **Listen to the speaker talk about her experience with her native language and culture. Create a chart like the one below to take notes. Try to note the reasons and examples that support the main ideas.**

TAKE NOTES My Life, My Language

Main Ideas	Details

2 **Read each question and circle the correct answer. Use your notes to help you.**

1. Where does the woman live?
   a. New Zealand   b. Greenland
2. What language did she learn in school?
   a. Maori   b. English
3. What language did her grandparents speak?
   a. Maori   b. English
4. How did she feel in her family?
   a. empty and different   b. happy and excited
5. Where do her children learn Maori language and culture?
   a. in elementary school   b. in language nests
6. What is a language nest?
   a. a pre-school   b. a home school

7. How many language nests are there now?

   a. a few hundred b. over 400

8. What are three Maori values that children learn?

   a. love, caring, and respect for elders b. hope, sharing, and family responsibilities

9. Who teaches the Maori adults their language and culture?

   a. linguists b. older Maoris

10. Where do they meet?

    a. in schools b. in neighborhood centers

11. What is / are the official language(s) of New Zealand now?

    a. English b. English and Maori

USE YOUR NOTES

Compare your notes with a partner's. How can you improve your notes next time?

Maori children celebrating with their grandmother

LISTENING SKILL

1 Listen to an excerpt from the lecture about language loss. What does the pronoun *they* refer to?

WOMAN: **They** decided to do something.

Recognizing and Understanding Pronoun Reference

Pronouns are words that represent other nouns. For example, *he, she, it, they, them, this, that,* and *these* are pronouns that can refer to people, things, and ideas. By using pronouns, speakers can speak about someone or something without repeating the name or idea they are referring to.

In the example, *they* refers to a group of Maori leaders who saw that the Maori language was endangered and decided to do something about it.

Listen to another excerpt.

Example

PROFESSOR: There are over 6,000 languages in the world, and some linguists think that about 50 percent could be extinct by the year 2100. Yes, that's a lot!

Explanation

In this example, the speaker uses the word **that** to refer back to the idea that 50 percent of the languages could become extinct.

2 Listen to the following excerpts from Language Loss. Write the meaning of the boldfaced words.

Excerpt One

a. Why do **they** want to do **that**? they = ________________

that = ________________

b. **That**'s a good point. that = ________________

Excerpt Two

c. When a language dies, all of **this** may be lost. this = ________________

Excerpt Three

d. I guess nobody speaks **them** or studies them. them = ________________

Go to **MyEnglishLab** for more skill practice.

CONNECT THE LISTENINGS

ORGANIZE

Work in pairs. Use your notes to list the examples from Listening Two for each idea from Listening One. Then compare your answers with a partner's.

USE YOUR NOTES

APPLY Review your notes from Listening One and Two. Use the information in your notes to complete the chart.

WHY ARE WE LOSING SO MANY LANGUAGES?	EXAMPLES FROM LISTENING TWO
1. Children don't learn the language in school.	**1.**
2. Children stop learning the language and only old people speak it.	**2.**
3. Children don't learn the culture.	**3.**
HOW CAN WE SAVE LANGUAGES AND CULTURES?	**EXAMPLES FROM LISTENING TWO**
1. Children learn the language and culture.	**1.**
2. The government makes the language official.	**2.**
3. Adults learn the language and culture.	**3.**

SYNTHESIZE

Work with the same partner. Student A, you are a student asking questions. Student B, you are the professor giving examples. Student A: Ask why we are losing so many languages. If the answer is not complete, ask a follow-up question such as "Could you give me an example?" Then ask about how we can save languages and cultures. Switch roles. Use the information from Organize.

Example

A: Why are we losing so many languages?

B: One reason is because children don't learn their native language in school.

A: Could you give me an example?

B: Before, in New Zealand, Maori children only learned English in school, so they couldn't speak Maori with their grandparents. Now, they learn Maori and English.

Go to **MyEnglishLab** to check what you learned.

3 FOCUS ON SPEAKING

VOCABULARY

REVIEW

1 Complete the conversation between two students with words from the box. Use the underlined phrases to help you guess the answers.

disappear	dominant	endangered	extinct	~~linguists~~

A: Have you heard of the Endangered Language Alliance?

B: No, what is it?

A: It's a project of people who study languages. It's a group of ___linguists___ (1).

B: What do they do?

A: They are studying ________________ (2.) languages that may die soon. And they do it in New York.

B: New York! Really? Why New York?

A: Well, English is the main language.

B: Right. English is the ________________ (3.) language.

A: Yes. But some linguists believe there are as many as 800 languages spoken in New York.

B: Eight hundred languages. Wow!

A: They call New York an "endangerment hot spot." New York is full of languages that are not going to be around in 20 or 30 years

B: Languages that will be ________________ (4.)?

A: Right. Over time, people will stop speaking the languages. The languages will slowly go away.

B: And they will ________________ (5.).

acquire	native language	official languages	preserve	replacing

A: That's right. The United Nations keeps a list of languages that might become extinct. UN experts and linguists think that a language will probably disappear in one generation or two. That happens when the number of people who use the language as a first language is too small.

B: In other words, when there are not enough people who use the language as a ______________ (6).

A: Right, and when no one is learning the language, children don't ______________ (7) it. For example, one language spoken in New York, Garifuna, is from Belize and Honduras in Central America. But people now speak Spanish and English instead, which are the dominant languages.

B: Spanish and English are ______________ (8) Garifuna?

A: Yes. And in many Central American countries, Spanish and English are the languages the government uses.

B: So English and Spanish are the ______________ (9).

A: Right. But Garifuna is now as common in New York as in Honduras and Belize where it is from. Many people moved to New York and still speak the language. Some people in New York want to save the language, so there are now classes in Garifuna.

B: Maybe they can ______________ (10) it, and they can do it in New York. They don't have to travel to far away countries.

A: Exactly!

2 Now practice reading the conversation aloud with a partner. Switch roles after item 5.

EXPAND

1 Read the article from a website about language preservation. Notice the boldfaced words and phrases. Try to guess their meanings.

Preserving the World's Languages

1 In 1999, the United Nations made February 21 International Mother Language Day to celebrate the many languages of the world and to encourage their preservation.

2 But preserving the world's languages is a big challenge. Languages are becoming extinct very quickly because people are starting to speak other languages, such as English. English is the dominant language of international business. Also, English and a few other languages are beginning to (1) **take over** popular entertainment, such as television, music, film, and the Internet. For example, more than 55 percent of websites on the Internet are in English. In many countries, students no longer learn in their (2) **mother tongue** at school. In addition, many parents encourage their children to learn the language of a more powerful community in order to get an education and find a good job. For these reasons, many children don't become (3) **fluent** in their native language, and many parents don't (4) **pass** their language **down** to their children. This is why linguists are (5) **making an effort** to preserve the world's languages before they are lost.

2 Write the number of each boldfaced word or phrase in the text next to its definition.

_____ a. native language

_____ b. give or teach something to younger people

_____ c. trying to do something; working towards a goal

_____ d. gain control of something

_____ e. speaking or writing very well in an easy, smooth way

CREATE

APPLY **Work with a partner. Role-play a conversation between the people in Situation 1 using the words in the box. Then switch roles to role-play Situation 2. Practice both role-plays, and then perform your best role-play for the class.**

Example

PARENT: Listen, I know that English is important, but I am worried that my children will lose their native language.

PRINCIPAL: I understand that you want to pass down your mother tongue to your children, but . . .

bilingual	fluent	mother tongue	preserve
endangered	generation	native language	take over
extinct	make an effort	pass down	

Situation 1

Student A: You are a parent. Your native language is endangered. You want your child to learn your native language at school, but the school only teaches English. You want the school to teach your native language.

Student B: You are the school's principal. You think all of the children should learn English at school because it is the dominant language in your community.

Situation 2

Student A: You are a parent. Your native language is endangered. You want your child to go to a community program to learn your native language, but your child does not want to go.

Student B: You are the child. You only want to learn English because all the children at your school speak it. You do not want to go to a community program.

Go to the **Pearson Practice English App** or **MyEnglishLab** for more vocabulary practice.

GRAMMAR FOR SPEAKING

1 Read the sentences and underline the verbs. Then answer the questions.

Fifty percent of the world's languages may disappear by 2100.
Linguists will try to preserve them.
Their cultures might die, too.

1. What time period are the people talking about? How do you know?
2. What are the verbs in each sentence? What form of the verb comes after *may, might,* and *will*?
3. Which actions are more likely to happen?

Modals of Possibility: *Will, May,* and *Might*

1. Use ***will*** to talk about something that is certain or that we think is certain in the future.	*Some languages **will** disappear.*
2. Use ***may*** or ***might*** for something that is possible, but not certain.	*They **might lose** their native language.*
3. To form statements with ***will, may***, and ***might*** • use will, may, and might plus the base form of the verb • use contractions of will ('ll) with pronouns • do not use contractions in affirmative short answers.	*Spanish **might replace** Garifuna.* NOT: *Spanish might ~~replaces~~ Garifuna* NOT: *Spanish might ~~to replace~~ Garifuna.* ***They'll** speak both Maori and English.* ***A:** **Will** they learn Maori in language nests?* ***B:** Yes, they **will**.*
4. To form a negative statement with ***will*** • use ***will not*** or ***won't*** *plus the base form of the verb.* • use ***won't*** in informal speaking and writing. • use ***won't*** in negative short answers. To form a negative statement with ***may*** or ***might***, use ***may not*** or ***might not.*** There are no contractions for ***may*** or ***might***. **5.** Use ***will*** to ask questions about the future.	*Many languages **will not survive**.* *In Greenland, students **won't lose** their native language.* ***A:** **Will** they lose their language?* ***B:** No, they **won't**.* *Maori **might not disappear**.* NOT: Maori ~~mightn't~~ disappear. NOT: Maori ~~mayn't~~ disappear. ***Will** you **pass down** your native language to your children?* *What language **will** you **learn** in school?*
6. ***May*** is a modal. ***May be*** is used as a verb in a sentence. ***Maybe*** (one word) is an adverb. It means "possibly." It comes in front of a subject and verb. If you use the adverb **maybe**, use **will** with the main verb. Do NOT use **may** or **might**.	*Maori **may be** replaced by English.* ***Maybe** people **will stop** speaking Maori.* ***Maybe** English **will** replace Maori.* NOT: *Maybe English ~~might~~ replace Maori.*

2 Complete the sentences. Choose the correct answer.

1. My children are learning two languages. They ________ bilingual.

   a. maybe become

   b. may become

   c. might becomes

2. Language nests ________ save the Maori language and culture.

   a. maybe might help

   b. may help

   c. may to help

3. Language programs ________ if people don't use the language in their everyday lives.

   a. mightn't work

   b. not might work

   c. may not work

4. If linguists create dictionaries and grammar books, maybe more people ________ the language.

   a. will study

   b. might study

   c. may not study

5. If young people don't learn a language, it ________ passed down.

   a. will not to be

   b. willn't be

   c. won't be

6. When the language becomes extinct, no one ________ it anymore.

   a. might speak

   b. will speak

   c. may not speak

3 APPLY Work in groups of three. Take turns asking each other the questions in the chart. Respond using *may, might,* and *will*. Give reasons or examples to support your responses. Write the other students' answers with reasons and / or examples in the chart. Report your answers to the class.

QUESTIONS	________ NAME	________ NAME
1. Do you think your native language will disappear, or will it be preserved for future generations?		
2. Will the children in your family be bilingual?		
3. Will your children speak the same language as your grandparents?		
4. Will you stop speaking your native language?		
5. Do you think new languages will appear in the future? Will another language replace English as the dominant language for business?		

Go to the **Pearson Practice English App** or **MyEnglishLab** for more grammar practice. Check what you learned in **MyEnglishLab**.

PRONUNCIATION

Using Contractions and Reductions of *Will*

When you speak, you can use the contraction *'ll* for *will*, and *won't* for *will not*.

Example One

Listen to the examples and repeat.

When my children start school, ***they'll*** *learn Maori.*

My children ***won't*** *forget Maori, because* ***I'll*** *speak it at home.*

Use contractions with pronouns and *will*.

Example Two

Listen to the contractions and repeat.

I'll	*he'll*	*it'll*	*they'll*
you'll	*she'll*	*we'll*	

When the word before *will* ends in a consonant, pronounce it /l/ and join it to the preceding word. The underlined words in the sentence below sound the same.

Example Three

Listen to the example and repeat.

Nick'll give me a nickel.

The contraction *'ll* is usually written only after pronouns. Even when the full form *will* is written, it is usually pronounced as a contraction.

Example

We Write: *What will you do?*

We Say: *"Whattul" you do?*

1 Listen and repeat the sentences. Use the contraction *'ll* for *will*.

1. When I have children, I'll make sure they speak Maori.
2. When she goes to school, she'll study only English.
3. If you go to Greenland, you'll hear two languages.
4. He'll visit his native country.
5. How will you learn the language?
6. If English takes over, the culture won't survive.
7. The children won't be able to speak to their grandparents.

2 Work with a partner. Student A, ask one of the questions. Student B, listen to the question, choose the correct answer, and read it aloud. Use the contractions *'ll* for *will*. Switch roles after item 4.

Student A

1. What will happen to Maori?
2. How will adults learn Maori?
3. What will children learn in language nests?
4. Who will teach the adults?
5. Will Maori children speak to their grandparents in Maori?
6. Where will young children speak the Maori language?
7. Why won't people speak Maori at work?
8. What will happen to Maori culture if the Maori language dies?

Student B

a. Yes, they'll speak to their grandparents.
b. Maybe English will replace it.
c. The children will learn the Maori language and culture.
d. They won't speak it there because English is the dominant language.
e. Maybe the culture will disappear.
f. They'll go to language classes.
g. Older Maoris will teach classes for adults.
h. They'll speak it at home and at school.

SPEAKING SKILL

Using Pauses Effectively

Effective presenters speak slowly and smoothly, pausing between their ideas. Pausing gives you time to think about what you want to say, and it gives the audience time to think about your ideas. To use pauses effectively in a presentation:

- Pause after transition words, such as *first*, *next*, or *for example*.
- Pause after key phrases, or when you use connecting words such as *and*, *but*, *or*, and *so*.
- Pause at the ends of sentences.
- Avoid using fillers (*uh, um*) between words or phrases. Instead, pause silently and look at your notes if necessary to remember what you want to say next.
- Practice your presentation several times. Record yourself, listen, and notice the parts where you get "stuck." Keep practicing until you feel confident. This will help you to speak more fluently.

1 Listen to the following excerpt from a student presentation about an endangered language. Notice how the student pauses briefly after the words and phrases marked with a / and at the ends of sentences marked with a //. Then work with a partner. Take turns saying the sentences out loud. Make sure to keep fillers (*uh, um*) out of your speech. Give each other feedback.

Next, / I'd like to talk about an endangered language / from North America / called Mohawk. // The Mohawk people live in Ontario, / Canada / and in New York, / in the United States. // Today, / there are about 3,000 speakers of Mohawk, / but only about 1,000 are fluent native speakers. //

2 Read another excerpt from the presentation. Put a / mark where you think the speaker should pause. Then listen and check your answers. Finally, work with a partner and take turns saying the excerpt out loud. Give each other feedback.

There are some programs to save Mohawk. For example, children can study it in school, or after school. There are also other resources, such as a weekly blog, and an app that people can use to learn vocabulary and pronunciation.

Go to **MyEnglishLab** for more skill practice and to check what you learned.

FINAL SPEAKING TASK: Oral Presentation APPLY

In this activity, you will prepare a 2–3-minute oral presentation about an endangered language. You will introduce the language, explain why it is endangered, and describe what is being done to preserve it.

PREPARE

1 Think of a topic. Choose an endangered language from the list below, or find another language to present about.

Cornish	Hokkaido Ainu	Quechua	Sare	Trumai
Gelao	Navajo	Remo	Sorbian	Ugong

2 Plan your presentation. Research and take notes about the language to answer the questions in the chart.

What is the name of the language?	
Where is it spoken? Name the place(s) and find it on a map. Who speaks it?	
What does the language look and sound like? Find a common word or phrase and learn to write it, say it, or find an audio example of someone saying it.	
How many people speak the language? How old are they?	
Why is this language endangered? Provide reasons and examples.	
What, if anything, is being done to preserve the language? Give examples.	
Do you think the language will survive? Why or why not? Give reasons and examples to support your opinion.	

3 APPLY **Use the vocabulary, grammar, pronunciation, and speaking skills from the unit. Use the checklist to help you.**

- ☐ **Vocabulary:** Read through the list of vocabulary on page 197. Which words can you include in your presentation to make it clearer and more interesting? Choose at least three words or phrases to use and add them to your notes.
- ☐ **Grammar:** Scan your notes for modals of possibility or future with *will*. Did you form the verbs correctly?
- ☐ **Pronunciation:** Record yourself practicing. Then listen to your recording. Did you pronounce the contractions of *will* correctly?
- ☐ **Speaking Skill:** On your outline, make a note of the places where you will pause. Practice reading your presentation out loud. Did you speak fluently? Then use your chart to make notecards to use during your presentation.

Topic: Mohawk

Mohawk = Native American nation
Ontario, Canada & northern New York

PRACTICE

1 Practice your presentation with a partner. Use your note cards and pause appropriately.

2 Give feedback to your partner.

- Did you understand your partner's ideas?
- Did your partner pause naturally in order to sound more fluent and give you time understand his or her ideas?
- What did your partner do well? How can he or she improve the presentation?

PRESENT

Take turns delivering a 2–3-minute presentation. Your classmates will listen, take notes, and ask you questions when you are finished.

LISTENING TASK

Listen to the other students' presentations. Take notes. When you are finished, discuss these questions:

1. Which language is the most endangered?
2. How will the culture and community be affected if this language disappears?
3. What else could people do to save these languages?

ALTERNATIVE SPEAKING TOPIC

APPLY **Work in a small group. Discuss the questions. Use the vocabulary, grammar, pronunciation, and speaking skills you learned in the unit.**

1. What do you think about learning English? How will it help you in the future?
2. Does your country require that you learn English in school? If so, what do you think about that policy?
3. Do you think learning English will threaten (hurt) your native language? Give examples, reasons, and explanations to support your ideas.
4. Do you think people should do more to preserve endangered languages? Why or why not?

CHECK WHAT YOU'VE LEARNED

Check (✔) the outcomes you've met and vocabulary you've learned. Put an X next to the skills and vocabulary you still need to practice.

Learning Outcomes

- □ **Infer a speaker's viewpoint**
- □ **Take notes on reasons and examples**
- □ **Recognize and understand pronoun reference**
- □ **Use modals of possibility: *Will / May / Might***
- □ **Use contractions and reductions of *will***
- □ **Use pauses effectively**

Vocabulary

- □ **acquire** AWL
- □ **bilingual**
- □ **disappear**
- □ **dominant** AWL
- □ **endangered (*adj.*)**
- □ **eventually** AWL
- □ **extinct**
- □ **generation** AWL
- □ **linguist**
- □ **policy** AWL
- □ **preserve**
- □ **replace**

Multi-word Units

- □ **came up with**
- □ **got together**
- □ **native language**
- □ **official language**

Go to **MyEnglishLab** to watch a video about endangered cultures, access the Unit Project, and take the Unit 8 Achievement Test.

EXPAND VOCABULARY

UNIT 1

Vocabulary

boring
dangerous
difficult
friendly
happy
hardworking
high-paying
indoors
interesting
low-paying
outdoors
a problem solver
safe
a team player
trustworthy
workaholic

Multi-word Units

be good with numbers
be good with my hands
have good communication skills
have good people skills
not want to have a boss

UNIT 2

Vocabulary

ace
bomb
cram

Multi-word Units

cut class
fall behind
figure out
hang out
hit the books
pull an all-nighter
the last minute

UNIT 3

Vocabulary

afford
bargain (*n.*)
bargain (*v.*)
cost (*v.*)

Multi-word Units

be worth
be worth it
get a good deal
pay an arm and a leg

UNIT 4

Multi-word Units

call something off
go out
I'll have to pass.
leave someone hanging
look forward to
sounds good
take a rain check
turn down

UNIT 5

Vocabulary

album
catchy
instrumental
track
vocals
volume AWL

Multi-word Units

turn up

UNIT 6

Vocabulary

admire
contribute AWL
generous
inspire
recognize
role model

Multi-word Units

do good deeds
get involved
have a good heart
make a difference

UNIT 7

Vocabulary

calories
encourage
mental AWL
physical AWL
workout
pattern

Multi-word Units

keep track of
stay fit

UNIT 8

Vocabulary

fluent

Multi-word Units

make an effort
mother tongue
pass down
take over

ACADEMIC WORD LIST VOCABULARY AWL

Words with an * are target vocabulary in the unit. The remainder of the words appear in context in the reading texts.

achieve*
acquire*
adult (*n.*)
affect* (*v.*)
appreciate*
assignment
attitude
available
chapter
communication
community*
computer
concentrate*
conduct* (*v.*)
construction
contribute*
convince*
create
creative*
cultural
culture
definitely
depression
design* (*v.*)
device
document* (*n.*)
dominant*
energetic*
environment*
eventually*
expert (*n.*)
factor* (*n.*)
file (n.)
final
finally
focus* (*v.*)
generation*
goal*
grade (*n.*)
illegal
income*
issues
item*
job
lecture (*n.*)
location
medical
mental*
monitor* (*v.*)
motivate*
negative*
network* (*n.*)
percent
perception
physical*
policy*
positive
professional*
react*
relax (*v.*)
relaxed (*adj.*)
relaxing* (*adj.*)
remove
research (*n.*)
researcher
respond
response
schedule (*n.*)
schedule (*v.*)
strategy*
stress (*n.*)
stressed (*adj.*)
stressful*
task* (*n.*)
technology
topic
tradition
volume*
volunteer* (*v.*)

GRAMMAR BOOK REFERENCES

NorthStar: Listening and Speaking Level 2, Fifth Edition	***Focus on Grammar, Level 2, Fifth Edition***	***Azar's Basic English Grammar, Fourth Edition***
Unit 1 Descriptive Adjectives	**Unit 5** Descriptive Adjectives	**Chapter 1** Using *Be*: 1-7 **Chapter 6** Nouns and Pronouns: 6-3 **Chapter 14** Nouns and Modifiers: 14-1, 14-2
Unit 2 Simple Present	**Unit 8** Simple Present: Affirmative and Negative Statements **Unit 9** Simple Present: *Yes / No* Questions and Short Answers **Unit 10** Simple Present: *Wh-* questions	**Chapter 3** Using the Simple Present: 3-8, 3-9, 3-10
Unit 3 Comparative Adjectives **Unit 4** *Can*, *Could*, and *Would* in Polite Requests **Unit 5** Simple Present vs. Present Progressive	**Unit 31** The Comparative **Unit 14** Permission: *Can* or *May* **Unit 17** Simple Present and Present Progressive	**Chapter 15** Making Comparisons: 15-1 **Chapter 13** Modals, Part 2: 13-4, 13-5 **Chapter 4** Simple Present vs. the Present Progressive: 4-5
Unit 6 Simple Past	**Unit 18** Simple Past: Statements with Regular Verbs **Unit 19** Simple Past: Statements with Irregular Verbs **Unit 20** Simple Past: Questions **Unit 21** Simple Past: Review	**Chapter 8** Expressing Past Time, Part 1 **Chapter 9** Expressing Past Time, Part 2: 9-1, 9-2, 9-3, 9-4, 9-5, 9-6
Unit 7 Modals of Advice and Necessity: *Should*, *Ought to*, and *Have to*	**Unit 29** Advice: *Should* and *Had Better* **Unit 30** Necessity: *Have to* and *Must*	**Chapter 13** Modals, Part 2: 13-1, 13-2, 13-3
Unit 8 Future Possibilities with *Will*, *May*, and *Might*	**Unit 23** *Will* for the Future **Unit 25** *May* or *Might* for Possibility	**Chapter 11** Expressing Future Time, Part 2: 11-1

AUDIO SCRIPT

UNIT 1: Offbeat Jobs

Listening One, Page 5, Preview

HOST: Good afternoon everybody, and welcome to *What's My Job?*— the game show about offbeat jobs. I'm your host, Wayne Williams. Today's first contestant is Rita, an office manager from Chicago, Illinois.

RITA: Hi, Wayne. I'm so happy to be here! Hi, Mom. Hi, Dad. Hi, Joe . . .

HOST: OK, Rita. Let's get started. You're going to meet some people who will describe their jobs. Then you can ask three questions to guess each person's job. You can win $1,000 for each job you guess correctly. Are you ready? Let's welcome our first guest, Peter. OK, Peter, can you tell us a little about your job?

Page 6, Listen

HOST: Good afternoon everybody, and welcome to What's My Job?— the game show about offbeat jobs. I'm your host, Wayne Williams. Today's first contestant is Rita, an office manager from Chicago, Illinois.

RITA: Hi, Wayne. I'm so happy to be here! Hi, Mom. Hi, Dad. Hi, Joe . . .

HOST: OK, Rita. Let's get started. You're going to meet some people who will describe their jobs. Then you can ask three questions to guess each person's job. You can win $1,000 for each job you guess correctly. Are you ready? Let's welcome our first guest, Peter. OK, Peter, can you tell us a little about your job?

PETER: Sure, Wayne. At my job, I work with food. My work is very interesting because I can enjoy good food and I can be creative.

HOST: That does sound interesting. OK Rita, go ahead and ask your three questions.

RITA: Do you work in a restaurant?

PETER: No, I don't.

RITA: Hmm . . . do you work in a bakery?

PETER: No, I don't. I work in a factory.

RITA: A factory?

HOST: OK Rita. Really concentrate now. It's your last question.

RITA: Hmm . . . Do you make food?

PETER: Yes, I help to make food.

HOST: OK. That's three questions. Now Rita, can you guess Peter's job?

RITA: Hmm . . . are you a chef?

PETER: No, I'm not a chef.

HOST: Ah, sorry Rita. So tell us, Peter. What do you do?

PETER: I'm a professional ice-cream taster.

RITA: A professional ice-cream taster?

PETER: That's right. I work in an ice-cream factory. I make sure the ice cream tastes good. I also think of interesting new flavors to make.

HOST: Gee, sounds like a difficult job, Peter. You taste ice cream all day and you get paid for it!

PETER: Yes, that's right. I'm lucky to have such a great job.

HOST: Good for you. So tell us Peter, is there anything difficult about your job?

PETER: Well . . . I guess so . . . For one thing, I can't eat all the ice cream. Otherwise, I'd get too full. I only taste a bit of ice cream and then I have to spit it out.

HOST: I see. Is there anything else that's difficult?

PETER: Let me think. Well, I have to be very careful to take care of my taste buds. For example, I can't eat spicy or hot foods.

HOST: Really?

PETER: Yes, and I don't drink alcohol or coffee . . . And I don't smoke, either. If I did those things, I might hurt my taste buds, and then I wouldn't be able to taste the ice cream very well.

HOST: Wow! You do have to be careful.

PETER: Yes, I do. In fact, my taste buds are so important that they are covered by a one million-dollar insurance policy.

HOST: One million dollars! You don't say!

Peter: That's right. You see, if I can't taste the ice cream, my company and I will lose a lot of money. That would really hurt my income.

Host: Gee, you do have a very important job, Peter. So how did you get started as an ice-cream taster? Did you go to ice-cream tasting school?

Peter: Oh, no. My family has been in the ice-cream business for a long time. I've always wanted to work with ice cream, too.

Host: That's great, Peter. Thank you very much for being on the show, and keep up the good work! OK everybody, it's time for a commercial break. But, don't go away!

Pages 7–8, Make Inferences

Excerpt One

Peter: Yes, and I don't drink alcohol or coffee . . . And I don't smoke, either. If I did those things, I might hurt my taste buds, and then I wouldn't be able to taste the ice cream very well.

Host: Wow! You do have to be careful.

Excerpt Two

Host: Gee, you do have a very important job, Peter. So how did you get started as an ice-cream taster? Did you go to ice-cream tasting school?

Peter: Oh, no. My family has been in the ice-cream business for a long time. I've always wanted to work with ice cream, too.

Page 10, Note-taking Skill

Exercise One

a. **Rita:** Do you work in a restaurant?

Peter: No, I don't.

b. **Peter:** I work in an ice cream factory. I make sure the ice cream tastes good.

c. **Peter:** Well, I have to be very careful to take care of my taste buds. For example, I can't eat spicy or hot foods.

d. **Peter:** You see, if I can't taste the ice cream, my company and I will lose a lot of money. That would really hurt my income.

Listening Two, Page 10, Comprehension

Job Counselor: Hello, I'm Nancy and I'll be your job counselor. I'm glad you've decided to come to this group; it's a good place to come to get ideas about new jobs or careers you might be interested in. It's helpful to listen to other people talk about their jobs when you're thinking of changing careers yourself. So, to begin, I'd like everyone to introduce themselves and tell us what your current job is and maybe why you are thinking of changing careers. I'll take some notes about what you say, which will help me suggest some possible new jobs. Hopefully, we can find the right job for you! OK. Let's start with you.

Mike: Hi, sure. My name is Mike and I'm a window washer.

Job Counselor: OK. Great. Why don't you tell me a little about your job?

Mike: Well, I wash office building windows, so I go high up in the air in a basket to reach the windows.

Job Counselor: Sounds scary to me! Do you like it? And if so, why?

Mike: Yeah, I really like my job because I enjoy being outdoors. I like to breathe the fresh air and look at the beautiful views of the city. It's really relaxing. I really don't think I could work indoors in an office or a store. And I earn a high salary . . . I make a lot of money. Window washing is a good job for me because I'm good with my hands. I don't like sitting in front of a computer all day. It was difficult for me to get started as a window washer. But I started my own business and I like that—working for myself—no boss, you know?

Job Counselor: OK . . . I'm just making some notes; like being outdoors, good with your hands, like being your own boss. OK. So why do you want a new job?

Mike: Well, my job is pretty dangerous. I have to be very careful not to fall out of the basket, and I have to be careful not to drop things on people below. I just think I'd like something a little safer. Also, I enjoy it, you know, but it's a lot of work and can be very tiring. I go home at night and just want to sleep!

Job Counselor: Hmm . . . dangerous, wants something a little safer. OK. Great. Let's hear from the next person. Please introduce yourself and tell us a little bit about your job.

Sarah: Hi, I'm Sarah and I'm a professional shopper. I go shopping for people who are busy and don't have time to shop. Basically, people give me a shopping list and some money, and I do the shopping for them.

Job Counselor: Well, if you like to shop, sounds like a great job.

Sarah: It has its good and bad parts. What's good about it is that I do love to shop and I really like to work with people. I'm also very good with money. I always find clothes that are on sale—you know—cheap. But, well, the bad part is that my job isn't that easy. I'm on my feet a lot, so my work is tiring. And it wasn't easy to get started as a shopper. I worked for many years as a salesclerk in a department store. Then I started to meet people who needed a shopper. So, when I had enough customers, I quit my job at the department store and started my own business. Now, I like being my own boss. However, I have to do everything myself and it's a lot of work and it can be very stressful, you know, making all the decisions myself. So, I wish I could just go to work, do my job, and then go home at night.

Job Counselor: Yeah, sometimes it's easier to work for someone else and let them have all the headaches! OK. Let's see . . . who's next? What's your name?

Page 12, Listening Skill

Example

Mike: It was difficult for me to get started as a window washer. But I started my own business and I like that—working for myself—no boss, you know?

Excerpt One

Sarah: It has its good and bad parts. What's good about it is that I do love to shop and I really like to work with people. I'm also very good with money. I always find clothes that are on sale—you know—cheap. But, well, the bad part is that my job isn't that easy. I'm on my feet a lot, so my work is tiring.

Excerpt Two

Sarah: I quit my job at the department store and started my own business. Now, I like being my own boss. However, I have to do everything myself and it's a lot of work.

UNIT 2: Where Does the Time Go?

Listening One, Page 29, Preview

College Counselor: Good morning, everybody. It's great to see you here today. You know, one of the most important factors in school success is having good study habits. So, I'd like to start out by asking you all a few questions about *your* study habits. Then later, I'll suggest some strategies that will help you study and manage your time better. So, how many of you like to multitask—you know, like surf the web, or chat with your friends while you study? . . . OK, I see a lot of you. . . . Well, I hate to say this, but research studies show that multitasking has negative effects on your school success. So, the first goal you should set for yourselves is to avoid multitasking while you study.

Page 30, Listen

College Counselor: Good morning, everybody. It's great to see you here today. You know, one of the most important factors in school success is having good study habits. So, I'd like to start out by asking you all a few questions about *your* study habits. Then later, I'll suggest some strategies that will help you study and manage your time better. So, how many of you like to multitask—you know, like surf the web, or chat with your friends while you study? . . . OK, I see a lot of you. . . . Well, I hate to say this, but research studies show that multitasking has negative effects on your school success. So, the first goal you should set for yourselves is to avoid multitasking while you study. Think you can do it?

OK, so now, let's talk about another bad study habit: procrastination. Imagine this situation: You get an assignment to write a research paper for your English class, and you have two weeks to finish it. How many of you think you'll start working on it the first day? . . . OK. . . . I see a couple of hands. How many of you will probably put it off for a few days? Be honest. . . . All right, who would put it off to the last day and then stay up all night trying to finish it? Ahhh, OK. Well, don't feel too bad. Researchers say that 80–95% of students procrastinate sometimes, and about 20% do it often. They also say that procrastination is getting worse. People are becoming more distracted and putting off their work more than they did in the past.

So let's talk about some strategies to help you avoid those problems and manage your time better.

OK, so the first thing you need to do is to set goals. That means, you need to think about all of the tasks you need or want to get done. Write them all down.

The next step is to put your list of goals in order from most important to least important. So, for example, your math homework needs to come before seeing that new movie, right?

The third step is to use a calendar to plan your time. Schedule all of your tasks, and be sure to give yourself plenty of time to do them. And be careful with big assignments, like that English paper. You can't do it all at once, right? No, you need to divide it into smaller tasks that you can do one at a time. Also, don't forget to schedule things like exercising, getting enough sleep, seeing friends. Those are important too! OK, so tell me, does anybody have any questions so far? . . . No?

OK, so, finally comes the hard part—avoiding distractions and getting your work done. But how can you do it? Well, there's no one right answer. You need to find what works for you. But, here are a few strategies you can try:

One idea is the "Do Nothing" strategy. This strategy has two rules. The first rule is, "You don't have to do your work." That's right . . . but there's another rule. The second rule is, "You can't do anything else." So, when your two choices are your work or nothing, it's easy, but the problem is it's so easy to get distracted . . . phones, friends, the Internet . . . right?

So another strategy is to remove all of your distractions: turn off your phone – hide it in another room if you have to. Put away the video games. Turn off your Internet. Do whatever you need to avoid distractions.

A third strategy is to promise yourself a reward when you finish your work. For example, tell yourself you can go to the party on Saturday after you get your homework done.

A final suggestion comes from Piers Steel, who is a researcher and a procrastinator himself. (In fact, he took 10 years to finish his study on procrastination!) He suggests this: Give some money to another person and tell the person that if you don't finish your work on time, they can give the money away. They can give it to a stranger, or even worse, to someone you *don't* like. Now that should keep you working!

Page 32, Make Inferences

Excerpt One

College Counselor: Imagine this situation: You get an assignment to write a research paper for your English class, and you have two weeks to finish it. How many of you think you'll start working on it the first day? OK . . . I see a couple of hands.

Excerpt Two

College Counselor: Also, don't forget to schedule things like exercising, getting enough sleep, seeing friends. Those are important too! OK, so tell me, does anybody have any questions so far? No?

Excerpt Three

College Counselor: OK, so, finally comes the hard part – avoiding distractions and getting your work done. But how can you do it? Well, there's no one right answer. You need to find what works for you.

Pages 35–36, Note-taking Skill

Example One

College Counselor: How often do you think students procrastinate? Researchers say that 80-95% of students procrastinate sometimes, and about 20% do it often.

Example Two

Man: There are many factors that lead to student success, such as choosing the right classes, having good study skills, getting help from teachers and counselors, and staying healthy and active. Another important factor is time management.

Exercise One

Excerpt One

Man: So what can you do to manage your time better? The first thing you need to do is to set goals.

Excerpt Two

Woman: How can you avoid distractions?

Man: One thing you can do is to put your phone away.

Woman: Right. Putting your phone away is a helpful way to avoid getting distracted while you work.

Exercise Two

Man: Multitasking has a negative effect on your ability to think and learn. Many research studies show that our brains are not able to concentrate on more than one challenging task at a time.

Listening Two, Page 36, Comprehension

Counselor: OK, so now, I'd like you to work together in groups to discuss your own study habits. Group leaders, I'll ask you to report back about your group's answers in a few minutes. Any questions? OK, go ahead and get started.

Annie: Hi, I guess I'm our leader. My name's Annie.

Sam: Hi, I'm Sam.

Justin: I'm Justin.

Annie: Hey . . . so why'd you guys decide to take this workshop?

Sam: Well, me, I'm here because . . . well, I'm not doing so well in school right now, and I need to improve my grades. My counselor said this workshop would help, but I don't know. I think we're wasting our time.

Annie: Really? You think so? I hope it's gonna be useful. I wanna go to medical school, so it's really important for me to do well in school. So, Justin, how about you?

Justin: Me? Well I'm here because my parents told me to sign up. They said I have to get straight A's, or else . . .

Sam: Whoa, are you kidding? That's some serious pressure.

Justin: Yeah, tell me about it.

Annie: OK, we'd better get started . . . So, our first question is, "Do you multitask while you study or attend class?"

Sam: Well, yeah, I do, for sure. I text my friends during class a lot, especially during long, boring lectures. It's hard to concentrate.

Annie: Yeah, it is easy to get distracted, especially if you have your phone or computer right there. Sometimes I surf the web when I'm working on the computer. How about you, Justin?

Justin: Me too. I also like to listen to music, and I chat online while I do my homework. And sometimes I take breaks to play video games.

Annie: Sounds like multitasking to me!

Justin: Well, doesn't everybody? I don't really think it's all that bad for you. I mean, we made it to college, right?

Annie: Well, yeah, I guess so. OK, so . . . our next question is, "Do you procrastinate?"

Sam: Well, yeah, I put off hard assignments. Sometimes I just don't know how to get started. And besides, there're so many fun things to do in college!

Annie: That's true, but for me, I hate putting things off. It's too stressful. Besides, I think you need to think about what you want to achieve after college. I try to think about my goal to become a doctor and that helps me focus on my school work.

Justin: Wow. You have a positive attitude. I put off work that I don't like to do, like writing papers. And, yeah, I guess I do waste time playing video games when I don't feel like studying.

Annie: Yeah . . . OK, so our last question: "Which strategies do you want to try?" Me, I'm definitely gonna set goals and schedule my time better.

Sam: Really? All that stuff about lists and schedules sounds like too much work! I do think I'll start putting my phone away during class though.

Justin: I need to stop procrastinating. But, I'll tell you I'm NOT gonna start giving my money away! Maybe I'll start giving myself a reward for getting stuff done . . . like buying myself a new video game!

Annie: Ha! Sounds like a great idea!

Page 38, Listening Skill

Exercise Two

Excerpt One

Sam: Well, yeah, I put off hard assignments. Sometimes I just don't know how to get started. And besides, there're so many fun things to do in college!

Annie: That's true, but for me, I hate putting things off. It's too stressful.

Excerpt Two

Annie: OK, so our last question: "Which strategies do you want to try?" Me, I'm definitely gonna set goals and schedule my time better.

Sam: Really? All that stuff about lists and schedules sounds like too much work!

UNIT 3: A Penny Saved Is a Penny Earned

Listening One, Page 53, Preview

Carol: Good morning, everyone. Let's get started . . . My name is Carol, and I'd like to welcome you to the City Barter Network. I'm glad you could all come to today's meeting. And I'm really happy to see so many people who are interested in joining our network. Now, there are a few things I'd like to do this morning.

Page 55, Listen

Carol: Good morning, everyone. Let's get started . . . My name is Carol, and I'd like to welcome you to the City Barter Network. I'm glad you could all come to today's meeting. And I'm really happy to see so many people who are interested in joining our network. Now, there are a few things I'd like to do this morning.

First, I want to tell you a little about bartering—what bartering is. Then I'll explain how you can barter in our network. Well, then, if you want to join, I'll sign you up as a member. Any questions? OK. Let's get started. First of all, does anyone know what bartering is?

Man 1: Bartering is trading stuff, right? Like, I trade my car for your computer, or something like that?

Carol: Well, that's one kind of bartering—exchanging one item for another item—but in our barter network, we only exchange services—things you can do for another person.

Man 1: Oh, I see.

Carol: Well, here's how it works. First, when you join the network, you sign your name on our member list and you list all of the services you can provide. Then every member gets a copy of the list or they can read it on our website.

Man 2: So, what kinds of services do members provide?

Carol: Well, most members provide services that a lot of people need like cooking, cleaning, or fixing things. But, ah . . . well, some people provide more unusual services like taking photographs, designing a website, or even giving music lessons.

Woman 2: Music lessons?! So, do you think I could get piano lessons? I've always wanted to learn how to play the piano.

Carol: Yeah, sure.

Woman 2: Wow! That's great!

Carol: It sure is! But remember that when you barter, you need to provide a service before you can get one . . . So that brings me to the next step, how to barter. After you become a member, another member can ask you to provide a service, to do something for them. For every hour of work you do for someone, you earn one Time Dollar.

MAN 1: So, you can earn money?

CAROL: Well, no, you can't. Time Dollars aren't real money. Basically, each Time Dollar just equals one hour of time that you spend providing a service. Later, you can spend your Time Dollars to get a service from someone else.

MAN 1: So all the members earn one Time Dollar per hour, no matter what kind of work they do?

CAROL: Yes. That's right. In our network, everyone's time is equal. No service is more valuable than another one. Oh, here, let me give you an example. A few weeks ago, another member needed some help cleaning his house. I spent three hours cleaning his house, so I earned three Time Dollars. Then last week, my computer broke and I needed to get it fixed. So I called another member who fixed it for me. He spent one hour fixing it, so I spent one Time Dollar. It was great! I saved money because I didn't need to pay anyone to fix it for me.

MAN 1: I have a question . . .What if you don't know how to do anything? I mean I don't really have any skills . . .

WOMAN 2: Hmm . . . can you walk?

MAN 1: Walk? Well, of course I can walk . . .

WOMAN 2: OK, it's a deal. You can do dog-walking! I need someone to take my dog for a walk when I'm not home. Why don't you do it?

MAN 1: Well, I suppose I could . . .

CAROL: Great! It looks like you're all ready to barter! But, let's get signed up first. Next, I'll pass out some forms . . .

Page 56, Make Inferences

Excerpt One

MAN 1: Bartering is trading stuff, right? Like, I trade my car for your computer, or something like that?

CAROL: Well, that's one kind of bartering—trading one thing for another thing—but in our barter network, we only exchange services—things you can do for another person.

MAN 1: Oh, I see.

Excerpt Two

MAN 1: I have a question . . .What if you don't' know how to do anything? I mean I don't really have any skills . . .

WOMAN 2: Hmm . . . can you walk?

MAN 1: Walk? Well, of course I can walk.

Page 58, Note-taking Skill

Exercise One

1. I spent three Time Dollars.
2. All services are equal.
3. The number of members in City Barter Network is going up.
4. I need a new computer and printer.
5. There are more than 25 services in our network.
6. For example, some people walk and feed dogs.

Listening Two, Page 59, Comprehension

MARK: Hi there. I'm Mark.

NATALIE: Oh hi. I'm Natalie. It's nice to meet you.

MARK: So, Natalie, tell me, why did you decide to join the City Barter Network?

NATALIE: Oh, well, I was looking for someone to fix my car. Luckily, I found somebody, and now I think I'm going to barter for piano lessons, too. How about you?

MARK: Well, I'm looking for people to barter with because I belong to another group called the Compact.

NATALIE: The Compact? What's that?

MARK: We're a group of people that made a compact—you know, like a promise . . . we promised not to buy anything new for a year.

NATALIE: No kidding! You aren't going to buy anything new for a whole year?

MARK: Well . . . actually we can buy new necessities, things, you know, that you need for your health and safety . . . for example, food and medicine.

Natalie: That sounds hard. So why did you decide to do it?

Mark: Well, we decided that we were spending too much money on things, you know . . . clothes, cars, electronics . . . we think most people just have too much stuff . . . stuff that they really don't need. We wanted to stop buying so much and learn to live with less.

Natalie: I see . . . But you need to buy some things beside food and medicine . . . How do you get the other stuff you need?

Mark: Well, we either borrow things from other people, or we buy things used at thrift stores . . . or we barter for the stuff we need.

Natalie: Huh . . . so how's it going? Are you keeping your promise?

Mark: Yeah . . .mostly . . . though sometimes we just have to buy something new when we can't borrow it or find it used . . . like, for instance, I needed to buy some new paint for my house. But that's it so far.

Natalie: Wow! I bet you're saving a lot of money! How many members are in the Compact?

Mark: It started out with only ten people but now there are thousands of members all over the world. . . . You should join us. You can do it online at our website.

Natalie: Well . . . thanks, but I don't think I could do it. I like shopping too much—especially for new clothes! But hey, good luck!

Page 60, Listening Skill

Exercise One

Carol: But remember that when you barter, you need to provide a service before you can get one.

Exercise Two

Excerpt One

Mark: Well, we decided that we were spending too much money on *things*, you know . . . clothes, cars, electronics . . . we think most people just have too much *stuff* . . . stuff that they really don't need. We wanted to stop buying so much and learn to live with less.

Natalie: I see . . . But you need to buy ***some*** things beside food and medicine . . . How do you get the *other* stuff you need?

Excerpt Two

Natalie: Huh . . . so how's it going? Are you keeping your promise?

Mark: Yeah . . .mostly . . . though sometimes we just *have* to buy something new when we can't borrow it or find it used . . . like, for instance, I needed to buy some new paint for my house. But that's it so far.

Page 68, Pronunciation

Exercise Three

1. Seven dollars and fifty cents
2. Eighty-three twenty-five
3. Three hundred and nineteen dollars and forty cents
4. Sixteen ninety-nine
5. One thousand five hundred dollars

UNIT 4: What Happened to Etiquette?

Listening One, Page 75, Preview

Host: Today our guest is Sarah Jones, a reporter who recently did an international study of manners. Welcome.

Sarah Jones: Thank you. It's great to be here.

Host: So, Sarah, why did you decide to study manners?

Sarah Jones: Well, I wanted to find out if what is happening to manners. I wanted to know . . . are people really becoming less polite? So, I decided to conduct a test to find out.

Host: Hmmm . . . I see. It seems like it'd be hard to ***test*** manners though. How did you do it?

Page 76, Listen

Host: Today our guest is Sarah Jones, a reporter who recently did an international study of manners. Welcome.

Sarah Jones: Thank you. It's great to be here.

Host: So, Sarah, why did you decide to study manners?

Sarah Jones: Well, I wanted to find out what is happening to manners. I wanted to know, . . . are people really becoming less polite? So, I decided to conduct a test to find out.

Host: Hmmm . . . I see. It seems like it'd be hard to test manners though. How did you do it?

Sarah Jones: Well, another reporter and I traveled to large cities in 35 different countries around the world and in each city we observed people's language and behavior to see how courteous they were.

Host: Hmmm . . . OK, so how did you conduct these tests?

Sarah Jones: First, we did a "door test," and then a "document drop," and finally, a "customer service" test. We did 60 tests in all—20 of each kind. In the door test, we wanted to see whether or not people would hold the door open for us as we entered or left a building. In the document drop, one of us dropped a file folder full of documents. We wanted to see if people would help us pick them up. And for the customer service test, we wanted to find out if people working in stores were polite—so we noticed if the cashiers were courteous and if they said "thank you."

Host: So, what did you find out?

Sarah Jones: Well, the results were really different depending on the city . . .

Host: OK, so tell us about the most courteous city . . .

Sarah Jones: OK, in the most courteous city, 90 percent of the people passed the door test.

Host: Wow! You mean to say 90 percent of the people held the door open for you?

Sarah Jones: Yeah, that's right.

Host: Well, I guess holding the door for someone is an easy enough thing to do.

Sarah Jones: Well, true, but sometimes people aren't sure if they should hold the door open . . . I mean, how long should you hold the door for someone who is behind you but still far away?

Host: Yeah, that's true. . . .

Sarah Jones: So, almost everyone held the door. But only 55 percent of the people helped us pick up our papers.

Host: Huh, only 55 percent? That's not very good. But, I can imagine that sometimes you just can't help. I mean, what if your hands are full?

Sarah Jones: Yes, but one woman had two cups of coffee on a tray and her keys and wallet in the other hand. She put everything in one hand and helped! The reporter wanted to help *her!*

Host: Huh, interesting! OK, now, what about customer service?

Sarah Jones: So, in the most polite city, we went to different locations of a popular coffee shop to test the cashiers, and it turns out that 19 out of 20 of them said "thank you."

Host: So did they just do it because they're being paid to be polite?

Sarah Jones: Well, that's true, they *are trained* to be courteous. But some said they do it because it shows respect.

Host: You know, what I'm curious about is why some people are courteous and some others aren't. Did you ask people why they were polite?

Sarah Jones: Yeah, actually, we did. *Most* people who passed the test said they were raised to be courteous; they were taught good manners when they were young. And some people said they just try to treat people the same way they want to be treated. They appreciate it when others take the time to help them when they need it, so they want to do the same. You know—they follow the "golden rule."

Host: Hmmm . . . So what did you learn about the different people in your study? Are some people more likely to help than others?

Sarah Jones: Yeah, this is where it gets interesting. We tested all kinds of people: young, old, men, women, business people, students, police officers . . . anyone and everyone! And actually, age or career didn't really matter, but we did find that men helped more often than women, especially in the document drop tests. In that test, men offered to help 63 percent of the time, compared to only 47 percent for women. Also, the men were much more likely to help me compared to the other reporter . . . who was male. So, it seems like men are more likely to help a woman than another man.

Host: Well, I suppose that's not so surprising. OK, so now, we've been waiting . . . of the 35 cities you visited, which city won—which one was the most polite?

Sarah Jones: Well . . . You're not going to believe this . . . It was New York City!

Host: You're kidding! New York certainly isn't known for good manners. I'm so surprised!

Sarah Jones: We were too, but New York won!

Page 78, Make Inferences

Excerpt One

Sarah Jones: So, almost everyone held the door. But only 55 percent of the people helped us pick up our papers.

Excerpt Two

Sarah Jones: In that test, *men* offered to help *63* percent of the time, compared to only *47* percent for *women*.

Page 81, Note-taking Skill

Exercise One and Two

Sarah Jones: First, we did a "door test," and then a "document drop," and finally, a "customer service" test. We did 60 tests in all—20 of each kind. In the door test, we wanted to see whether or not people would hold the door open for us as we entered or left a building. In the document drop, one of us dropped a file folder full of documents. We wanted to see if people would help us pick them up. And for the customer service test, we wanted to find out if people working in stores were polite—so we noticed if the cashiers were courteous and if they said "thank you."

Listening Two, Page 81, Comprehension

Host: Now is the time for listeners to call in and tell *us* what *they* think. We've just heard about an interesting study of manners. So the question for our listeners is, why do you think there's a lack of manners? Caller one, you're on.

Caller 1: Hi. Well, I learned how to behave at home . . . from my parents. I think that's where a lot of people learn manners. But nowadays, parents are too busy; some moms or dads are raising children alone or have two jobs and just aren't home much. So there's less family time and that's where you learn manners—from your family, at home.

Host: Yeah, good point. Parents don't spend enough time with their kids, teaching them good manners. Well, let's see what other callers have to say. Who's next?

Caller 2: Well, I live in a large city and one thing I notice is there are people living here from all over the world. When I walk down the street, I hear people speaking three or four different languages.

Host: So it's because we don't all speak the same language? That's why people are rude?

Caller 2: No, not that. Manners are cultural, right?

Host: Right. Sure.

Caller 2: And what's polite in one culture might not be polite in another. So when many people live together, sometimes it's hard to know what's right and wrong . . . I mean, sometimes I can't tell if someone is being rude, or if they just learned to behave differently in their own culture. It gets confusing.

Host: Yeah, that's true. It is confusing when different cultures follow different rules of etiquette. OK. Let's take one more call.

Caller 3: Why are people rude? Electronic devices. I think it's because of cell phones, texting, and the Internet.

Host: Well, you certainly have a strong opinion!

Caller 3: Look, everywhere you go you see people talking on cell phones or texting; they're having a conversation with someone who isn't even there!

Host: Well, maybe, but cell phones and texting are very convenient.

CALLER 3: Sure, but people have forgotten how to talk with someone face-to-face. Also, people expect an immediate response and they don't see a need to be courteous; they just write short messages. They forget to say things like, "how are you" and "thank you."

HOST: I don't know. I like getting a fast response. Sometimes it's nice to not have a long conversation.

CALLER 3: Look, I have a cell phone and I use text messages and I think they are useful. But I think people use them too much. Electronic devices have made us more separate; now we spend more time on our devices and less time with real people.

HOST: Well, we're out of time, but to wrap up: we need more family time, a better understanding of our different cultures, and more face-to-face time . . . certainly some things to think about! That's all for now, until next week.

Page 82, Listening Skill

Exercise One

HOST: Well, we're out of time but to wrap up: we need more family time, a better understanding of our different cultures, and more face-to-face time . . . certainly some things to think about! That's all for now, until next week.

Exercise Two

Excerpt One

Part 1

CALLER 2: And what's polite in one culture might not be polite in another. So when many people live together, sometimes it's hard to know what's right and wrong. I mean, sometimes I can't tell if someone is being rude, or if they just learned to behave differently in their own culture. It gets confusing.

Part 2

HOST: Yeah, that's true. It is confusing when different cultures follow different rules of etiquette.

Excerpt Two

Part 1

CALLER 1: Hi. Well, I learned how to behave at home . . . from my parents. I think that's where a lot of people learn manners. But nowadays, parents are too busy; some moms or dads are raising children alone or have two jobs and just aren't home much. So there's less family time and that's where you learn manners—from your family, at home.

Part 2

HOST: Yeah, good point. Parents don't spend enough time with their kids, teaching them good manners.

UNIT 5: The Sounds of Our Lives

Listening One, Page 97, Preview

HOST: Next, I'd like to welcome today's guest, neuroscientist Leila Amari. She's here to talk to us about sounds and how they affect us. Welcome, Dr. Amari.

DR. AMARI: Thanks for having me.

HOST: So, we all know that the world's full of sounds. Some we want to hear, and some we don't.

DR. AMARI: Yes, our sound perception is always at work, even when we sleep—you can't close your ears, after all. Our brains are always checking for sounds in our environment, so we can know what's happening in our environment. And all these sounds have a big effect on our body, our mind, and our emotions.

Page 98, Listen

HOST: Next, I'd like to welcome today's guest, neuroscientist Leila Amari. She's here to talk to us about sounds and how they affect us. Welcome, Dr. Amari.

DR. AMARI: Thanks for having me.

HOST: So, we all know that the world's full of sounds. Some we *want* to hear, and some we don't.

DR. AMARI: Yes, our sound perception is always at work, even when we sleep—you can't close your ears, after all. Our brains are always checking for sounds in our environment, so we can know what's happening in our environment. And all these sounds have a big effect on our body, our mind, and our emotions.

Host: Can you give us an example?

Dr. Amari: Sure, let's listen to this: [sound of an alarm clock beeping]

Host: Whoa! Now, I'm awake!

Dr. Amari: Made you jump, didn't it? You felt surprised because sudden loud sounds like that alarm clock are a warning to us that something's happening, and our bodies respond immediately.

Host: Yeah, by jumping out of bed!

Dr. Amari: Right, the sudden sound surprises you, and your heart beats faster. Actually, a study done by the National Institute of Health in Japan showed that if you wake up to the sound of an alarm clock, it may be bad for your heart. You may want to wake up to light instead.

Host: What do you know? Well, you should tell that to the people who make car alarms. So, does a sound have to be sudden or loud to stress us out?

Dr. Amari: Oh, no, there are other factors, like pitch. What do you notice about this sound? [sound of breaks squeaking]

Host: Ouch! What is it?

Dr. Amari: Squeaky bicycle brakes! That sound is high-pitched. Our ears are most sensitive to sounds high in pitch. Like that alarm clock, or a baby crying, they get your attention. They're so annoying, they can even be used to scare people away. One company in the U.K. developed an electronic device called the Mosquito that uses high-pitched sounds to keep young people from hanging out in public places.

Host: Only young people? How does that work?

Dr. Amari: Well, as we get older, we lose our ability to hear sounds that are very high in pitch. So when some shopkeepers wanted to stop young people from hanging out near their stores—an inventor named Howard Stapleton got the idea to create a device that plays high-pitched sounds—that only people around the ages of 13 to 25 can hear. Shopkeepers place it outside their stores, and the sound is so annoying to young people that they stay away.

Host: Wow. So, I guess there's one good thing about getting older. We can hang out wherever we want to!

Dr. Amari: Good point! OK, Here's another example . . . [sound of a lion roaring]

Host: Oh! Don't want to get too close to that one!

Dr. Amari: That's right—the sound of a lion roaring probably makes you feel scared—even if you've never been chased by a lion before.

Host: Why is that?

Dr. Amari: It's because a lion's roar is not only loud, but it's low in pitch, and that sends a message to your brain that something big—and maybe dangerous—is nearby. So, your heart beats faster, you breathe more quickly, and your body gets ready to fight or run. We call this the "fight or flight" response. It's our body's way of getting us ready to fight, or run away from danger.

Host: Well, I can see how that is helpful if you're being chased by a lion!

Dr. Amari: It sure is. But noises aren't so helpful when we aren't actually in danger. For example, loud sounds in our environment, like the sound of airplanes flying overhead, can also cause us to feel stressed and anxious.

Host: Hmmm. So, sudden, loud, high- or low-pitched sounds can bother us. Are there other factors?

Dr. Amari: Yes, really any unwanted sound can be annoying. What do you think of this? [sound of a mosquito buzzing]

Host: Oooh, an actual mosquito! That is annoying.

Dr. Amari: Sure is! That sound of a mosquito probably reminds you of the annoying feeling of mosquitos buzzing in your ear, or leaving you covered in bites. Our brains make a strong association between sounds and emotions—in this case the sound of the mosquito and the feeling of being annoyed.

Host: Wow. So sound really can have a negative effect on us. But sound can create positive feelings too, right?

Dr. Amari: Of course! The world's full of pleasant sounds. How about this? [sound of running water]

Host: Ahhh . . . Now that's more like it!

Dr. Amari: Better, right? A lot of people are relaxed by the sound of water running down a stream. Other nature sounds, like the sound of the ocean, or rain falling can be relaxing too. If you are feeling stressed, listening to these peaceful sounds helps you to stop focusing on your own thoughts and worries, and that helps you to relax.

Page 100, Make Inferences

Excerpt One

Dr. Amari: Howard Stapleton got the idea to create a device that plays high-pitched sounds—that only people around the ages of 13 to 25 can hear. Shopkeepers place it outside their stores, and the sound is so annoying to young people that they stay away.

Host: Wow. So, I guess there's *one* good thing about getting older. We can hang out wherever we want to!

Excerpt Two

Dr. Amari: Of course! The world's full of pleasant sounds. How about this? [sound of running water]

Host: Ahhh . . . now *that's* more *like* it!

Dr. Amari: Better, right? A lot of people are relaxed by the sound of water running down a stream.

Page 103, Note-taking Skill

Exercise One

Excerpt One

Dr. Amari: Actually, a study done by the National Institute of Health in Japan showed that if you wake up to the sound of an alarm clock it may be bad for your heart.

Excerpt Two

Dr. Amari: . . . the sound of a roaring lion probably makes you feel scared.

Excerpt Three

Dr. Amari: . . . the sound of airplanes flying overhead, can also cause us to feel stressed and anxious.

Excerpt Four

Dr. Amari: . . . listening to these peaceful sounds helps you to stop focusing on your own thoughts and worries, and that helps you to relax.

Listening Two, Page 103, Comprehension

Presenter: Good afternoon. I'd like to start with a question: How does music affect you? Well, music can change your mood, right? Music can make us feel happy, sad, excited, or relaxed. But there are other ways that music affects our minds and our bodies, and can help us improve our everyday lives.

One way? Exercise. [sound of upbeat music with dance beat] Want to get up and move your body? Well, there's a reason for that. Research shows that listening to music with a strong rhythm before and during exercise can make you feel more energetic and exercise longer. In one study, when people ran with music, they were able to run longer without feeling tired. Why? One reason is the rhythm of the music. When we hear a musical rhythm, we use the same parts of our brain that help us to move our bodies. So, if we move to the beat of music with a strong steady rhythm, our movements become easier, and our bodies feel less tired. And of course listening to your favorite upbeat music improves your mood and keeps you moving longer—it sure helps get me through my morning jog!

OK, so how about when you work or study? Is music a good idea? Well, the answer is—maybe. Music can have a positive *or* a negative effect on our ability to concentrate on a task. It depends on the type of music, the kind of work you are doing, and *you*. We all know that noise, especially the sound of people talking, can be a distraction. So, if you need to concentrate on a *difficult* task, like studying for a test, you should avoid listening to music with lyrics. The words can distract you. On the other hand, some music *without* lyrics may help you to remember better. One study found that people remembered better when they listened to happy music. It may be that their brains made a connection between the new information and the positive feelings created by the music – and that helped them to remember. So music *could* help you to study better. But which music should you choose? Well, that depends on *you*. What makes you feel good?

Another memory strategy? Make your *own* music. In another research study, students were better able to remember new vocabulary words by *singing* the words instead of saying them. Just don't try that in the library!

So music can help us get things done, but it can also help us relax. Do you ever feel anxious or have trouble sleeping? Studies show that listening to relaxing music before going to bed can help us to fall asleep faster and sleep better. Here's some of my favorite bedtime music. [sound of quiet music] It's not too loud, and not high in pitch either. Also, it has a slow, regular rhythm. Researchers say that listening to music with a regular rhythm of about 60 beats per minute can help to slow down your breathing and your heartbeat. This makes your body feel relaxed, so you sleep better.

So, music is not just something that makes us feel good. If you use it right, it can change your life for the better. Thank you.

UNIT 6: Everyday Heroes

Listening One, Page 121, Preview

Announcer: What does the word "hero" mean to you? Maybe you think of superheroes or famous people who do great things. But what about every day ordinary people who help others? Are they heroes too? We begin tonight's program in New York where Brad Peck has the story of the ordinary man that many people are now calling a hero.

Reporter: It was a Tuesday afternoon at about 12:45, and subway riders were waiting on the platform for their train to arrive.

Woman 1: I was standing there waiting for my train, when suddenly, a young man fell down on the platform. A man and two women went over and helped him to get up, . . . but then he fell down again—right onto the tracks!

Page 122, Listen

Announcer: What does the word "hero" mean to you? Maybe you think of superheroes or famous people who do great things. But what about everyday ordinary people who help others? Are they heroes too? We begin tonight's program in New York where Brad Peck has the story of the ordinary man that many people are now calling a hero.

Reporter: It was a Tuesday afternoon at about 12:45, and subway riders were waiting on the platform for their train to arrive.

Woman 1: I was standing there waiting for my train, when suddenly, a young man fell down on the platform. A man and two women went over and helped him to get up, . . . but then he fell down again—right onto the tracks!

Reporter: The young man who fell on to the tracks that day was 20-year-old college student, Cameron Hollopeter.

Woman 1: So, this guy was just lying there on the tracks, and he couldn't get up. And then I saw that a train was coming! . . . And then this man—I couldn't believe it—he just jumped down, right onto the tracks!

Reporter: The man who jumped onto the tracks was Wesley Autrey, a 50-year-old construction worker, who was waiting for a train with his two young daughters, ages 4 and 6. When he saw Mr. Hollopeter fall, he reacted immediately. He left his daughters with a woman on the platform, then jumped into the subway tracks to help Mr. Hollopeter.

Woman 1: So, at first, he tried to get the young guy back onto the platform. But he couldn't do it. So, he pushed him into the small space between the tracks . . . and he lay down on top of him and held him down to keep him under the train. The train was coming fast into the station, and I . . . I just covered my eyes and waited. I thought they were both going to die!

Reporter: The subway train arrived just six seconds after Wesley Autrey jumped down on the tracks. Five cars passed over the top of the two men, less than two inches above Mr. Autrey's head, before it came to a stop.

Woman 1: It all happened so fast. I was afraid to open my eyes, but then I heard the man's voice from under the train, calling out "We're OK!" They were both OK! It was amazing—the train passed right over both of them!

Reporter: By acting quickly and holding the man down under the train, Wesley Autrey saved Cameron Hollopeter's life. Richard, another subway rider who saw what happened, praised Mr. Autry's actions.

Man: It was such a brave thing to do. I was just standing there on the platform, I couldn't move. It took a lot of courage for him to jump onto the train tracks like that. That guy should definitely get a reward for what he did.

Reporter: Another subway rider, Emily, was concerned about the risk Mr. Autrey took by leaving his two young daughters behind when he jumped onto the tracks.

Woman 2: I thought about those two young girls . . . They saw their daddy jump onto the tracks. I thought—would they lose their daddy right then and there? Oh my gosh . . . I'm just glad it turned out all right.

Reporter: Later, when Mr. Autrey was asked why he did it, he said he just saw someone who needed help, and he did what he felt was right. He also thanked his mother, saying that she raised him to believe we should help people whenever we can. He didn't worry about getting hurt; he just thought about saving Cameron Hollopeter from that train.

Announcer: So, it seems Wesley Autrey doesn't see himself as a hero—just an ordinary guy who did the right thing. That may be true, but people in this community are now calling Wesley Autrey "the Subway Hero."

Page 124, Make Inferences

Excerpt One

Woman 1: The train was coming fast into the station, and I . . . I just covered my eyes and waited. I thought they were both going to die!

Excerpt Two

Woman 1: It all happened so fast. I was afraid to open my eyes, but then I heard the man's voice from under the train, calling out "We're OK!" They we both OK! It was amazing—the train passed right over both of them!

Excerpt Three

Woman 2: I thought about those two young girls . . . They saw their daddy jump onto the tracks. I thought—would they lose their daddy right then and there? Oh my gosh . . . I'm just glad it turned out all right.

Page 126, Note-taking Skill

Exercise One

Woman: Well, in my opinion, there are four characteristics of a hero. First of all, heroes help others in need. . . . In addition, heroes make the choice to help out because they want to, not because it is required, or because someone told them to do it. Third, heroes help others even when there are risks. . . . Finally, heroes help others even when there is no reward for their actions.

Exercise Two

Man: Did you hear what happened on the subway?

Woman: No, what happened?

Man: Well, first, a young guy fell down on the tracks. . . .

Woman: Oh, no!

Man: I know, scary, huh? But right after he fell, this man—they call him the Subway Hero—he jumped on the tracks to save him. Then he held the young guy down between the tracks. Next—within seconds—the train came into the station . . . but it didn't hit them! They're both OK!

Woman: That's amazing!

Listening Two, Page 127, Comprehension

PROFESSOR: Today, I'd like to talk about altruism. Altruism simply means "showing an unselfish concern for others." In other words, altruism means caring for and helping others without thinking about ourselves. So, altruism can mean doing something brave, such as saving someone from a fire. . . . Or it can mean doing something simple, like holding the door open for a stranger, or giving a homeless person some money to buy food. The important point is that you're showing concern for others. Does that make sense?

The problem is that many people don't volunteer to help others—especially in dangerous situations. In fact, most people just do nothing. Research shows that only about 20 percent of people will take risks to help others. We also know that some people are more likely to help others in their everyday lives. But, why is that? Why do some people help out and others don't? Well, we don't know for sure, but there's research that shows several possible factors.

One possible factor is the situation we are in. For example, we are much more likely to help someone we know, like a friend or family member, than a stranger. We are also more likely to help when we are alone compared to when we are in a crowd. For example, if an accident happens, most people usually watch and wait for other people to help out first, but if no one else is there, they are more likely to do something.

Another possible factor is our genes. One study in Germany found that people who have a certain gene are more likely to help others, for example by giving money to those in need. So, maybe some people're just born to help others.

A third possible factor is our personality—the kind of person we are. For example, research shows that people who have positive attitudes, people who expect good things to happen, are also more likely to help others. This could be because they expect that things will turn out OK.

Finally, it may also be the way we are raised. Some people are raised by their families to help others, to feel responsible for others, and to show concern for them.

OK, so those are some of the factors that explain altruistic behavior. So, now, let's look at some different kinds of altruism . . .

Page 128, Listening Skill

Example, Exercise One

WOMAN: . . . heroes help others even when there are risks. This means that heroes will help even in situations where there is a chance that they will get hurt or something bad will happen to them as a result of their actions.

Exercise Two

Excerpt One

PROFESSOR: Today, I'd like to talk about altruism. Altruism simply means "showing an unselfish concern for others."

Excerpt Two

PROFESSOR: A third possible factor is our personality—the kind of person that we are.

Excerpt Three

PROFESSOR: Research shows that people who have positive attitudes, people who expect good things to happen, are also more likely to help others.

UNIT 7: Take Care of Yourself

Listening One, Page 147, Preview

HOST: Good afternoon and welcome to "Talk of the Day." Today we're talking about health care—and our topic is self-care. "Self-care" simply means doing things to take care of your own health.

HOST: I have two guests joining our discussion today. My first guest is Anita Burman. Her company, Self-Care Technology, creates digital products for self-care. Welcome Anita.

ANITA: Thank you for having me.

HOST: My second guest is Carlos Perez, a nurse and public health expert. Welcome to the show.

CARLOS: Glad to be here.

Page 148, Listen

Host: Good afternoon and welcome to "Talk of the Day." Today we're talking about health care—and our topic is *self*-care. "Self-care" simply means doing things to take care of your own health.

Self-care is becoming more popular these days, especially with young people. And why is that? Well, one reason is the high *cost* of health care. Doctor visits are expensive. Today more people turn to self-care in order to stay healthy and avoid getting sick. And when they *do* get sick, they often turn to the Internet rather than a doctor or nurse to diagnose their problems. Another reason for self-care? Technology. More people are using phone apps and wearable devices to monitor and manage their health problems. Americans spend ten billion dollars a year on self-care products. And that number is growing.

I have two guests joining our discussion today. My first guest is Anita Burman. Her company, Self-Care Technology, creates digital products for self-care. Welcome Anita.

Anita: Thank you for having me.

Host: My second guest is Carlos Perez, a nurse and public health expert. Welcome to the show.

Carlos: Glad to be here.

Host: So, let's talk about online health information. More than one-third of Americans now use health websites for advice when they get sick—that's over 97 million people a year. Do you think this is a good idea?

Anita: Absolutely! As you said, there is a lot of health information available to people online. I think it's great that more people are using the Internet to educate themselves and stay healthy.

Host: So, you think this is a good thing. Carlos, how about you?

Carlos: Well, of course it's a good thing if people want to educate themselves and take care of their health . . . but it's important that they get the right information. There are a lot of websites and blogs that give out *bad* health advice. And websites that diagnose health problems are often wrong. For example, online symptom checkers . . .

Host: Symptom-checkers?

Carlos: Right. These are websites where you can choose from a list of symptoms, and the website diagnoses your health problem. They might *seem* like a good idea, but they're usually *wrong.* In fact, a study by Harvard University showed that these symptom checkers are correct only 34 percent of the time. And an *incorrect* diagnosis can lead to a dangerous situation, especially if you have a serious illness or chronic disease and don't get the right treatment. Doctors and nurses have the education and experience needed to diagnose health problems, and they can suggest the best treatment for each person.

Anita: Well, sure, I think we can agree that people ought to see a professional to diagnose a serious problem. But even then, technology can help patients *and* doctors work together to *manage* their health problems. Digiceuticals, for instance.

Host: Digi*what?*

Anita: Digi*ceuticals.* Digiceuticals are phone apps that doctors and patients can use together to manage health problems. This is how they work: First, the app gets information from the patient. Sometimes it asks questions, but often the app works with a wearable device that monitors the patient to get information, like their heart rate or blood sugar levels. Then the app gives patients and doctors advice about how to manage their health problem. Digiceuticals can be used for all kinds of health issues. And often the app can be used instead of medication, which is great for the patient.

Host: Wait, so you mean that people can use a phone app instead of taking medication?

Anita: Yeah, that's right. For example, people who have trouble sleeping can use an app that will help them sleep better by making changes to their sleep habits, which is much healthier and cheaper than taking sleeping pills. Digiceuticals are great for people who need to manage a chronic health problem.

And of course there are plenty of other apps that we can *all* use to stay healthy—for instance, apps can help you to improve your exercise habits, diet, stress levels—you name it.

Host: So, in other words, apps can help us create better health habits?

Anita: Right. And that's good for everyone, don't you think?

Host: I suppose so . . . Carlos, what's your take on this?

Carlos: Well, again, I agree that we should all try to develop healthy habits, but I advise patients to work with a doctor if they want to make any big changes to their diet or exercise habits. Your doctor can help you to understand any risk factors you may have and can help you create a plan that's safe and healthy. Otherwise, you might end up getting hurt or sick. But once you and your doctor agree on a new plan—then, sure, if an app will motivate you, then go for it!

Host: OK, so let's hear from our listeners. What's your experience with self-care? . . .

Page 150, Make Inferences

Excerpt One

Carlos: . . . a study by Harvard University showed that these symptom checkers are correct only 34 percent of the time. And an *incorrect* diagnosis can lead to a dangerous situation, especially if you have a serious illness or chronic disease and don't get the right treatment. Doctors and nurses have the education and experience needed to diagnose health problems, and they can suggest the best treatment for each person.

Excerpt Two

Anita: . . . Then the app gives patients and doctors advice about how to manage their health problem. Digiceuticals can be used for all kinds of health issues. And often the app can be used instead of medication, which is great for the patient.

Page 153, Note-taking Skill

Exercise One

1. Self-care is becoming more popular with young people.
2. For example, many young people use technology and get health information on the Internet.
3. Our guest is Carlos Perez, a nurse and public health expert.
4. It's important that people with diabetes take their medication.
5. You should see a doctor to diagnose a health problem.

Listening Two, Page 153, Comprehension

Host: Welcome to "Talk of the Day."

Caller 1: Thanks for taking my call. I want to thank the nurse for talking about the dangers of self-diagnosis. I had my own experience with this. Two years ago, I had stomach pains. So I went online to check my symptoms. Pretty soon, I was convinced that I had cancer! And I put off seeing a doctor because I was afraid of the cost—and to be honest I thought there was no cure, and it was too late to get help.

Host: Oh, no! Then what?

Caller 1: Well, I started spending more time with my family because I actually thought I was going to die! And I worried—a lot. I was feeling really anxious. Finally, I went to see a doctor, and guess what? It turned out that I didn't have cancer after all. My doctor was able to treat my problem, and now, I'm fine. I should have seen a doctor sooner.

Host: Wow. So I'll bet you won't self-diagnose anymore.

Caller 1: That's right! Never again. Now when I need health advice, I always check with my doctor.

Host: Thanks for your call. OK, here's our next caller. Hello?

Caller 2: Hi, well, I use a digital app to manage my asthma, and I think it's great!

Host: An app for asthma?

Caller 2: Yes. My asthma inhaler monitors my breathing and how much medication I'm using. Then the app creates reports with information about my health. When I see my doctor, we talk about the reports and my doctor uses the information to make changes to my treatment. Thanks to the app, I now need less medication than before . . . and when I do need medication, my app reminds me to take it. That helps me to prevent asthma attacks, and I feel better, too.

Host: That's great! So it sounds like you're a fan of digiceuticals. Let's hear from another caller. Hello, you're on Talk of the Day.

Caller 3: Hi, well I suffer from depression, and I use an app that I like. It asks me questions to monitor my mood. It gives advice and exercises that help me to deal with my problems and motivate me to take care of myself.

Host: That's great.

Caller 3: Yeah, and I use another app that connects me to online counseling.

Host: Online counseling? How does that work?

Caller 3: Well, you sign up through an app. It connects you to a counselor that you can text. My counselor checks with me to see how I'm doing, and I can also text her whenever I'm feeling down and get advice.

Host: So, how do you like it?

Caller 3: Well, it's really convenient—I don't have to make an appointment and go to an office. I can just text my counselor whenever I feel like I need help. And it's cheaper than meeting a counselor in person too. Though, I think it would feel more personal if we could meet face-to-face. You know, sometimes I think she doesn't understand me very well through text messages.

Host: Well, thanks for sharing your experience. OK, we have another caller on the line . . .

Pages 154–155, Listening Skill

Exercise One

Anita: . . . But even then, technology can help patients *and* doctors work together to manage their health problems. Digiceuticals, for instance.

Host: Digi*what?*

Anita: Digi*ceuticals.* Digiceuticals are phone apps that doctors and patients can use together to manage health problems.

Exercise Two

Excerpt One

Carlos: There are a lot of websites and blogs that give out *bad* health advice. And websites that diagnose health problems are often wrong. For example, online symptom checkers . . .

Host: Symptom-checkers?

Carlos: Right. These are websites where you can choose from a list of symptoms, and the website diagnoses your health problem.

Excerpt Two

Anita: . . . And often the app can be used instead of medication, which is great for the patient.

Host: Wait, so you mean that people can use a phone app instead of taking medication?

Anita: Yeah, that's right. For example, people who have trouble sleeping can use an app that will help them sleep better by making changes to their sleep habits, which is much healthier and cheaper than taking sleeping pills.

UNIT 8: Endangered Languages

Listening One, Page 174, Preview

Professor: Good morning, everybody. Today, I'd like to talk about endangered and dead languages. So . . . who did the reading for today? Hm . . . I see . . . *some* of you did. . . . Then who can tell me what a dead language is?

Student 1: Um . . . Is it a language that nobody speaks anymore, you know, like Latin?

Professor: Yeah, that's right. Now, how about an endangered language? Jessica, what do you think?

Student 2: An endangered language? Well, uh . . . maybe it's a language that might die?

Professor: Right. An endangered language is a language that may die or become extinct soon. There are over 6,000 languages in the world, and some linguists think that about 50 percent could be extinct by the year

2100. Yes, that's a lot! So, many linguists want to preserve these dying languages.

Page 175, Listen

PROFESSOR: Good morning, everybody. Today, I'd like to talk about endangered and dead languages. So . . . who did the reading for today? Hm . . . I see . . . *some* of you did. . . . Then who can tell me what a dead language is?

STUDENT 1: Um . . . Is it a language that nobody speaks anymore, you know, like Latin?

PROFESSOR: Yeah, that's right. Now, how about an endangered language? Jessica, what do you think?

STUDENT 2: An endangered language? Well, uh . . . maybe it's a language that might die?

PROFESSOR: Right. An endangered language is a language that may die or become extinct soon. There are over 6,000 languages in the world, and some linguists think that about 50 percent could be extinct by the year 2,100. Yes, that's a lot! So, many linguists want to preserve these dying languages.

STUDENT 2: So, why do they want to do *that?* There are so many languages! Isn't it easier when people speak the same language anyway?

PROFESSOR: Well, that's a good point. Having fewer languages *is* more convenient for communication, but there are good reasons to save endangered languages. When a language dies, part of the culture can die, too. Now this doesn't *always* happen. For instance, the Manx people on the Isle of Man in the Irish Sea lost their native language, but they've kept many parts of their culture and traditions as Manx. But when a language dies it usually has a big effect on the culture. Think about what is expressed through language: stories, ceremonies, poetry, humor, a whole way of thinking and feeling. When a language dies, all of this may be lost. So, culture is lost. Also, history and knowledge are passed down through language, so when the language disappears, important history and knowledge may be lost, too. So that's why people care about language loss. All right . . . moving on . . . Now, how do you think languages become endangered and extinct?

STUDENT 3: Well, I guess nobody speaks them or studies them.

PROFESSOR: Yes. And there are several reasons why languages can become endangered. One reason is sometimes the government makes it illegal to teach the language in school. For example, before 1987, it was illegal to teach the Hawaiian language in Hawaii's public schools. It was difficult for children to acquire Hawaiian. As a result, that language became endangered. But, starting in 1987, new programs began to teach the Hawaiian language. Today, there are more than 2,000 students enrolled in these programs. So now, many children have the chance to learn Hawaiian and preserve it for the future.

In another situation, if one community has more power than another community, the less powerful community often feels it must learn the language of the more powerful or dominant group. Two things can happen in this situation. In one case, the more dominant language replaces the other language. One example is the case of Native American languages spoken in what is now the United States. Once, there were hundreds of Native American languages. Now, more and more people speak English, and not the native languages. Many of these languages have become extinct.

So, sometimes a community totally replaces their native language with another language. Or, the less powerful community can keep their native language and learn the other language, too. An example of this is in Greenland where students learn Kalaallisut and Danish. They are bilingual; they learn both languages, so they won't lose their native language. Also, Kalaallisut was made an official language in Greenland, along with Danish. This can help save endangered languages for future generations.

STUDENT 3: So . . . Are people doing anything else to save the dying languages?

PROFESSOR: Yes, linguists help create community programs where people can study the language and learn about the culture. Also, they try to preserve as many endangered languages as they can. They make videotapes, audiotapes, and written records of language with translations. They also study the vocabulary and rules of the language and write dictionaries and grammar books.

OK, that's a lot of information for one lecture! We talked about endangered and dying languages and why it's important to save languages, how languages die, and how people can save endangered languages. Great! So for next time, please read chapter ten.

Page 177, Make Inferences

Excerpt One

Professor: Yes. And there are several reasons why languages can become endangered. One reason is sometimes the government makes it illegal to teach the language in school. For example, before 1987, it was illegal to teach the Hawaiian language in Hawaii's public schools. It was difficult for children to acquire Hawaiian. As a result, that language became endangered. But, starting in 1987, new programs began to teach the Hawaiian language. Today, there are more than 2,000 students enrolled in these programs. So now, many children have the chance to learn Hawaiian and preserve it for the future.

Excerpt Two

Professor: So, many linguists want to preserve these dying languages.

Student 2: So, why do they want to do that? There are so many languages! Isn't it easier when people speak the same language anyway?

Page 180, Note-taking Skill

Exercise One

Excerpt One

Professor: Having fewer languages *is* more convenient for communication, but there are good reasons to save endangered languages. When a language dies, part of the culture can die, too. Now this doesn't *always* happen. For instance, the Manx people on the Isle of Man in the Irish Sea lost their native language, but they've kept many parts of their culture and traditions as Manx.

Excerpt Two

Professor: And there are several reasons why languages can become endangered. One reason is sometimes the government makes it illegal to teach the language in school. For example, before 1987, it was illegal to teach the Hawaiian language in Hawaii's public schools.

Page 181, Comprehension

Woman: I am Maori, living in New Zealand. In school, I learned and spoke English. This is because English was the official language. Everything was taught in English in school. That was the government policy. I only heard Maori when I was with my grandparents. I could understand a little Maori, but could not speak it. I could not have a conversation with my grandparents because they did not speak English.

When I was in school, I knew that I was not learning the Maori culture. As a result, I felt separated from my grandparents. I felt empty inside and different from my family. Maori is an endangered language and if children stop learning it, it will eventually die. I do not want to see Maori disappear. So now that I am an adult and have children of my own, I decided I wanted my children to learn their native language. I found a preschool that teaches children Maori before they enter school where they will learn English. The schools are called "language nests." Language nests began in 1981, when a group of Maori leaders saw that Maori was endangered and dying. They decided to do something. They did not want to wait for the government to do anything, so they got together and came up with the idea of preschools where children can learn Maori. Now, there are over 400 language nests and more than 9,000 children go to school at language nests. Language nests are a big part of Maori education.

Through the language nests, children learn about the values and traditions of the Maori culture. For example, we have a strong belief in love, compassion, caring, hospitality, family responsibilities, and respect for elders. Also, children learn our Maori stories, which are a big part of our tradition. So, children learn about Maori culture, as well as the language.

We are also trying to help adults learn Maori. For instance, I now attend classes that meet in a neighborhood center, where the teachers are all older Maoris, usually grandparents. Another way adults can learn is by attending week-long classes. In these courses, no English is spoken all week! Everything is Maori. Now there are many more adults who speak Maori, and this encourages our children who are also learning Maori. Language classes have really helped to preserve Maori.

Also, in 1987, the government recognized Maori as the official language of New Zealand, with English, too. This will also help preserve the Maori language.

Page 183, Listening Skill

Exercise One

Woman: Language nests began in 1981, when a group of Maori leaders saw that Maori was endangered and dying. They decided to do something.

Exercise Two

Excerpt One

Professor: So, many linguists want to preserve these dying languages.

Student 2: So, why do they want to do that? There are so many languages! Isn't it easier when people speak the same language anyway?

Professor: Well, that's a good point.

Excerpt Two

Professor: Think about what is expressed through language: stories, ceremonies, poetry, humor, a whole way of thinking and feeling. When a language dies, all of this may be lost.

Excerpt Three

Professor: Now, how do you think languages become endangered and extinct?

Student 3: Well, I guess nobody speaks them or studies them.

THE PHONETIC ALPHABET

Consonant Symbols			
/b/	be	/t/	to
/d/	do	/v/	van
/f/	father	/w/	will
/g/	get	/y/	yes
/h/	he	/z/	zoo, busy
/k/	keep, can	/θ/	thanks
/l/	let	/ð/	then
/m/	may	/ʃ/	she
/n/	no	/ʒ/	vision, Asia
/p/	pen	/tʃ/	child
/r/	rain	/dʒ/	join
/s/	so, circle	/ŋ/	long

Vowel Symbols			
/ɑ/	far, hot	/iy/	we, mean, feet
/ɛ/	met, said	/ey/	day, late, rain
/ɔ/	tall, bought	/ow/	go, low, coat
/ə/	son, under	/uw/	too, blue
/æ/	cat	/ay/	time, buy
/ɪ/	ship	/aw/	house, now
/ʊ/	good, could, put	/oy/	boy, coin

CREDITS

VIDEO CREDITS

Unit 1: Pearson Education
Unit 2: Crash Course Study Skills/BO Clips
Unit 3: Pearson Education
Unit 4: Rick Ray/Shutterstock
Unit 5: Sci Show Psych/BO Clips
Unit 6: ABC News Internet Ventures
Unit 7: Pearson Education
Unit 8: Pearson Education.

PHOTO CREDITS

Cover
Kochneva Tetyana/Shutterstock; Pla2na/Shutterstock.

Frontmatter
Page vi (pp. 2–3): Marco Aprile/Shutterstock; vii (p. 4): Cavan Images/Getty Images; vii (p. 9): Dolgachov/123RF; ix (p. 14): Adadem/Shutterstock; x (p. 21 left) Antonio Guillem/Shutterstock; x (p. 21 right): BlueSkyImage/Shutterstock; x (p. 22): Cecilie_Arcurs/E+/Getty Images; xi (p. 24): Pressmaster/Shutterstock; xiv (Unit 1 opener): Marco Aprile/Shutterstock; xiv (Unit 2 opener): Akhenaton Images/Shutterstock; xv (Unit 3 opener): Tzido Sun/Shutterstock; xv (Unit 4 opener): Dean Drobot/Shutterstock; xvi (Unit 5 opener): Oomka/Shutterstock; xvi (Unit 6 opener): Greg Vote/Vstock/Getty Images ; xvii (Unit 7 opener): Blazej Lyjak/Shutterstock; xvii (Unit 8 opener): Viiviien/Shutterstock.

Unit 1
Pages 2–3: Marco Aprile/Shutterstock; 4: Cavan Images/Getty Images; 9: Dolgachov/123RF; 11 (left): Ljupco Smokovski/Shutterstock; 11 (right): Strauss/Curtis/Corbis/Getty Images; 14: Adadem/Shutterstock; 15 (top): Dolgachov/123RF; 15 (bottom): Mind and I/Shutterstock; 16: Zurijeta/Shutterstock; 21 (left): Antonio Guillem/Shutterstock; 21 (right): BlueSkyImage/Shutterstock; 22: Cecilie_Arcurs/E+/Getty Images; 24: Pressmaster/Shutterstock.

Unit 2
Pages 26–27: Akhenaton Images/Shutterstock; 28: Jannis Tobias Werner/Shutterstock; 29: Commercial Eye/The Image Bank/Getty Images; 36: Maskot/Alamy Stock Photo; 39: Rawpixel.com/Shutterstock; 40: PeopleImages/E+/Getty Images; 42: New Africa/Shutterstock; 47: Stylephotographs/123RF.

Unit 3
Pages 50–51: Tzido Sun/Shutterstock; 52 (Roman coin): Claudio Divizia/Shutterstock; 52 (Chinese banknote): Ashmolean Museum/Heritage Image Partnership Ltd/Alamy Stock Photo; 52 (bank cheque): Universal History Archive/Universal Images Group/Getty Images; 52 (Harvard): Marcio Jose Bastos Silva/Shutterstock; 52 (ATM machine): Barbara Alper/Archive Photos/Getty Images; 54: Hero Images/Getty Images; 57: SpeedKingz/Shutterstock; 59: Ian Allenden/123RF; 62: Studioimages7/Shutterstock; 64 (top left): Brenda Carson/123RF; 64 (bottom right): TIvanova/Shutterstock; 66 (left): Zamollxis/12RF; 66 (right): Martin Sookias/Pearson Education Ltd.

Unit 4
Pages 72–73: Dean Drobot/Shutterstock; 74: Tyler Olson/Shutterstock; 75: Africa Studio/Shutterstock; 84 (top left): Pixelheadphoto digitalskillet/Shutterstock; 84 (bottom right): BlueSkyImage/Shutterstock; 85 (top right): Vernonwiley/E+/Getty Images; 85 (bottom right): Elnur/Shutterstock; 86: Mangostar/123RF; 87: Spohn Matthieu/PhotoAlto Agency RF Collections/Getty Images.

Unit 5
Pages 94–95: Oomka/Shutterstock; 96 (left): JohnnyGreig/E+/Getty Images; 96 (right): OLJ Studio/Shutterstock; 96 (background): Marina Dehnik/Shutterstock; 98: Tanwa Na Thalang/123RF; 99 (top): Khlungcenter/Shutterstock; 99 (bottom): Veniamin Kraskov/Shutterstock; 103 (left): Shutterstock; 103 (right): Maridav/123RF; 106: My Good Images/Shutterstock; 108–109: Argus/Shutterstock; 111: Hemant Mehta/123RF; 113: Smile photo/Shutterstock; 114 (left): Shuttertsock; 114 (right): Andrey_Popov/Shutterstock.

Unit 6
Pages 118–119: Greg Vote/Vstock/Getty Images; 120: Gordon Chibroski/Portland Press Herald/Getty Images; 121: Inspired By Maps/Shutterstock; 122: Nicks Brooks/AP Images; 125: Hedgehog94/Shutterstock; 127: Shutterstock; 130: Shutterstock; 131 (chimpanzees): Sam DCruz/Shutterstock; 131 (rats): Ilia Shcherbakov/123RF; 131 (gorillas): Dennis van de Water/123RF; 132: Michael Matthews/Alamy Stock Photo; 138: Gregory James Van Raalte/Shutterstock.

Unit 7
Pages 144–145: Blazej Lyjak/Shutterstock; 146: Roman Yanushevsky/123RF; 147: Andrey_Popov/Shutterstock; 151 (girl with inhaler): Bubutu/Shutterstock; 151 (beach scene): Ximagination/123RF; 151 (therapy session): Shurkin_son/Shutterstock; 153: Andrey Suslov/Shutterstock; 155: GBALLGIGGSPHOTO/Shutterstock; 158: CREATISTA/Shutterstock; 159 (sports equipment): Markspirit/123RF; 159 (meditation): Nick Moore/Alamy Stock Photo; 159 (sleep): Vladimir Godnik/Getty Images; 162: Extreme Media/E+/Getty Images; 166: Shutterstock.

Unit 8
Pages 170–171: Viiviien/Shutterstock; 179: Matej Kastelic/Shutterstock; 182: Jessie Casson/DigitalVision/Getty Images.

ILLUSTRATION CREDITS

ElectraGraphics, Paul Hampson, Dusan Petriçic

NOTES

NOTES

NOTES

NOTES